DEMOCRATIC
PHILOSOPHY
and the
POLITICS of
KNOWLEDGE

Richard T. Peterson

DEMOCRATIC PHILOSOPHY
and the
POLITICS of
KNOWLEDGE

The Pennsylvania State University Press
University Park, Pennsylvania

Richard T. Peterson is Professor of Philosophy at Michigan State University

Library of Congress Cataloging-in-Publication Data

Peterson, Richard T.
  Democratic philosophy and the politics of knowledge / Richard T. Peterson

    p.   cm.
  Includes bibliographical references and index.
  ISBN 0-271-01544-6 (cloth: alk. paper)
  ISBN 0-271-01545-4 (pbk. : alk. paper)
  1. Philosophy. 2. Democracy. 3. Liberalism. 4. Postmodernism.
5. Political science—Philosophy.   I. Title.
B65.P43   1996
700'.1—dc20
[101]   95-23637
                                                                 CIP

Contents

For Carolyn and my mother,
and in memory of my father

Acknowledgments

The influence, help, and support of many teachers and students, friends, and colleagues have left their mark on this work. Mitchell Franklin, Marvin Farber, and V. J. McGill were teachers whose insight, scholarly erudition, and political integrity showed me that a critical ideal for intellectuals still can be taken seriously. Anatole Anton preserves that spirit and has offered much helpful criticism and support. Steve Esquith has read many versions of parts of this text and has offered countless useful suggestions; his help has been invaluable. Among my colleagues in the Philosophy Department at Michigan State University, I thank especially Charles McCracken and Rich Hall for their encouragement and friendship. Clint Goodson, Roger Meiners, Mark Sullivan, Kevin Kelly, Jim McKee, and Rick Hill are colleagues at Michigan State whose insights have helped along the way. Others who have read parts of this text and generously offered suggestions include Richard Schmitt, Thomas McCarthy, Linda Alcoff, and Fred Evans. Doug Kellner and Bill Martin made helpful observations on the manuscript as a whole. Sandy Thatcher at Penn State Press has been most supportive; my copyeditor, Keith Monley, helped mightily in moving this text toward readability. Finally, I thank the many students who have been perhaps unwitting but nonetheless indispensable collaborators in developing the ideas presented here.

Part One

The Idea of Democratic Philosophy

Chapter 1

Philosophy and Politics

A Democratic Philosophy?

Is there, or should there be, such a thing as a specifically democratic approach to philosophy? The possibility or even desirability of philosophy remains a debated question. But perhaps the fact that challenges to philosophy and traditional philosophical ideas are today especially vigorous can be taken as a sign of a persisting interest in philosophical issues, an interest often pursued outside academic philosophy. Professional philosophers have themselves been affected not only by arguments in other disciplines (e.g., over method and theory in natural and social sciences, over uses of expertise in professions, over language in linguistics and literary criticism) but also by the challenges of social movements (e.g., by feminism's identification of the workings of power in language and culture, by minorities' contestation of persisting inequalities and differentiation, and by ecologists' claims about animal rights and the fate of the environment). Before we can draw any conclusions from the extent or nature of present philosophical activity, however, we need to have a more definite idea of what counts as philosophy as well as what relation the fate of philosophy so under-stood might have to politics, and particularly to democratic politics. All of these ideas remain of course highly contested. In working toward specific understandings of them, the following discussion aims to show ways that arguments about the nature of philosophy, politics, and democracy are closely interconnected.

What follows is an essay, in the literal sense of an attempt or experi-ment, in which I propose historical understandings of philosophy and politics and with these understandings work toward a democratic conception of philosophy. Because specialized knowledge now plays a crucial role in the language and practice of politics, philosophical reflection on knowledge has a direct, if abstract, relation to politics and to the prospects of democracy. I try to make good on this claim in a discussion that is not complete or detailed enough to warrant being called systematic, yet that is developed in the belief that the attempt to think systematically remains valuable and important. This belief goes against the grain not just of mainstream academic philosophy but also of much of the criticism of the mainstream. Rejection of systematic thinking is often confused with challenges to the intellectual errors that have made many of the ideas and aims of the philosophical tradition problematic. At this point it is premature to elaborate on what I take to be a defensible and necessary kind of systematic reflection or to anticipate my criticism of common rejections of the tradition. But in connecting these themes with the linkage of philosophy and politics I mean to imply that a certain kind of systematically oriented thinking about rationality is necessary not just for thinking about philosophical issues bearing on democracy, but for engaging in a democratic practice of philosophy itself. Moving toward an idea of such a democratic practice is a major aim of this essay.

Philosophy and Politics

To bring out more clearly the aims of the following study, I begin with the question of philosophy's relation to politics. The idea that philoso-phy might have an inherent relation to politics or that the practice of philosophy might itself be political (that is, that there might be a specifically democratic or nondemocratic practice of philosophy) breaks with the prevailing view that philosophers should stand apart from specific social interests and conflicts, even when they are discussing political themes. This is a moral requirement as well as a claim about the conditions of successful philosophical work. On this view, philosophers who do not keep their distance from politics risk forfeiting their intellectual vocation and in any case will not contribute genuinely philosophical insights. This opposition to pursuing philosophy politically is conjoined with the historical claim that genuine philosophical achievements of the past were not directly political. If, then as now, philosophers have political motives and make politically loaded assumptions, and even if their work contributes to political realities in various ways, still, pursuing philosophy in a directly political way risks losing its distinctive intellectual achievement. Thinking that proceeds this way, proponents of this view might claim, will lead to philosophy that is either shoddy or fraudulent, and probably both.

In view of the susceptibility of intellectuals to political and economic corruption, such a resistance to politicized philosophy is compelling. Further, there are too many cases of philosophers being in over their heads when they have turned to politics (consider Plato and Heidegger) for us to have much confidence in the mixing of philosophical and political judgment. Warnings about reductionism are persuasive as well, since, if philosophy can in some way contribute to politics, it will surely be on the basis of distinctively philosophical insights. Otherwise, why bother with philosophy?

One can acknowledge such considerations, and yet not believe that they rule out the need to think about philosophy in political terms. All such considerations are to some extent circular so far as they presuppose ideas of philosophy and politics. The traditional, if vague, ideas with which the discussion has proceeded so far rule out a linkage between the two virtually by definition. Philosophy ceases to be philosophy once it becomes politicized, because then it is no longer following uniquely philosophical considerations. Whether we reject a politically defined project for philosophy today, or feel dissatisfied with a political reading of past philosophy, we do so on the basis of a normative conception of philosophical activity. This conception posits uniquely philosophical considerations, both in subject matter and in the kinds of rules or validities to be observed in philosophical work. On this conception, there is a distinctive philosophical activity and its distinctiveness would be lost if it were to be treated as a variant of politics. Regardless of how one might work out such a view, the point remains that one cannot proceed with this theme without a normative conception of philosophy, and developing such a conception requires that one come to terms with traditional ideas of the autonomy of philosophical theory and method and that one do so in the light of the various challenges that have been mounted to the tradition.

Since my concern is with the relation of politics to philosophy, similar points could be made about any conception of politics we might adopt. I shall postpone that set of considerations and instead develop a few observations from my discussion to this point. First, it does not follow from there being a distinctive philosophical activity that this activity might not simultaneously have a political dimension. This political dimension might or might not characterize accomplishments that can be considered also in their specifically philosophical aspects. Second, any normative conception of philosophy itself needs to be elaborated and defended in view of the various challenges that have been made to received notions of philosophical theory and method. It is an open question, too, how the rejection of traditional ideas of autonomous philosophical theory and method might bear on the relation between philosophy and politics. To put the point more positively, any position on the relation of philosophy and politics requires a notion of philosophy and should not avoid contemporary debates over the possibility of philosophy. Later I approach these debates by referring to discussions of postmodernism.

If we affirm the possibility and desirability of a distinctive philosophical reflection without positing a freestanding philosophical theory or autonomous method, the relation between such philosophy and politics still needs to be explained. It is possible to conclude, I will argue, that pursuit of philosophical outcomes, which have to be judged in specifically philosophical terms, at the same time carries out political functions that can be judged in a distinctively political way. Such a conclusion is compatible with, and requires, a historical conception of both philosophy and politics and of their interrelationship. One can distinguish philosophical and political aspects of practices within a reflection that is itself simultaneously philosophical and political. I argue that an explicit overlap of these functions is inherent in the project of a democratic philosophy.

How one can make such an argument in a way that respects concern about a direct politicization or analytical reduction of philosophy is a major preoccupation of the discussion that follows. For now, suffice it to say that discussions of the relation between philosophy and politics proceed today in a setting in which traditional understandings of philosophy have given way without being followed by agreement on what, if anything, should replace them. Today, to make philosophical arguments for relations between philosophy and politics is to argue for the viability of philosophy. So we have all the more reason to guard against a reductive treatment of philosophy.

We can explore ways the political connections of philosophy might affirm and extend distinctively philosophical reflection by noting implications that would follow from showing that philosophy always has been political. If we could establish an account of philosophy along these lines and thus fill out the social and historical character of philosophical work, we would undermine appeals to the traditional separation of philosophy from politics discussed earlier. Against the argument that such accounts in the end are antiphilosophical, we could respond that resisting them on general principle is itself antiphilosophical. If philosophy has always been political, then exploring how this has been so must count as an unavoidable problem for those who aspire to philosophical insight, even if the prospects for rescuing distinctively philosophical insight are uncertain.

Toward a Political Understanding of Philosophy

Those who resist thinking about philosophy in political terms make use of ideas of philosophy and politics that are themselves open to question. Similarly, many who seek to trace the political dimension of philosophy make use of insights developed by critics of traditional philosophy. To work toward a conception of philosophy that both preserves distinctively philosophical work and reflects on its political functions, I refer to features of contemporary debates over philosophy.

One line of argument involves more or less internal criticisms of traditional assumptions and claims. Probably the most influential of these in the past generation of Anglo-American philosophers has been the challenge to various aspects of traditional ideas of immediate knowledge and formal reason. These debates have in turn reopened the question of the distinctiveness and potential of philosophical argumentation. Perhaps the most influential combination of these themes has been found in the work of Richard Rorty (1979). In some respects these challenges seem to restage battles fought long ago. For example, the criticism of immediacy and formalism developed by Hegel staked out terrain that dialecticians and theorists of hermeneutics and of deconstruction have worked over for decades.

But another dimension of the contemporary debate over the tradition places recent philosophical arguments in a more contemporary light. This has to do with what we may call attempts at therapeutic demystification. From this point of view, the standing of intuition or formal reason is less a matter of theoretical dispute than a question about the nature and value of theory as such. And what is at issue regarding theory is not so much the powers or pretensions of abstract thought as the effects of theory in culture and politics. Refuting theoretical mistakes is not enough to free us from the confusions and mystifications to which theory contributes. This point can be pressed as the critique of ideology, where features of theoretical thinking (e.g., the abstract individual subject of epistemology and much liberal theory) organize social perceptions appropriate to specific class interests (e.g., those of the privileged groups of capitalism), but in recent years such criticism has been reworked by representatives of social movements. Now traditional ways of thinking (e.g., instrumentalist logic) are treated as organizing standpoints and practices appropriate to specific kinds of power (e.g., those of patriarchy, of Eurocentric culture, or of a technological will to power over nature). Theoretical refutation of traditional ideas here is part of a larger project of exploring and attacking their influences and attempting to shape suitable alternatives.

Such critics try to explain the persistence of traditional patterns of thought in terms of their ongoing attractions and functions as reconstructed in the various critical frameworks. Traces or variants of ideas may persist even when the intellectual justification for their originals has long faded, in part because these ideas are serving political functions. Criticism of this sort faces the difficulty that identification of such functions does not eliminate the intellectual problems for which discredited notions were developed. Already in the nineteenth century Marx and Nietzsche had created the problem how far their demystifications of the tradition freed them from the need for some kind of philosophical clarification and justification of their claims. This question takes on a more explicit and sustained form in the work of such twentieth-century successors of these thinkers as Adorno, Heidegger, and Derrida. Philosophically minded challenges to the tradition cannot for long sidestep questions about their own philosophical commitments and aims and so about how sharply they break with the tradition they bring into question.

Hermeneutical thinkers like Gadamer (1975) have pointed out that a well-founded suspicion of specific traditional ideas does not justify or require a complete break with the tradition as a whole. Such a break is not only impossible but perhaps even unthinkable, since familiar notions of radical rupture are themselves part of the modern tradition of criticism and display their debt to tradition once they attempt to state the aims or means of such a break. But acknowledgment of the unavoidable continuity with a tradition whose claims about reason and being are nonetheless widely discounted may only lead to an acceptance of paradox or withdrawal from theoretical discussion altogether.

Skepticism about theoretical reflection is in fact widespread among contemporary intellectuals. Aside from doubts about the basis for such reflection, such skepticism treats concern with the philosophical tradition as artificial and irrelevant, as little more than a self-indulgent exercise on the part of privileged intellectuals. On this view, theoretical reflection on rationality at best diverts attention from concrete and meaningful problems. One difficulty with this skepticism is that it tries to short-circuit the Enlightenment culture of which it is a part by ignoring the issues that can be raised about its own commitments. Another problem is that this skepticism turns its back on legitimate political questions that have been raised about the work of intellectuals and other experts; these questions themselves have an epistemological dimension. I shall explore these themes in detail, so it may suffice for now simply to identify a paradoxical effect of this skepticism, one that ties in with the issue of dogmatism raised earlier.

Consider a political consequence of skepticism about reflection on rationality in contemporary intellectual life. What seems a healthy distrust of certain kinds of abstraction becomes an impediment to reflection on the social being and effects of intellectual practices so far as these are themselves bound up with normative claims. Reflection on such claims is inseparable from examination of the claims to authority by experts in a world in which expert influence is central to the differentiated workings of power. In the absence of philosophical reflection on the authority claims made by specialists, this authority becomes a matter of professional certification and institutional recognition, which can at best provide a partial examination of the normative basis for expert functions. Professionalization inserts intellectuals into institutional settings that organize their activities in functions whose social utility makes reflective justification seem superfluous.

The struggles over the social role of knowledge justify a certain skepticism about reflection when that reflection ignores the most important grounds for knowledge having become problematic. But the status of philosophy should not be decided by the impossibility of foundationalism and transcendentalism or the illusions fostered by covert attempts to revive traditional philosophical strategies. Rather, philosophy should be examined for its capacity to respond to the historical doubts about actual knowledge in the light of its contributions to various forms of domination and inequality. In contrast to earlier debates, the issue today cannot seriously be posed as that of the reality or power of human knowledge, and the challenge to rationality does not come mainly as theologically motivated skepticism. The issue today is not the reality of knowledge, but the nature of its universality and objectivity. The most important skepticism philosophy encounters consists of the various claims that knowledge is a power specific to particular interests and perspectives. There are many variants of this view, which I later link to debates over postmodernism. For now, I label this the theme of knowledge-power.

Skepticism about knowledge today, then, requires a reflection that examines the relations between cognitive achievement and the organization of power relations. If philosophy is possible as a response to skepticism, it must be one that addresses issues of universality and objectivity as these arise in the various ways knowledge is politically charged. Since its own claims project universalistic aims of some kind, philosophy has to reflect on its own activity within the debates over knowledge and power. This very insertion of philosophical activity in reflexive debates about knowledge-power gives it a political character.

If philosophy today is inherently political, it must attempt to be democratic: this is not just a matter of general principle, but has to do with the need to confront forms of power that operate within knowledge, that is, within intellectual work generally. The aim of the following study is not to construct such a philosophy so much as to trace some of its tasks and possible strategies. I draw from a variety of authors, movements, and debates and interpret many of them as contributions to a democratic tendency that proceeds in a variety of contexts and on many different levels of abstraction in identifying and combating the construction and use of knowledge for undemocratic ends. The idea of a "tendency" is meant here in a loose enough sense to accommodate significant disagreements, and the identification of such a tendency is by no means itself a matter of common understanding. But with this interpretive idea of democratic philosophy I hope to contribute to a clearer sense of some of the lines along which democratic conflict exists and must develop. Thus my general aims are to identify the nature of the democratic project in philosophy, to note and advance some of the contributions that have been made to it, and to make explicit some of the problems and dilemmas that this project faces.

At this point in the discussion, the relevant senses of philosophy and politics remain undeveloped. Nevertheless, I can make some preliminary claims about the kind of reflection that is appropriate to making philosophical sense of issues of knowledge and power. Such a philosophy must be critical and hermeneutical, it must take issues of rational validity seriously, and it must be able to place such issues within a historical context in which democratic change has definite content. Let me anticipate general features of the discussion that follows by saying something about each of these dimensions of democratic philosophy.

(1) Saying that such philosophy must be critical and hermeneutical follows partly from the idea that democratic philosophy pursues reflection proper to tendencies within intellectual and political life that concern themselves with ways in which knowledge is associated with domination and the mystification of social powers. As I have spoken of it, democratic philosophy is itself an interpretation of various kinds of critical activities. These in turn are understood to involve interpretive reconstructions that identify and examine the content, effects, and conditions of specialized knowledge and associated forms of expertise. Democratic philosophy, then, has to do with both democratic and undemocratic forms of intellectual representation, and it aims to place its own activity within the scope of its critical interpretations.

(2) Though concerned with historical issues of interpretation and critique, philosophy understood along the lines I am sketching follows the characteristically modern concern with rationality and knowledge. Abandoning foundationalist and transcendental strategies, it cannot hope to secure guarantees against skepticism, whether aimed at the very possibility of knowledge or at its universalistic claims. But this does not undercut the possibility of philosophy if it is true that the relevant skepticism today is not the challenge to the possibility of

modern knowledge but rather the questioning of the objectivity and universality of knowledge claims as these bear on issues of power. What arguments can plausibly confront such skepticism remains to be seen, but there is no a priori basis for ruling out the promise of hermeneutic and critical approaches.

In more positive terms, democratic philosophy is in part concerned with the validity of claims about the social world and the practices that help make it up. To understand the politics of philosophy in a way that respects what is distinctively philosophical, we must think about a politics that is concerned with issues about the claims to authority of social practices, including those generating and making use of specialized knowledge. The politics of philosophy, then, in part has to do with representations and claims about expertise as these do or should occur in public discussion. A democratic philosophy would explore not only the corresponding issues of power and inequality but also issues about philosophical discussion itself, now understood as having a political force.

In negative terms, democratic philosophy seeks to avoid accounts that reduce away the orientations of agents to validity claims. It aims to preserve the standpoint of agency, yet to break with the immanence of philosophical subjectivity that characterizes not only the tradition but persists in the work of such critics of the tradition as Heidegger and Derrida.

(3) A critical and interpretive reflection that would preserve agency without absolutizing subjectivity must pursue a conception of historical being in which subjectivity plays a constitutive but not autonomous role. Such an "ontological" contextualization of subjectivity is the aim of a kind of historical materialism, though it is one that yields various criticisms of Marx. Materialism here involves not simply a heuristic acknowledgment that all forms of awareness presuppose and are often blind to various aspects of social being, but more specifically a commitment to the analysis of subjectivity as figuring within practices and the various objectifications that characterize them. Hegel is the source of this kind of materialism so far as it treats experienced forms of subjectivity and objectivity as aspects of historical activities that must be conceived in terms not prejudiced by modern metaphysics. There are a number of important contemporary Hegelian materialists in this sense. Two who are important sources in my discussion are Habermas and Foucault.

Beyond the contextualization of subjectivity, this materialism confronts issues of historicity. This term refers us to relations to past and future as these organize important features of the present. Historicity is a problem because present social practices are constructed with determinate relations to past and future (as can be seen in such disparate cases as economic growth imperatives on the one hand and the persistence of national and racial identities on the other). A political understanding of historicity must make critical sense of prevailing forms of historical consciousness as well as propose a democratic sense of the historical present. While making democratic sense of historical possibilities, it must avoid the presuppositions of teleological philosophies of history.

A philosophy pursued along these lines will not be able to assert the necessity of rational claims traditionally sought by philosophers when responding to skepticism. The historical and materialist aspects of this critical and interpretive reflection imply reliance on historical and empirical disciplines and on argumentation understood to be bound in important ways to its historically specific settings. Nonetheless, such reflection need not embrace the historicism associated with postmodern philosophical views. Historical arguments are available that allow us to defend appropriate universalistic claims concerning the validities at issue in debates about knowledge and power. In particular, the historical perspective afforded by a philosophical idea of the division of labor conjoined with a communications ethic understood in historical and political terms provides sufficient universality to sustain the needs of a democratic philosophical reflection.

Philosophy as Social Practice

Thinking about philosophical issues in political and historical terms means thinking about social practices. This holds for the issues of knowledge and rationality facing democratic philosophical reflection as it holds for thinking about philosophy itself. Carrying through on the idea of democratic philosophy means conceptualizing issues of knowledge and power in social terms that will make it possible to see how the practice of philosophy itself figures within social life. That is, the social practice of democratic philosophy involves appropriate conceptualizations of intellectual activity just as the social practices of philosophers in the past typically and appropriately (given the politics of which those practices were a part) involved conceptualizations that minimized the social and political character of intellectual activity.

Knowledge or intellectual activity as social practice refers to patterns of activity involving experienced, if not consciously explicit, orientations to norms on the part of individuals associated in formal and informal ways within various social institutions. The problems and commitments of such practices have a historical objectivity that transcends individuals and that contributes to the relations between these practices and other practices in society. The emphasis on practices sustains what I earlier characterized as the materialist aspect of this philosophical reflection, just as the orientation to norms bears on its concern with validity issues.

A convincing reconstruction of intellectual activity as social practice must confront many difficult conceptual problems and soon becomes enmeshed in issues of social theory that go well beyond what this study attempts. Issues about the interrelations of social practices, institutions, and social structure are touched upon only in respects that are most crucial for this discussion and even then are treated in very general terms. I explore the conceptualization of intellectual practices mainly by adapting linguistic ideas that seem appropriate and fruitful.

In particular, I draw from linguistic themes developed by Habermas, Foucault, and Bakhtin. The formative and communicative features of language provide conditions for specifically intellectual forms of achievement, for the coherence of corresponding social practices, and for the means by which intellectual practices practically affect other social practices. A linguistic approach to intellectual activity allows us to explore its interpretive dimensions, its validity orientations, and the insertion of its conceptual dimension in the historical objectivity of interacting social practices.

The use of language theory to treat intellectual practices, including philosophy, as social practices should help to expose the specifically political dimension of this activity. For example, a linguistic conception of intellectual practice can approach political functions that, in traditional terms, are both internal and external to specifically conceptual or theoretical concerns of philosophy. My discussion considers a number of ways intellectual practices serve political functions.

A philosopher like Descartes may be thought politically influential so far as his metaphysical and epistemological ideas affect the political understanding of liberalism. A communications reconstruction of Descartes's intellectual activity would explore the effects of his texts as utterances in an unfolding discussion of human capacities, self-experience, motivation, and so on. It might similarly explore the ways his ideas and arguments go on to inform the public language of expertise in societies increasingly given to conceiving social problems not just as issues for experts (which they have been for thousands of years) but as issues for an expertise couched in the language of modern scientific abstraction. Such a reconstruction of the politics of Cartesianism would explore not only the influence of specific ideas or arguments on later reasoning, but also the effect the language of Descartes's reasoning has on the language with which later intellectuals characterize their achievements and assert their authority.

Of course, it is difficult, if not impossible, to assess the influence of a single thinker with regard to the general ways in which intellectuals understand themselves and present their achievements and claims to others. The fact that Descartes's specific influence soon blurs into the influence of a tendency of thinking in which he plays only one part does not diminish his political contribution, though it raises questions about how best to understand the publics in which such political functions are played. The point here is that once placed in a communications perspective, Descartes's philosophical work may serve as the focus of research beyond the philosophical issues that most directly concerned Descartes. At the same time, in following his influence in such areas as the social self-understanding of intellectuals, we would not be departing from Descartes's own preoccupations, since he so explicitly aimed to make the work of the new sciences respectable and secure.

These references to Descartes make clear that in any exploration of the politics of philosophical work it is not easy to separate influences that bear on theoretical issues from influences that bear on the self-reflection and social presentation of theorists. A somewhat different philosophical influence in political contexts might be traced to a thinker like Locke, who takes part in policy debates of his day. One need not concentrate on Locke's political theory to consider how his epistemological or metaphysical ideas enter political discussion, since the politics of his ideas figures as well in his participation in debates over taxes or in issues of colonial administration (see Wood 1983). Patterns of reasoning, claims about the practical relevance of reflective abstractions, theoretical notions of motivation and decision making, and so on, all inform a language that in turn contributes to the shaping of ensuing debates and the self-understandings of the participants in them.

With these schematic claims, I am anticipating the lines along which a reconstruction of political dimensions of philosophical activity can proceed. I have suggested that a linguistically minded account makes such a reconstruction of philosophy as a politically charged social practice possible. In general the aim is to think about various respects in which it is possible to think of philosophy and other intellectual work as mediating activity. With the interpretive and communicative functions of philosophy, I have touched upon respects in which philosophical reflection takes place in contexts of conflict and debate to which philosophers contribute concepts, patterns of argumentation, theoretical possibilities, and so on. These contributions may serve a political function within philosophical debate narrowly construed so far as they contribute to a social understanding for the immediate circle of specialists. This political function is more apparent so far as it contributes to a wider social understanding of rationality and expertise, including forms of self-understanding and social presentation on the part of experts of all sorts.

The distinction here between what is internal and what is external to specifically philosophical debate is not necessarily clear or stable. It is not obvious that once beyond the realm of professional discussion we have for that reason departed from philosophical discussion. Further, it is not clear that once we have moved from philosophical issues as traditionally understood, we have left behind philosophical problems or reasoning. With a communications reconstruction of philosophical practice and with the idea of philosophical mediation, we not only see how traditional argumentation can be reconstructed in its political dimensions, we may also see how specifically philosophical functions have been and can be served without corresponding to received self-understandings of philosophy. I have touched on some of these in referring to the use of philosophical ideas in the social understanding and self-presentation of intellectuals. When social scientists appeal to notions of cognitive autonomy developed by modern philosophers of knowledge, are they making nonphilosophical (but political) use of philosophical ideas? Or are they tacitly involving themselves in a debate over their authority claims, a debate whose politics cannot be so easily separated from live philosophical questions?

In speaking earlier of democratic philosophy as a trend of contemporary criticism I already offered an answer to this question. If minority critics of mainstream social science challenge claims about objectivity and method, this involves them in more than a repudiation of specific strategies and uses of research. It also involves them in debates over rationality both as it bears on specific intellectual problems and as it bears on the presuppositions and functions of social science in a racially divided society. Insofar as such critics question the self-understanding of proponents of value-free social science, they also question the philosophical construction of the elements of that understanding. Implicitly they contribute to the formulation of alternative understandings.

This suggests that exploring a conception of philosophy as mediating activity may contribute to a normative conception of democratic philosophy. In particular, the critical reconstruction of claims about rationality within political contexts raises the question of the philosophical component of political questions about expertise. From a democratic perspective, these questions imply that the philosophical aspects of certain political questions may require a democratic political participation in philosophically consequential discussion.

The idea of philosophical mediation, then, reveals a host of issues that bear on the intersection of philosophy and politics. And this kind of reflection may broaden our understanding of politics and philosophy both. But a consideration of some general features of the historical setting in which this discussion takes place had better precede consideration of the specifics of philosophical mediation.

Paradoxes Regarding Knowledge and Politics Today

Any attempt to explore the democratic potential of contemporary United States confronts two paradoxes. First, virtually all aspects of social experience are affected by politics, yet there is a diminishing public interest in political questions. A second, related paradox concerns the cultural response to the continuing extension of the place of specialized knowledge in social life: as we rely increasingly on systematically organized knowledge, irrationalist themes assume a deeper hold on our culture. Because politics and knowledge are so closely

intertwined, these paradoxes together indicate a profound ambivalence toward modern social capacities. Let me say something more
about each of these paradoxes in turn.

Depoliticization and the Growth of Political Practices

That the role of politics has increased can be seen in the increase of
activity devoted to assessing and regulating social life. In addition to
classical liberal concerns with protection of property and person,
defense of the nation, and pursuit of the "general welfare," many
aspects of human agency have today become the focus of political
intervention. Institutional practices now cultivate forms of individual
and collective identity, articulate practical goals, examine and super-
vise social relations, and measure and promote human capacities. We
find the pursuit of these concerns in all sorts of institutional settings
beyond their traditional location in the family: in education, work,
health care, marketing, and the military.

What is novel about our time is not the existence of such activities
but their magnitude. And if it seems strange to speak of them as
politics, that may only be a measure of the inadequate extent to which
we have made them an object of public discussion. "Politics" seems an
appropriate term to describe the direct exercise of power regarding
issues of wide social concern. In any case, it is not only because they
receive insufficient public attention that it is worthwhile making an
issue of such practices. In addition, they represent exercises of power
for which there is by and large no effective means for establishing
responsibility and regulation. In many cases, these activities exist
outside formally political institutions. Frequently, when they do figure
within political institutions they are not the focus of conventional
political concern, but are made matters of bureaucratic and professional expertise.

Another reason to explore the political aspects of such practices
is that their emergence has coincided with the decline of conventional
political activity to which I have already alluded. These tacitly political
practices are part of a wider evolution of socially reflexive activities.
But there has not been a corresponding development of appropriate
forms of social understanding and regulation. Instead, in recent years
political discourse on the cultivation of democratic capacities has declined. This decline can be seen in diminishing participation in elec-

tions, highly selective and abstract statement of important social is-sues, reliance on advertising and marketing techniques funded on a massive scale by vested interests, and so on. My suggestion is that the decline of conventional electoral politics and the rise of new un-acknowledged politics is more than a coincidence. Part of the burden of the following discussion is to show how these developments figure within a wider impasse in contemporary political life, one that is marked by significant forms of alienation as well as by new kinds of democratic possibility.

Irrationalism and the Growth of Specialized Knowledge

The other paradox of contemporary politics, though a matter of cul-ture, bears nonetheless on the understanding and practice of politics. It is a truism of contemporary social commentary that science and tech-nology contribute to qualitative changes in the character of modern society. There is no consensus about the nature or implications of these changes, but within them the role of all sorts of abstract knowledges and methodical rationalities is beyond dispute. The computer has become the emblem of this new age, but the cognitive and technical dimensions of it are far wider. They include not only other sophisti-cated technologies but also many social techniques that are charac-terized more by distinctive refinements of reasoning and social interaction than by specific forms of hardware or software (e.g., man-agement and other interactive strategies). I have already touched upon some of these developments in speaking of new forms of politics. In whatever way we understand them, social powers of all sorts are increasingly promoted through forms of knowledge and rationality.

The paradox in this regard lies in the coincidence of these develop-ments with a deepening cultural irrationalism. Modern culture has always exhibited a deep ambivalence about commitments associated with the Enlightenment. The classic statements of rational method were developed in confrontation with theology and skepticism. But at issue today is not the cognitive powers of secular reason so much as their value. Irrationalism today assumes many forms, from shopping-mall astrology to postmodernist assaults on the Enlightenment tradi-tion. In between we find the more dangerous forms of this distrust of rationality: the loss of confidence in rational debate of common issues, the ironic attitude of the educated classes to their acquired powers, the loss of relation to the task of forging common social identities and values. The point is not mainly to criticize these tendencies as self-indulgent or morally misguided. Rather, we need to explore how they reflect fundamental difficulties in modern society and the evolution of human capacities. We need to examine the paradox that these developments accompany social development that is experienced as driven by science and technology. The paradox has to do with social relations to reason, but is at the same time a profoundly political matter.

These conjunctions of more politics and less political consciousness, more knowledge and less respect for knowing, figure within a period whose dominant sociological interpretation concentrates on the growing importance of abstract knowledge. Theories of the "postindustrial society," the "knowledge society," and so on, emphasize the cultivation, distribution, and control of specialized competencies in production and in economic activity more generally as well as in culture (see Bell 1976a). Critics on the Left and on the Right both speak of a "new class" whose claims, power, and frustrations are bound up with its cultural capacities and their function in the evolving social order (e.g., Konrad and Szelenyi 1979; Gouldner 1979; Steinfells 1979). Regardless of the merits of specific sociological and political interpretations, the historical trends they emphasize must be acknowledged: industry is increasingly dependent on new forms of high technology; nonindustrial services play a growing economic role; struggles over the construction and control of information are increasingly important in politics; and cultural activity is changing with the evolution of new media.

It is not difficult to propose an account of these paradoxes: our political culture may be declining precisely because it is overloaded by the extension of unacknowledged politics. Conventional politics becomes discredited as it fails to grapple with the exercises of power that are confronted in everyday life. And irrationalism is not an implausible response to the experience of a reason associated with powers that frequently seem as arbitrary as they are irresponsible. Familiarity with some kinds of rationality quite understandably breeds contempt. But accounts of this kind do not get us very far toward a conception of these paradoxes that is conducive to political and cultural ways out of them. At stake is a viable future for democratic thought and practice. The retreat from confidence in politics and in modern rationality amounts to a crisis of democratic culture.

Such a crisis comes at a time when the idea of democracy has a special urgency. This is evident in the reconstruction of formerly Communist societies. The nature and practice of democracy is also an urgent issue elsewhere, for example, Latin American countries attempting to replace authoritarian institutions. The difficulties exhibited by Western democracies in understanding and responding to these changes illustrates how uncertain the practical conditions and implications of democracy are for them too.

The aim of this study is to contribute to the discussion of an appropriate democratic politics in the context that underlies the paradoxes I have mentioned so far. A guiding claim, which I hope the argument supports, is that the problem of knowledge, and of philosophical reflection on knowledge, today assumes a direct political importance. It is important for any approach to politics, but especially for a democratic approach, since at issue is the status of the universal capacities that are required for a democratic polity.

Chapter 2

Political Impasse
and Liberalism

Impasse and Structure

The paradoxical standing of politics and rationality in contemporary societies contributes to an impasse in political life. "Impasse" here means an incapacity not only to find political solutions to outstanding difficulties but also to find the terms in which to articulate those difficulties in a concrete and illuminating way. The notion of impasse seems appropriate because the retreat from conventional politics coincides with deepening social problems that have a structural character. The idea of an impasse implies not simply the existence of difficult or unresolved problems, nor does it have exclusively to do with persisting injustices and oppressions. Rather, use of this idea implies that specific issues count as symptoms or expressions of problems with the framework in which social action takes place, and so with the ability of society to maintain itself as a stable process. Impasse is reflected in a society's repeated failure to resolve problems that represent threats to its constitutive institutions. Poverty and racism are symptoms of an impasse if they reflect a crisis in society's ability to reproduce itself under changing circumstances. Violence, whether as international conflict, street crime, or intrafamilial strife reflects an impasse if it figures in the disintegration of institutions where alternative ways of organizing social life cannot be found. Analogous claims hold regarding economic issues (e.g., the international debt crisis, unemployment in the Third World) and ecological problems (e.g., global warming, contamination of the food supply, and depletion of the ozone layer). The ecological case illustrates how society's inability to look to the future with hopeful expectation or with reasonable provision for coming generations constitutes a political impasse.

I shall not try to prove that such an impasse exists today, but I hope to make the idea intelligible and its application plausible. As I have already suggested, the idea of an impasse is not precisely or exclusively a matter of seemingly insoluble problems. It is also a matter of the quality of problems, and of society's capacity to respond to them. That such an impasse exists today may be reflected by phenomena I have already cited, for example, the tendency for politicians faced with ecological issues to seek short-term solutions while avoiding systemic questions and the challenge of a long-term vision. Similarly, it is a matter of the retreat from conventional politics to which I have already alluded—the decline of participation in voting, the increasing domination of political discourse by marketing techniques, and the general drift toward politics as spectacles of which citizens become the easily distracted yet anxiety-ridden consumers. But perhaps even these are merely symptoms.

Conceiving Structure

Impasse, more than the failure of individuals, suggests the inadequacy of existing forms of agency, institutions, and practices. An impasse implies fundamental structural problems with extant and possible kinds of political agency. A political impasse is bound up with general conditions of political life and with our capacity to understand as well as to act upon them.

Structure per se, however, is difficult to define precisely. Structure concerns the most general organizational features of society; it is as I employ the word here, a more general concept than that of institution or practice, and may be analyzed in terms of either or both of the latter. To emphasize structure, institutions, and practices in this way is not to neglect individuals but to treat them relationally and historically. Emphasizing structure does not deny that individuals can, through reflection, conflict, and choice, act in ways that modify the relations in which they live. But it does imply that this activity takes place in constructed situations, and asserts that the terms of such activity are historical products. The distinction between different levels of relational analysis (structure, institution, practice) permits a conception of constitution and change as contexts for individuality.

Structure so conceived, then, is not an aspect of social life that operates entirely independently of the awareness of individuals. Nor is it some variant of ideas of organization derived from Saussure's linguistics. The structural thinking I mean to pursue is not "structuralist" in that sense, though I do not mean to exclude the usefulness of structural or semiotic ideas for specific problems. Thinking about structure may entail the use of linguistic ideas precisely because structure does involve forms of social awareness as they are embedded in social objectivities that transcend and sometimes overwhelm consciousness. Structure, in this sense, is that quality of a society that enables it to draw upon, condition, and undercut the conscious action of individuals. Structure organizes both what individuals can do and what it is unthinkable for them to do. Thus structure incorporates what Marx talks about when he advocates a materialist approach to history that places agency always within conditions and relations that constrain, inform, and distort social understanding.

In this light, the form particular issues take and the implications of their being resolved or not depend on structural features of society as a whole. Pursuing a historical use of the idea of structure, I suggest that the relevant structural features today are ones that characterize modern society as such. On this view, the political impasse we now confront is one that has to do with some of the most general features that make our society modern. One implication of this claim is that the impasse of politics is in part an impasse of the quality and forms of contemporary politics. A structural perspective is required to grasp the impasse of contemporary politics as a historical phenomenon of modern society. Structural reflection allows us to pursue the question of what is specific to modern politics and what is needed for a politics that is consciously responsive to contemporary structural change.

Institutional Differentiation

The features I have in mind as characteristic of modern structure are undergoing fundamental evolution. The impasse of politics emerges from this evolution and contributes to it.

During the rise of modern society the prevailing institutional framework included market economies that were relatively independent of traditional political and cultural regulation. With markets came political states that accepted exclusion from direct regulation of production and consumption while defending political as well as economic rights for individuals. In contrast to feudalism, both economy and state became for the most part free of explicit or systematic dependence on religious principles, even for legitimacy. At the same time, cultural evolution gave rise to new forms of art, both elite and popular, that had no official relation to the rest of social life. The differentiation of market, culture, and politics provides the institutional framework in which modern politics establishes its specific powers and resources and faces the official limitations on what it may do. As I noted earlier, this framework has facilitated the burgeoning of practices whose political qualities it cannot recognize explicitly. More generally, there is today a growing overlap and blurring of boundaries between economics, culture, and politics that changes the terms of modern action.

National Organization of Society

All three spheres—market economy, secular liberal state, and private culture—contributed to nationhood as the paradigm for society's most general institutional organization and for its most general collective identity. The state has been tailored to a national market and provides political culture as well as a framework of power that subordinates regional and minority identities and practices. This structural feature of modern society becomes increasingly vulnerable as institutions and practices increasingly become multinational, transnational, or regional in orientation. Though the unity of modern national societies has always been exaggerated, even where it has been most completely embodied, and has frequently been contested, contemporary challenges to the national organization of social life seem to represent qualitatively new developments. Nationally oriented culture is challenged by regional, minority, and religious movements on the one side and by multinational mass culture on the other. The coherence of nationally organized economies and the power of nation-states to act in relation to them is weakened by a commerce organized by multinational corporations in whose strategies for production and marketing national factors are but one of a variety of considerations. The legacy of industrialization imposes another kind of cross-national reality to which the agency of the nation-state is ill suited to respond: ecological damage requires the response of international agencies.

Orientation to Labor and Growth

Within the modern institutional framework nations seek to advance productive wealth as the precondition and sign of social well-being. From being the precondition of social existence, labor in the modern period became, in an unprecedented way, the focus of intellectual and moral concern as well as of political strategies. Though this is in many respects an outcome of the institutional imperatives of a capitalist market economy, it is not solely a matter of economic life, as can be seen from the evolution of technologically oriented science on the one hand and the rise and vicissitudes of the work ethic on the other. In our period, consumption has assumed as much importance as production, with a myriad of paradoxical results. But however unstable a mix this may seem to construct, it serves an abiding orientation to the imperative of economic growth. And this is an imperative that today is increasingly invoked in the most disparate institutional spheres of society.

The modern orientation to labor and growth may not seem to be "structural" in quite the same sense as the institutional or national organization of modern society, or it may seem to be inherent in the components of the modern institutional framework. But because these features of modern society are so crucial for issues of politics, they deserve separate emphasis.

The Historical Fact of Structural Change

In general, the structural aspects of modern society I have identified are so closely interrelated that it would be difficult to explore any one of them without encountering the others. This can be illustrated by reference to the modern market economy. Its emergence within the institutional framework of modern Europe was inseparable from the rise of national economies and the culture of work and acquisitiveness. But the distinctions between these structural aspects of the modern world are worth drawing because they each raise distinctive issues in the present political setting.

First, the institutional differentiation proper to the modern world has been altered as economics, politics, and culture have come to overlap and interpenetrate in ways that compromise long held ideas and ideals of institutional integrity without restoring premodern forms of social integration. The mixed economy involves systematic state intervention in the market, even as debates over policy seem more than ever influenced by appeals to economic necessity. The evolution of the culture industry has helped make the marketing of culture an important sphere of economic activity, and has helped transformed the forms of public political debate. Since forms of what I earlier described as unacknowledged politics figure prominently in these developments, it is reasonable to link structural changes on the level of institutional differentiation to fundamental issues about politics.

Second, though the nation-state remains a key institution in domestic and global politics, it has come to be rivaled on both levels by institutions and practices that are both super- and subnational in significant respects. Multinational corporations, international economic agencies (e.g., the IMF, World Bank), military-political power blocs (e.g., NATO), as well as regional combinations that overflow specific national boundaries (e.g., national and ethnic identities in Africa, Arab nationalism, regional movements in the former USSR), all illustrate the growing importance of institutions and social identities that do not coincide with national organization. The difficulty of regulating multinational corporations and the instability of existing political structures in the face of regional movements illustrate the political problems associated with this decline in the nation-state.

Finally, while it may seem odd to speak of the changing significance of labor and economic growth in a world plagued with unprecedented poverty and hunger, the fact remains that traditional understandings in these areas are rapidly losing their applicability. In part this has to do with the value of labor as individual activity and as a universal need. In part it has to do with the promise of economic growth for ensuring human well-being. Environmental trends provide one basis for rethinking standard conceptions: the environment can no longer tolerate growth in the by-products of industrial production (carbon dioxide and global warming, pollution of the water supply, etc.). Growth measured by conventional economic terms cannot accommodate survival needs in these regards. But conventional notions of growth have been found wanting in other respects too. Within advanced economies, these conceptions can only be sustained by a credit-driven economy that promotes consumerism. Today the credit structure is in crisis, and the satisfactions of endless increases of consumption are in doubt. Sociologists (e.g., Bell 1976b) speak of the clash of consumerist motivations with the work ethic. Dissatisfaction with the quality of work raises issues of need measured by the quality of activity as opposed to the acquisition of things. Lest these concerns be regarded as solely the privilege of the world's minority living in the advanced industrial societies (though undoubtedly they are that too), it should be remembered that it is doubtful whether the application of advanced technologies needed to modernize underdeveloped economies can ever accommodate full employment. Though the issues are very different in different parts of the world, familiar ideas of growth and employment do not provide adequate terms for mapping a viable future. It is hardly necessary to note that contemporary political discourse has hardly begun to register the seriousness of the issues rethinking labor and growth imply.

Each of the structural aspects of the modern world thus is a site both of significant change and of profound and for the most part unconfronted political questions. If these questions are not stated in terms of the structural complexes of which they are a part, political action that addresses them will be seriously compromised in its coherence and effectiveness.

Nevertheless, to speak of a political *impasse* is to take the discussion a step further. Structural change could alter the terms of politics without undermining political agency in a fundamental way. But my claim is that confronting the issues posed by structural change requires addressing both structure and politics directly. Structure, as I have conceived it, already involves the historical nature of politics, and the changes I have described have had the effect of compromising existing forms of politics without providing adequate alternatives to them.

I have spoken of structure as the most general ways society positively shapes and negatively constrains historical forms of human activity. I have identified aspects of structure that contribute to what is distinctive of the modern period and that are undergoing changes important for contemporary politics. It is in relation to this structural change that I have characterized a contemporary political impasse.

Politics today by and large does not acknowledge the extent or depth of structural issues and so does not provide the medium for reflective, and therefore for democratic, response to these structural issues. To say this is not to deny that there is any political response at all to structural issues, or to suggest that a political impasse results in structural stasis. Rather it is to observe constraints on the forms possible structural change may take, and to suggest corresponding distortions of political life. An impasse of politics is not an absence of politics, any more than the absence of democratic regulation of structural change excludes such change.

Politics, Interpretation, and Knowledge

Using ideas of structural change and political impasse, I have described the context in which democratic reflection finds itself today. To further illumine the link between such politics and philosophy necessitates consideration of other features of the contemporary political scene, in particular, features of liberalism. This is not only because liberalism is the dominant framework of political understanding, but also because it embodies the prevailing synthesis of philosophical and political understanding to which democratic reflection must turn its critical scrutiny.

Liberalism today is marked by a combination of institutional triumph and political exhaustion. The triumph is found in the hegemony of free-market conservatism in much of the West and in the rise of the market ideal in the East. The fundamental liberal claim that human fulfillment follows from a politics that enables the free play of market forces has not been so widely honored since the nineteenth century. But in other respects liberal politics is in profound disarray: explicit political discourse has degenerated; numerous forms of power have emerged in practices that escape scrutiny or accountability in received political forms; and the philosophical foundations of liberalism have been widely repudiated. The connection between economic liberalism and political democracy becomes ever more obscure.

Perhaps the condition of contemporary liberalism can be understood by contrasting the triumph of specific liberal slogans with the problematic standing of liberalism as the dominant culture of modern politics. If we think of liberalism as such a culture, it is not surprising that it has become problematic, given the transformation of so many of those structural features of the modern world for which liberalism has provided a political understanding. Liberalism historically has been a politics of societies organized as nation-states, yet, as I have noted, a host of developments has brought into question the promise of the nation as the focus of collective identity and as the main organization of political power: transnational corporations, the international division of labor, regional power blocs, minority, feminist, and fundamentalist movements, global communications, and international mass culture. Liberalism also presupposes the institutional differentiation of economics, politics, and culture, yet these spheres have come to overlap and merge in ways that make each an immediate practical component of the others; today the study of one sphere separate from the others is methodologically indefensible. A third historical feature of liberalism as the political culture of modernity is its understanding of the central human vocation as being some form of labor and its commitment to a progressive transformation of nature that aims at a perpetual increase of productivity and economic growth. The impossibility today of full employment and the ecological consequences of unending growth have made these assumptions untenable. Structural change brings fundamental commitments of liberal political understanding into question.

To speak of liberalism as a political culture is to emphasize its development of the dominant political interpretations in which social conditions and lines of political action are conceived. As such a culture, liberalism has been distinguished by its reliance on modern philosophy. That is, liberalism understands the world as open to objective knowledge that can be applied effectively and produce desirable and morally defensible ends. Agents are potentially rational subjects, and action is best pursued on the basis of reflectively conceived strategies. Conceptualization and reasoning that represent the world are both possible and can become central to culture generally. On this account, liberalism is a rationalist understanding of human action; it interprets the evolving division of labor along rational lines and articulates the role of specialists and leaders in terms of rational capacities and authority. Liberalism, like modern philosophy more generally, provides a self-understanding for modern intellectuals, an understanding that treats public power as a kind of knowledge-politics.

The broad historical thesis that provides the background for my more specific arguments, then, is that it is not just socialism or the politics of the welfare state that have been overwhelmed by recent historical change. The more general impasse of contemporary political understanding is embodied in the inadequacies of liberal knowledge-politics. The passing of the structural presuppositions of liberalism may, on this claim, also be the passing of the conditions for the political application of the specific cognitive style promoted by modern philosophy.

In this light, the postmodernist challenge to the philosophical foundations of liberalism can be construed as an important historical symptom of an impasse that is both political and intellectual. In fact, I argue that rather than provide a critique of liberalism, postmodern irony about subjects, representation, and totality both illustrates and extends the impasse of liberalism. In exploring this claim, I argue that postmodernism not only consists of philosophical arguments or cultural practices, but figures in the evolution of contemporary politics as such. Postmodernism from this angle is an aspect of contemporary liberalism, the practical self-understanding, so to speak, of the impasse of knowledge-politics.

Political Understanding and Liberalism

If it is true that modern abstract knowledge figures importantly in the way modern structure is registered in social consciousness, then it may be plausible to draw a connection between inadequately grasped structural change and such reactions against modern Enlightenment as occur in discussions of postmodernism and arguments over knowledge-power. This is a preliminary hypothesis, but one that characterizes the kind of interpretive reflection that is a necessary feature of democratic philosophy. Historical interpretation is part of the practical work of a philosophy that places itself in a critical relation to the role of modern philosophy in shaping modern political understanding.

The Idea of Political Understanding

Politics is inherently interpretive: political activity must make sense of the realities it hopes to influence. Reliance on modern epistemological ideas has allowed political thought to suppress or minimize this interpretive side of politics. And casting itself in terms of theoretical knowledge, whether as philosophical theory or political science, modern political reflection has also minimized its own interpretive and its own political commitments. One consequence of this self-conception has

been a distortion of the ways knowledge functions within policy formation and decision making. Adopting a contemplative understanding of
theory contributes to understanding practice as applied knowledge.

What is lost is not just clarity about the interpretive side of politics
but recognition of the social nature of that interpretation. Within the
interpretive process, social relations are organized as well as portrayed. Power that may be exercised in this process is ignored in the
cognitivist understanding of politics. The suppression of the interpretive side of politics affects the nature of political action itself. When
political interpretation has been conceived as theoretical knowledge,
the practical side of politics, the relation of interpretation to practice,
has assumed technological form and has opened itself to the criticisms
of such thinkers as Arendt (1958) and Habermas (1970).

Their critique of liberalism states traditional concerns about contrac-
tualism, possessive individualism, abstract reason, and so on, in terms
of the treatment of forms of action and relations to social worlds. For
example, Arendt criticizes the reduction of social action to versions of
labor, and Habermas shows how liberals have tended to obscure social
interaction by thinking of action in exclusively instrumental terms.
According to this line of analysis, one of the resulting deficiencies of
liberalism is its inability adequately to conceptualize or appreciate
social and political bonds and their reliance on meaning, in the senses
both of communication and of culture. A consequence of this inability
is liberalism's failure to conceptualize either social "worlds" or political
"publics," ideas important for reflecting on the political impasse as
well as for conceiving a democratic response to it.

Their importance lies in their relation to the theme of social or
political understanding. Once we acknowledge the function of objectivistic knowledge as a form of political understanding, we have to
develop a conception of what is being understood and to see that it is
itself a medium of meaning. To emphasize understanding is to acknowledge that social experience is linguistically organized. Our relations to others not only involve communication, but turn on the ability
to assume or achieve common understandings about social conventions, purposes, and values. The idea of a network of meanings and
assumptions provides us with a preliminary idea of what constitutes a
specifically social world. It is not just the sum of individuals pursuing
their needs, but involves the medium of their reciprocal awareness and
dependence as well as that of power and ideology. The problem with

objectivistic knowledge is precisely a reductionism that blinds it to the specific features of these properties of worldhood.

Worldhood in this sense denotes a distinctively social reality. The distinction between world and public parallels the distinction between social being in general and specifically political existence and experience. Political understanding, then, figures as the capacity to interpret social experience and orient action in political terms. At issue is not some essence of politics but historically evolving forms of social judgment in which tradition mediates our relation to existing problems.

Political understanding thus implies a concern with common affairs. But here there is a great deal of ambiguity, both because public affairs can be approached in highly indirect ways and because ostensibly public orientations can be strategies for self-interest. These ambiguities are all the greater because of the political impasse, which does not result so much in an absolute decline of politics as in the emergence of covert forms of political action and the diversion of political energies into indirect and often narrow paths.

In this light we may distinguish politics in the full sense as that political action which constitutes a public. Such a politics involves a special relation to worldhood and to common issues. Politics establishes a culture of public discussion, of common definitions and concerns. As such it is an idealization that is all the more valuable for its being detached from actual practice. With this ideal we can note salient features of covert politics and of diverted political energies as well as of initiatives that may redefine important aspects of political life.

We need to distinguish a public from a world. Both are contingent and fragile constructions. World is more general and may contain publics. On the other hand, the breakup of publics may threaten the integrity of a world. Worlds are constituted by common meanings that extend beyond, but provide a necessary background and resource for, political action and the publics it may be able to construct.

In relation to publics we may distinguish aspects of political understanding: Horizontally (relations within the present) we actively respond to each other in acts of mutual recognition, interaction/communication. Social reality is relational in ways that may be captured with the idea of the collectively generated and generating play of social appearances, where this term is not meant to hint at the existence of a more profound, though hidden, reality. In contrast, the vertical dimension (situating the present in relation to past and future) sets our present interactions in relation to tradition on the one hand and future possibilities on the other. Tradition may be fragmented and the future uncertain. Received meanings may be little more than shells over compulsive ongoing demands of social systems. But under certain circumstances, political construction through appearances makes possible action that, for Arendt, permits humans in community to raise themselves above the animal functions of material reproduction. Liberalism and socialism have, for her, typically failed to sustain any recognition of the construction of a social world in these respects.

Political understanding involves the construction of a social world, of a common identity and shared experiences in relation to ongoing issues. The metaphor of a story, a narrative, brings out features of shared experience but also of the effort to keep lives in some kind of desirable interrelation. The construction of narratives is the constitution of contexts of meaning and can be seen against the contrasting erosion of meaning inherent in structural change that threatens the integrity of worlds and publics. The metaphor breaks down so far as the story is not constructed from outside the developments it depicts and is not constructed from the standpoint of its having an end. But the teleological aspect is important for the unification of social life around common tasks or problems. The evolution of political understanding is inseparable from debates over the identification and progress of such tasks and problems. Thinking of politics in terms of narrative is relevant for democracy but also for stating issues about the evolution of political understanding today. The idea of a narrative is of course a simplification. Social life is a complex of narratives that overlap, intersect, break off, undergo drastic changes and revisions, and so on. Their development is inseparable from the evolution of political judgment.

Philosophy and Political Understanding

In my argument, philosophy itself is to be seen both as a dimension of political understanding and as an important contributing factor to the evolution of political understanding in society as a whole. From this perspective, philosophy must grasp itself as a practice that promotes interpretive effects in definite social circumstances. While this conception follows the idea of a historical evolution of social structure and social understanding, it clashes with the traditional account of philosophy developed in the modern period. The epistemological understanding of philosophy pursues the ideal of context-independent knowledge and conceives philosophy as being independent of social and historical factors. An interpretive self-understanding of philosophy, on the other hand, conceives philosophy's work as context responsive and philosophy itself as situated in historical conditions as an agent interactive with other practices.

This interpretive conception implies a philosophy concerned with a political understanding responsive to structural change and critical of intellectual practices that contribute to an obscuring of political dilemmas. At the same time, forging an adequate political response is a practical task that cannot be accomplished by theoretical reflection on its own. But breaking with the epistemological tradition implies a philosophy that is not purely contemplative. How are we to understand philosophical practice and its bearing on politics? For philosophy simply to identify itself with political practice is not only to obscure what philosophy's specific promise may be, but also to risk returning surreptitiously to the role of a cosmic legislator. The question is, how can specifically philosophical practice contribute to the wider practical problems of contemporary politics?

Answering this question may depend on emphasizing the shared interpretive functions of philosophy and politics and on exploring these functions in a way that bears on the historical problems facing politics: problems rooted in structural change. The break with philosophy as contemplative knowledge neither implies a neglect of its highly abstract and reflective character nor a rejection of its cognitive and rational aspects. At the same time, this break implies incorporating into the idea of philosophy a dependence on other practices, a fallibility, and a perspectivism. Philosophy is neither autonomous nor self-validating nor free of particularities of interest and experience.

To say that philosophy is interpretive, however, is not to say that philosophy is *merely* interpretive, as though it comprised simply overblown opinion. For interpretation itself makes rational, or universalizing, claims. Interpretation is the cultural function of philosophy as an abstract and encompassing form of social sense making. And this sense making observes and cultivates standards of rationality and criticism by which it can be assessed. This "cultivation" is not a matter of creation from whole cloth but an elaboration on the achievements of other practices, for example, in science, but not only there. In any case, the specific sense making in which modern philosophy has engaged not only draws from but is practically keyed to the specific features of the modern world.

Liberalism as Epistemologically Encoded Understanding

Liberalism as Conceived Here

My claims about political understanding and the role within it of philosophy have remained very general, despite the references to specifically modern conditions and practices. More particular claims about political understanding entail elaboration of the relation between it and abstract knowledge. By emphasizing liberalism's characteristics as a knowledge-politics, I have already suggested a conception of liberalism that supplements traditional conceptions of it as individualist, concerned with freedom, tied to market society, and so on. I suggested that in key respects abstract social knowledge is a primary form of modern social understanding and that liberalism incorporates ideas about such knowledge into its construction of modern political understanding.

Liberalism, like modern philosophy in general, underplays its own interpretive role. And in so doing, it fails to explore the extent to which politics constructs political understanding and the political agency of which understanding is a part. This feature of liberalism, more than parallel with modern philosophy, is a feature also of modern philosophy. One could put the point somewhat differently and speak of the extent to which modern philosophy is part of modern politics. Philosophy's suppression of its interpretive character may be itself an aspect of modern philosophy's political function.

Emphasizing the overlap of liberalism with modern philosophy throws light on the relation between the challenge to epistemological philosophy and the impasse of contemporary politics. If philosophy is itself part of political life, then the debate over postpositivist philosophy is simply a moment in the larger political discussion. If philosophy has shaped modern political understanding in important ways, then politics has a philosophical dimension. Philosophy becomes interpretive as politics seeks a wider understanding of itself.

Epistemology and Knowledge-Politics

From this perspective, the epistemological reconstruction of abstract knowledge as autonomously functioning pure theory provides an organizing framework for the modern understanding of society and politics. That is, it depicts modern structure in a certain way and constructs a corresponding notion of social experience and political action. As epistemological reflection, modern philosophy assumes the role of the self-reflection of rational subjects. It constructs a notion of knowledge that implies a metaphysics, a relation of subjects to objects, and corresponding forms of action and communication. The metaphysics implied is one of fixed objective necessities confronted by subjects with a certain rational potential, and the communication between subjects is conducted on the basis of such knowledge.

The metaphysics of modern philosophy thus offers a specific construal of the structural differentiation of modern institutions and the resulting experience of structure. Similarly, it offers terms in which to understand the composition of the modern social collective (either atomistically or as the projection of the individual subject onto the whole). With its absolutization of reified objectivity, it treats structural tendencies, like the growth requirements of the market economy, as necessities inscribed in the objective world.

The experience of structural objectivity is thus ratified by philosophy as being necessary and as possessing the means for rational insight and action. The form of practical reason follows: it involves the application of objectively determined necessities as the means for seeking desired or morally justified goals. But what is implied is not just the *form* of action but the necessary resources for genuinely rational action, namely, rational theoretical insight into the workings of the objective world. And this implies social content beyond the structural features already cited: only those equipped with such insight will be qualified to act politically. This in turn makes room for hierarchy and a division of labor, for power relations. In the context of these relations objective knowledge remains awareness of socially constructed dynamics: the insight of specialists is a relation to social activity as a whole.

Thus a differentiated social world underlies the epistemological and metaphysical conceptions of modern philosophy as incorporated into liberalism. It is a world in which the political construction of a public receives scant explicit attention, even though the political interpretations of liberalism contribute precisely to the construction of such a public.

Liberalism can be seen as fostering certain narratives, certain themes and styles—for example, the narrative of society as a nation, of a kind of politics, of economic participation in certain terms. Thus the idea of narrative can be used for distinguishing different kinds of political understanding as well as for identifying a key element of political understanding as such. And perhaps the political impasse can be equated with the decline of certain kinds of narrative and with the capacity to frame political narratives altogether. Differences and conflicts within political understanding can be approached in these terms. Fundamental differences may be linked to different narratives. They may be tied to different access to or experience with the preconditions of narrative construction, and may oppose those who reject "grand narratives" against those still engaged in traditional meaning schemes. More significant are differences between the narrative perspectives of those who wield power and those of the majority who participate in at best passive ways. The fact of this divergence is of concern to a democratic view and points to issues of power and ideology that accompany concern with social appearances in class society.

Political Understanding
and the Philosophical Tradition

To identify interpretive functions in liberalism is to go beyond the limits of liberalism's epistemologically couched self-understanding. It is to identify political functions that liberalism carries out without acknowledging that it is doing so. This emphasis on interpretation is at once an analysis of what liberalism has historically been and a critique of liberalism's account of politics. Widening our sense of politics becomes important in a period of change that affects the conditions and practices of politics.

While the emphasis here has been on various dimensions of the political understanding liberalism has provided, the aim has also been to stress that this political understanding has in important ways taken the form of philosophical argument about knowledge. Liberalism does not just borrow from modern epistemology, it assimilates this philosophy into the social and political understanding it provides for the modern world and the working of the modern political public. In fact, the epistemological project, conjoined with the metaphysics it develops in the modern period, already amounts to an interpretive scheme proper to a society in which abstract knowledge plays a key constitutive role. Over the past century, the idea of modern philosophy as an interpretive scheme proper to a specific historical world has been a theme of many of the most influential thinkers. They have sometimes seen themselves as philosophers, sometimes as the grave diggers of philosophy, and sometimes have never resolved their ambivalence about philosophy: philosophy as ideology, as perspective, as worldview, as wish fulfillment, as ontological forgetfulness, as linguistic confusion, as fantasy of knowledge-power, as phallocentrism, and so on.

So there is nothing new in treating modern philosophy as a form of interpretation despite its aspirations to pure theory. But as this list of intellectual positions makes clear, to treat philosophy as interpretation is to raise questions not only about the character of this interpretation (what is being interpreted? who is interpreting? what does interpretation yield? etc.), but also about its relation to the rational aims of the Enlightenment tradition. To treat of philosophical reflection as interpretation is not inherently to relativize it out of rational existence. Interpretations may have cognitive value, and they may inform rational practice. But an interpretive scheme that denies its own interpretive character cannot be expected to be clear about the precise nature of its rational accomplishments. Thus we may expect that historical forms of social awareness couched in the language of modern philosophy will be open to challenge.

In the discussion of liberalism in the next chapter, I consider how modern philosophy contributes to various types of social consciousness spread throughout modern society. For the moment let me touch upon only one aspect of this analysis so as to develop the programmatic aims of the argument as a whole. I referred above to the tacit social hierarchy built into modern philosophical claims about knowledge. If a certain discipline and capacity is required to realize the human cognitive potential, then so far as society requires abstract knowledge, only individuals with the required capacity and discipline will be qualified for key positions of authority. Mill argues thus for the composition of his legislative commission (1972, chaps. 5 and 10), as Hegel does for the qualifications of his civil servants (1991, 328–36). So far as liberalism builds these ideas about knowledge into its account of the distribution of social tasks, it makes key claims of modern philosophy into aspects of modern political understanding in general and into the self-consciousness of modern political intellectuals in particular. And so far as it provides such grounds for holding positions of authority, modern philosophy helps remove the choice of officeholders and the nature of their functions from distinctively political scrutiny: they are measured by impersonal reason rather than political discussion.

This idea implies a sociological claim about philosophy itself, namely, that it is a social practice that, among other things, constructs the self-understanding of modern intellectuals, particularly with regard to the interrelation between their cognitive practices and their social authority. Such a construction figures as one aspect of the interpretive work of modern philosophy: it construes knowledge and the activity that generates it in a way that contributes to the understanding by intellectuals of their place in the modern social world and of their relation to the modern political public. This claim is consistent with a general tendency in the interpretivist turn in philosophy, that knowledge is to be seen as practically conditioned. But whether this approach is consistent with a reconstruction of rational capacities remains to be seen. Its critical side will be compromised if it proves to be a path to the self-defeating logic of the theses of knowledge-power or postmodernism.

Suggesting that philosophy be conceived as a practice that, among other things, contributes to the self-understanding of intellectuals is to portray philosophy as a kind of social mediation. Working out the nature and extent of this mediation as carried out by modern philosophy requires further exploration of its relation to liberalism. As such, the relation between philosophy and the structural features of modern society must be depicted socially as well as conceptually.

Philosophy understood in this way offers historical perspective on the problem of a postpositivist reflection that incorporates the insights of theories of knowledge-power and postmodernism without sacrificing continuity with the Enlightenment. Democratic philosophy must be conceived and developed as democratic mediation in the context of the interrelation of knowledge and social structure, expertise and the evolution of social agency. Philosophical interpretation must be treated in the setting of mediating functions, and a critical relation to that interpretation is possible only upon careful consideration of the issues and terms of mediation. Before turning to the problem of understanding specifics of modern philosophy in this light, it may be helpful to say more about the context of mediation, namely, the modern division of labor. With my discussion so far, I have in effect claimed that the division of labor should become a key philosophical idea.

Chapter 3

Democratic Philosophy: Democratic Mediation?

Pursuing the Idea of a Democratic Philosophy

I began with the question of a specifically democratic approach to philosophy. I have tried to establish a context for this question by discussing aspects of recent social, political, and intellectual history. The issue of a democratic approach to philosophy is posed in a setting in which politics itself is at issue and in which the need to rethink democracy is urgent not only because of the difficulties encountered by democratic movements but also because of the depth of conflict over the nature and scope of politics itself. Intimately conjoined with these conflicts are debates over rationality, debates that have to do ultimately with definitions of what is historically possible. My thesis, then, is that debates over philosophical questions are frequently connected to debates over politics and that a democratic politics needs a democratic philosophical reflection. The need to think of philosophy in social terms confronts us, further, with the question whether democratic philosophy is not as much a matter of the democratic practice of philosophy as it is a matter of reflection on conceptual issues that concern democratic politics. Because of the close relation between philosophy and the evolution of politics, exploring the idea of a democratic philosophy means rethinking the nature of philosophical activity, past and present.

What democracy means here remains undeveloped. The task of the study itself is partly to fill out some of the assumptions and objectives of a democratic philosophy, but it may be clear already that I am assuming that a democratic approach is promising and necessary for confronting ways politics and rationality have both become problematic in our setting. Conceptually and practically, democratic philosophy is committed to understandings and practices of rationality consistent with a democratic organization of social powers. On the one hand, this includes a commitment to Enlightenment ideals that steers between the dogmatism of the tradition (a dogmatism regarding the relations between knowledge and power) and the irrationalism of contemporary historicisms, including many that go under the heading "postmodernism." On the other hand, democratic philosophy as understood here is committed to a politics that is democratic not only because of the bankruptcy of justifications for hierarchy. Rather, it assumes the political value of that combination of rights, popular powers, and forms of solidarity that constitutes the core of the radical democratic tradition. An objective of the present study is to show that one reason the idea of a democratic philosophy is warranted is that it is possible to combine a historically minded commitment to aspects of Enlightenment universalism with such a political standpoint. Indeed, it is the argument here that in important respects these features of democratic philosophy are mutually illuminating.

"Radical democracy" is not sufficiently vague a term to escape the challenge posed by postmodernism to modern projects of social criticism and change, a challenge that is inseparable from postmodernism's historicizing attacks on Enlightenment conceptions of rationality. The capacity of democratic philosophy to respond to this line of challenge depends partly on the adequacy of its own response to issues about knowledge and power. Whether the present discussion is fruitful in this regard can only be judged on the basis of the argument as a whole. At this point, it may be useful in the light of these issues to develop in still tentative fashion the idea that a critical relation to Enlightenment requires thinking of rationality as embodied in social practices. More specifically, we need to consider further what it means to speak of philosophy, democratic or otherwise, as a social practice.

Philosophy as Intellectual Mediation

In what follows, the idea of mediation plays a key role for discussing how intellectual practices figure within the social relations of which they are an active part. As a way of contextualizing intellectual work—that is, embodied reason in its specialized forms—the idea of mediation has special critical force when applied to philosophy. It has this force because of the traditional inclination of philosophers to treat reason and their own activity as independent of social conditions. We need not claim that this feature of the philosophical tradition has been simply a matter of self-indulgence or willful mystification. Philosophers fought for the distinctiveness of rational procedures against theological and irrationalist cultural forces and thus defended not only science but political and intellectual freedoms by constructing one-sided accounts of these procedures. The intellectual problems with this kind of defense of rationality have become more obvious as the opponents of Enlightenment have changed. When the opponent is no longer those who deny the power of reason but those who assert the malignancy of this power, then a decontextualizing approach no longer serves the cause of Enlightenment and freedom.

With the idea of mediation I seek a conception that avoids traditional illusions about the autonomy of reflective reason without missing the importance of philosophical understanding in modern society. On the one hand, my conception must be explicit in its avoidance of the inflated view of philosophy found in a thinker like Husserl (1970), who traced the social crisis of the thirties to the crisis of Western reason. But on the other hand, my conception must be explicit in its avoidance of the dismissive attitude of those like Rorty, who want to walk away from reflective debates over reason, as though these were not inherent features of the modern world and part of conflicts over freedom and democracy.

Intellectual work considered as mediation contrasts with traditional notions of theory both with regard to the relation between reflection and other social activities and with regard to the nature of that reflection. To speak of mediation is to break with both contemplative and autonomous conceptions of intellectual work. Mediation makes this break as a matter of logic, so far as this implies that we cannot entirely separate the rational achievement of intellectual practices from their social functions. This does not deny that there are rational functions served by abstraction from social relations both in specific kinds of intellectual work and in specific aspects of philosophical reflection.

The interrelation between conceptual abstraction and the social being of rational activity obviously is extremely complicated. To begin with, concern with philosophy as mediation implies that even the highest forms of abstraction always occur within historical contexts of social interaction and can be assessed for their role in those contexts. Just as explicit abstraction from social content does not ensure that such content has been eluded, so, too, relative levels of abstraction do not guarantee any specific degree of importance or effectiveness. To avoid exaggerated estimates of the role of philosophy, a program that emphasizes the importance of philosophy as mediation does not assert any correlation between levels of abstraction employed in intellectual practices and degrees of historical importance or effectiveness. The decision to think of philosophy as mediation leaves open how we are to assess the various functions philosophy serves. Certainly, this historical question cannot be answered by equating high levels of abstraction with primacy within intellectual work or society more generally. Forms of abstraction that yield logical primacy do not imply anything definite about the actual role of these abstractions in communicative relations.

The term "philosophy as mediation" may call to mind Hegel's treatment of relations as being bound up with activity, for example, his account in the *Logic* of the interrelations of concepts as pathways of the activity of thinking. To speak of intellectual practices like philosophy as mediation maintains this Hegelian linkage of conceptual relations and activity so far as the conceptual products of specialized intellectual reflection figure within practices that organize features of social life. Of course the connections between conceptual relations and activity has to be treated in a way that avoids the logicizing reductionism inherent in Hegel's idealism. And, further, to speak of intellectual activity as mediation is to focus on what for Hegel would be only one of many mediations. Nonetheless, the term usefully evokes activity that figures within a continuum of activities, without beginning or end, without a founding act of intuition or a completing step into spiritual or intellectual quiescence.

Philosophical mediation, then, is activity operating within both conceptual and social relations. For example, interpretive functions of philosophy mediate between epistemological theory and political activity. I have treated liberal philosophy as involving a contribution to political understanding by virtue of its recasting of epistemological ideas in the political context, contributing to a distinctively modern political metaphysics proper to a social sphere in which abstract knowledge has a host of applications.

Reference to liberal philosophy in fact evokes a number of specific mediations. Liberal political theorists mediate between the activity of modern epistemologists and modern political leaders and social scientists. In some exceptional cases, like that of John Locke, these mediations may be carried out within the activity of a single individual (see Wood 1983). But whether the process occurs within an individual or among individuals, sometimes across great social distances, it is a matter of ideas being reworked as they are taken from one context and reconsidered within the conceptual relations of another. Two aspects of this process can be underlined here. One concerns the extent to which this is a matter of a positive intellectual construction, a reworking or novel production. The other concerns the extent to which this is a matter of language, the extent to which this reworking is a linguistic process changing the kind of language used in a specific sphere. I move more systematically to the linguistic side of mediation in Part Two.

If we think of intellectual activity as figuring within social practices, we can think of these features of mediation as practical operations among such practices. One thesis I explore is that philosophers engage in mediations that bring various intellectual practices into new relations or that contribute to modifications of one intellectual practice on the basis of appropriations from other intellectual practices. Locke (1980), for example, brings conceptual features of modern epistemological thinking into reflection on legitimate power and the institutional features of the modern state. Certainly it is not only philosophers who engage in mediations of this kind, but their role is distinctive so far as it involves reflective work on very general ideas that come to figure in a host of specific practices.

Philosophy may mediate between intellectual practices, or it may mediate, directly or indirectly, between practices of intellectuals and of nonspecialists—citizens. This is one way of thinking about the evolution of the philosophical features of modern political culture. If within the political language and practice of citizens there figure reflections on ideas about rationality, human capacity, and the necessities structuring the world, these indicate the influence of specialized philosophical activity, itself mediated through various specialist practices in education, journalism, literature, and politics itself.

The idea of mediation, then, involves specific mediational activity of philosophers, but also the further mediations made possible by that activity. Thus philosophers as mediators operate within a complex network of interactions characterized by various appropriations, reworkings, and transformations. To speak here of interaction is to imply the value of a communications approach to such mediation. As a philosophical reflection, the pursuit of such an approach is directed in part toward the rational character of these various dimensions of mediating activity. In this way I pursue a social approach to philosophical reflection on rationality, even as this involves reflection on philosophy itself.

Appropriation and reworking, comprehension and interpretation: these various characterizations of mediating activity pertain to thinking about interrelations both across social space and across social time. Mediation operates between contemporaneous practices and between past and present. In both respects it contributes to the articulation of practical relations to the future in ways characteristic of a given historical differentiation of activity. Though I have emphasized the conceptual and linguistic side of mediation, it also can be applied to the rethinking or even the avoidance of structural conditions. Mediation as interpretation can rework other interpretations as it develops new understandings of nature, social institutions, and structural possibilities.

Intellectual Concerns of Democratic Philosophy

When measured against traditional conceptions, philosophy treated as one among several mediating intellectual practices offers a way to avoid inflated conceptions of theory. This treatment answers political as well as intellectual concerns, but it by no means eliminates difficult political and intellectual problems. Rather, democratic philosophy's problem of reconstructing philosophy along with a complex of other mediating practices presents distinctive difficulties.

As I have described it, a democratic approach to philosophy constructs rationality in social terms and does so by reconstructing abstract knowledge in terms of the social practices in which it figures. I have shown some ways the idea of mediation can be used to think about such practices, and in particular have considered ways this idea can be used in thinking about philosophy as a social undertaking. When we think of philosophy as a mediating practice we are placing the philosophical discussion of conceptual issues about rationality within a wider communicative setting, but we do not thereby exclude attention to these issues or deny that their discussion is important. Indeed, rather than reduce away the force of what have traditionally been understood as specifically philosophical concerns, the conception of philosophy as mediating practice is meant to explore aspects of this force.

Since this approach to philosophy presupposes the failure of foundationalist and transcendental thinking, it does carry with it some assumptions (so far mainly negative) about the kinds of arguments that philosophy can pursue in discussing rationality. With the idea of mediation we are adding to the conceptual stock of such arguments even as we are developing a way of reconstructing what has gone on in historical processes of argumentation. As I have noted, this intersection of argumentation and self-reflection is inherent in philosophical discussions of rationality, though this intersection assumes a somewhat novel form in the present discussion. In any case, this is a twofold claim I can present now only as a programmatic feature of this study. First, this kind of social approach is by no means a reductionism that undercuts what is distinctive about philosophical argumentation. On the contrary, it seeks to emphasize the importance of such argumentation by finding a historical way to make sense of it. In doing so it brings out features of specifically philosophical activity that have been ignored by most philosophers. Second, this approach is itself part of a philosophical argument and so means to contribute to normative understanding of rationality. So far as such understanding is concerned, the aims of the present study are restricted to clarifying the validity of philosophical claims that have to do with political understanding. But my programmatic claim is that this kind of reflection on philosophical activity is compatible with and can contribute to a wider range of normative concerns that organize different philosophical specializations.

Denying that a social conception of philosophy undercuts the distinctive force of its theoretical arguments implies not only that philosophy must be taken seriously as a practice with universalist aims (as a reflection asserting claims to universal validity) but also that treating philosophical arguments historically does not preclude taking seriously their concern with universal features of human rationality. Once we take philosophy to be a mediating activity, issues of history and universal validity have to be posed in a way that addresses or accommodates philosophy as such a practice.

In rejecting reductionism, I am denying that there is a contradiction between conceiving intellectual practices (embodied reason) as involved in relations of power and taking seriously their argumentation about universal validities. To say that a specific kind of knowledge is an exercise of power is not to say that its claims to validity are thereby removed from scrutiny. For now these are simply negative claims against conclusions sometimes drawn from insights into the workings of knowledge and power. I emphasize these claims here in order to distinguish what I take to be a democratic approach to philosophy from various forms of skepticism that respond to oppressive forms and uses of rationality. The point is that willingness to enter into argument with traditional philosophy while at the same time historicizing such philosophy by treating it as mediating practice means that democratic philosophy posits the need for and the possibility of a defensible perspective on issues the tradition has addressed with its disembodied conception of rationality.

Given its opposition to reductionism and historicism, what kind of relation to issues of validity is open to democratic philosophy? If it tries to avoid contemporary variants of skepticism, it must nonetheless find a way to honor the universalistic commitments of philosophical reflection without reverting to the foundationalist and transcendental strategies of the epistemological tradition. I take this to imply the avoidance of dreams of autonomous philosophical theory arguing from a purely philosophical necessity. (Part Two takes up features of a historical philosophical theorization that would steer between skepticism and traditional argumentation.)

Democratic philosophy poses questions pertaining to the intersection of two kinds of validity issues that have usually been kept apart. We may distinguish these as internal and external to the concerns of intellectual practices, or as having to do with theoretical issues rather than political issues. Such a distinction is at first glance easier to maintain for the natural sciences than for at least some of the social sciences. My main concern in this study is with its standing for philosophy. Can an account of intellectual mediation help us see ways in which the politics of an intellectual practice informs its properly theoretical concerns without simply reducing theory to politics (or without falling into the more familiar, traditional tendency to reduce politics to theory)?

Answering this question requires an account of the rationality of intellectual mediation in general and of democratic mediation in particular. I argue that the fruitful outlines of such an account are available in the social uses of language theory found in such thinkers as Foucault, Bakhtin, and especially Habermas. I consider issues about the development of this account in Parts Two and Four. Here I will continue with my more programmatic discussion.

Questions of theoretical and practical validity are connected to a theme on which I have already touched, namely, the respects in which philosophy is interpretive it its functions. I have noted the claim that philosophical interpretation figures within the formation of political understanding. While emphasizing the interpretive (and hermeneutic) features of philosophy points to ways of rethinking the history of philosophy, it also charts a course for democratic reflection. Reconstruction of intellectual practices is itself an interpretive undertaking that, in the kind of reflection I have in mind, contributes to historical narratives that make sense of past intellectual practices and places them in relation to contemporary debates. In so doing such narratives situate the initiatives of democratic intellectual practices, including philosophy. I take such a narrative to be a specifically (though not exclusively) philosophical reflection. It tries to make sense of what reason has been and what it might be. It also bears on normative concerns about intellectual work by informing our consideration of how intellectuals should function in the present and future.

Such narrative reflection characterizes the work of the three contributors to democratic philosophical reconstruction on whom I rely most directly in Part Two. Bakhtin's concern, as well as that of his collaborator Volosinov, with the performative features of language is explicitly connected with reflections on the role of intellectual work (especially literature and philosophy) in relation to the evolution of language and social organization (see Bakhtin 1981; Volosinov 1973). Both of these thinkers challenge authoritative and dogmatic intellectual voices and are committed to the freeing up and recognition of a plurality of voices within a revitalized public. They proceed in part through a reconstruction of writing over the past several centuries. Habermas's concern with communicative rationality is tied to a rethinking of modernity and the role within it of specialized forms of thinking and acting (see Habermas 1984, 1987b). His historical account is explicitly joined to a conception of philosophical mediation that would counteract mystifying forms of specialization. Foucault, perhaps the most historicist and

least normatively inclined thinker of this group, nonetheless repeatedly developed narrative contextualizations of his work and connected
these to ideas about how critical intellectuals should proceed within
the world of knowledge-power (see Foucault 1980, "Truth and Power").

The kinds of localized conceptual concerns pursued by most philosophers are thus placed by democratic reflection in a setting that both
informs specific reflective concerns and brings out philosophical features of the social reality of knowledge. To say that it should do so from
a democratic standpoint is to say that it tries to make politically relevant
a sense of rationality and so places itself in explicit relation to political
norms. One normative problem for democratic philosophy, then, has
to do with the idea of democracy itself. We need to develop a conception that bears specifically on the questions of knowledge-power that
trouble contemporary reflection.

Would such a democratic conception also speak to reflection focusing on specific conceptual issues over cognitive and technical activities
of specialists? How would it bear on the normative conception of
philosophical and other intellectual mediation? These latter issues are
my more direct concern in this project, though I take up relations to the
other issues as well. The interrelations of these issues reflect features of
Habermas's communication theory on which I rely in developing my
account of democratic philosophy. For now it is enough to say that I
develop connections between his ideas of democratic reciprocity and
collaboration in a way that speaks both to themes of democratic politics
in general and to the role within such politics of democratic intellectual
mediation. I hope to reveal relations between this idea of practical
rationality and theoretical questions about the standing of democratic
reflection itself.

I take Habermas's conception of discursive rationality to be both
illuminating and incomplete. His account of the discursive redemption
of validity claims does capture aspects of traditional understandings of
truth and rightness, and his emphasis on the process of discursive
redemption underlines the unavailability to us of an account of rationality that appeals to substantive givens and points of departure
(whether conceived in the order of reality or that of thought). At the
same time, discursive redemption is an overly abstract idealization
insofar as it departs from actual processes in which theoretical and
practical rationality is both exercised and reflectively validated. The
argument that follows does not for the most part rely on accepting

Habermas's communications account, though I do draw on other and related features of his theory in discussing the conceptualization of intellectual practices. In Part Four I defend a somewhat historicized version of his conception when I discuss the standing of the normative aspects of the concept of democracy with which I work.

Political Concerns of Democratic Philosophy

Having discussed some of the aims of a democratic philosophical reflection on rationality, we now turn in a preliminary way to the relation of such philosophy to politics. Although my discussion of democratic philosophy's concern with normative issues about validity had to do with politics, the question now is less about how to re-construct the rationality of such politics than about its bearing on power issues. This returns us to the theme of specifically democratic philosophical mediation. My historical account of a contemporary political impasse in the face of structural change allows for one way of considering the relation of philosophy to politics. Democratic philoso-phy might contribute to a political understanding that approaches structural change in terms adequate to outstanding questions of power, including those specific to intellectual mediation. To explore what such a contribution might involve, we need to discuss the relation of such philosophy to political understanding, and we need to consider why such a philosophical contribution would be appropriate to the conditions of political impasse. Inherent in this latter problem is the question why a democratic response is appropriate to the dilemmas of structural change.

Democratic Philosophy,
Democratic Political Understanding

I proceed from the thesis that modern political understanding has in part been shaped by the mediations of modern philosophy. For exam-ple, political understanding contains assumptions and claims about rationality, and these are claims that draw from specialist debate. The criticism of modern politics and the criticism of modern philosophy go hand in hand. Modern political understanding is at an impasse so far as contemporary politics fails to address structural change. My thesis has been that this impasse is marked by a decline of conventional forms of politics conjoined with a growth of various kinds of tacitly political activity. The ambiguous presence and role of politics is not of course exclusively a problem of philosophical reflection, but there is a philosophical dimension to the obscuring of our relation to politics. Making sense of politics requires making sense of practices in which modern forms of rationality play crucial roles. The problem of political understanding includes the problem of making adequate sense of rationality as it operates in actual and possible political practices.

To approach this point from a different angle, we may say that an adequate political response to structural change requires appropriate philosophical reflection and mediation. Such reflection is thus engaged with the twofold problem of making political sense of structural change while articulating an explicit and adequate politics. The twofold reflective task of philosophy—having to think about itself as it thinks about issues of rationality—is paralleled in politics. Philosophy contributes to the way politics makes sense of the world while making sense of itself.

This is a philosophy that places the conceptual concerns of reflection on reason within reflection on rationality as embodied in intellectual practices. In doing so such philosophy reconstructs conceptual features of its own mediating activity. The political role of such philosophy consists partly therefore in contributing to a political understanding in which the social dimensions of rationality are explicit. Its mediations simultaneously address issues of intellectual mediation as these in turn bear on the different forms of power relations and conflicts informing structure and structural change.

Democracy, Change, and Reflection on Embodied Rationality

If we accept, at least for argument's sake, that philosophy may contribute to a democratic political understanding, we then can consider how the social understanding of rationality I am associating with democratic philosophy can contribute to the development of an adequate political response to contemporary structural change and the conflicts over the meaning and possibilities of such change. I approach this question by way of the more general issue of why overcoming the political impasse and responding adequately to political change requires or is even possible for a democratic politics. My response to this more general issue provides some basis for discussing the role in democratic politics of the philosophical reflection I have been associating with democratic mediation.

Why Democracy?

It is not obvious that deepening and radicalizing democracy represents the best prospect for responding to the problems posed by structural change. The contrary view is more or less an article of practical faith in contemporary politics so far as it exhibits the technocratic and meritocratic forms that inform the prevailing conservatism. More openness, more participation, more responsibility on the part of officials—all these represent destabilizing threats to those who think of the problem of politics as that of steering a perilously complex society through new and uncertain waters (for a much-cited statement of this kind of thinking, see Crozier, Huntington, and Watanuki 1975). Democracy is not rejected so much on normative as on what are taken to be practical grounds. In fact, technocratic and meritocratic perspectives are informed as much by a liquidation of practical discourse, including its normative aspects, as by a sense of the magnitude of problems facing massive and intricate social processes (e.g., see Habermas 1987b, sec. 6, "Intermediate Reflections: Systems and Lifeworld"). But even if democratic criticism can show that such undemocratic views tend toward circularity—they define away normative politics and define in what counts as relevant forms of stability—the fact remains that the terms of action are in fact dangerously obscure in a period of great technological force and fractured common understandings.

One line open to democratic criticism is to locate the conservative content in technocracy and meritocracy and to gauge the possibilities that can be opened up by challenging that content. Doing so can quickly bring forth issues of power connected with intellectual mediation, since the inclination of the technocrat is to conserve the position of experts if not to place them entirely above scrutiny. In Part Two, I approach this antidemocratic impulse as it bears on conservative relations to the division of labor.

More generally, I argue that intellectual and practical democratization of intellectual mediation concerns us with various features of a philosophically developed idea of the division of labor. What technocracy says against democracy is what it has to say for the division of labor, and what it sees as a threat in democracy is a denial of the necessity of at least some crucial features of the division of labor. The issues for democracy are not just matters of general structures of governing, but bear on all the kinds of power that are organized in the division of labor, including those having to do with race and gender as well as class.

The question for the democrat has then to do with confronting this kind of conservatism and exploring how to construct an alternative relation to issues about the division of labor. Among other things, issues of structural change are open to democratic alternatives because of the relation between these issues and the division of labor. My argument is that democracy presents a viable response to structural change because the problems posed by structural change can only be addressed by addressing the division of labor and that the division of labor is increasingly conflict ridden because it is proving increasingly difficult to stabilize the power relations it organizes.

These claims cannot be adequately elaborated, much less justified, in this introductory section. The study that follows aims in part to offer a coherent and plausible statement of them. Some reasons, however, stand out for associating structural change and the division of labor. In fact, connections between such change and the organiza- tion and distribution of agency have already been made in issues raised by social movements.

First, issues about the national organization of social life have linked battles over opportunities for individual and group development (col- lective identities) with attacks on existing forms of national unity (liberal nationality). This is not just a matter of minorities asserting sub- and cross-national identities as they fight over powers exercised through education, job opportunities, cultural politics, and so on. It is also a facet of feminist politics; it can be found in some fundamentalist challenges to scientific and professional authority; and so on. While such movements may not focus on the division of labor as such, they chip away at its seeming naturalness and necessity, and they often question the credentials and authority of those who occupy positions of influence and prestige within it.

Next, the institutional differentiation of modern society has been linked to issues about the division of labor. The evolving intersection of economics, politics, and culture and new corresponding forms of dif- ferentiation provide sites for conflict over various kinds of specializa- tion and expertise. The politics of medicine is a case in point, as is the politics of the mass media. One can again point to the role of movements in these conflicts, for example, over abortion rights, over access to health care, over news coverage, and over the control of images. If the division of labor has not explicitly defined the larger stakes of these battles, they have perhaps shaken the stability with which it has heretofore reproduced itself and evolved.

Analogous and closely related points can be made about ways movements have connected modern society's adoption of the growth imperative and the corresponding centrality of labor to the division of labor. It is not just that the division of labor is inevitably called into question once issues of production and consumption associated with growth are pursued, as they are by ecologists and movements in the Third World. The political nature of labor and working conditions has been broached by movements concerned with safety, quality of life, and so on. In all these cases, the definition of specialized tasks, as well as those who frame these definitions, comes into question.

These brief references show that structural change and the division of labor have been connected in the setting of various specific conflicts proper to democratic politics. Of course, how we are to understand this connection and what kinds of change are possible in matters of structure or the division of labor remain open questions. Simply acknowledging these further questions refers us to the problematic relation to politics I have associated with the impasse of contemporary politics. Here philosophy connects with the theme of the division of labor.

Politics, Philosophy, and the Division of Labor

How does the theme of the division of labor bear on locating covert politics and making the development of political understanding a crucial theme? This concerns both the decline of conventional political involvement and the emergence of unacknowledged politics. For my purposes, these questions have to be answered in a way that illuminates the role of philosophy in a democratic critique of the division of labor.

Initiatives of social movements indicate what I take to be democratic impulses within the context of the political impasse described earlier. These initiatives have democratic promise in contesting aspects of the division of labor reified and mystified by the apostles of technocracy and meritocracy. These reifications and mystifications contribute to the persistence of the political impasse by cloaking contestable features of social structure as interpreted and reproduced within the division of labor. Making the division of labor an issue means simultaneously challenging conservative defenders of expertise and opening up political discussion of structural changes. Thus exploring the division of labor provides access to the covert politics of expertise and offers the prospect of new definitions of political issues and processes.

Now, let me conclude this programmatic discussion by returning to the place of philosophy in all of this. To recall language used earlier, this is the problem of democratic philosophical mediation. Such mediation would be concerned with mediations that advance a democratic reflective relation to rationality within political culture. If modern politics involves a philosophically mediated understanding of rationality, then democratic politics presupposes its own appropriate understanding of rationality. What would make a democratic understanding as advanced by such mediation appropriate would be a reflection that makes democratic sense of the division of labor as the framework in which specialized intellectual mediations function in the reproduction between citizens of relations of domination.

Philosophy that identifies and makes explicit the intellectual mediations proper to modern power relations may itself have a democratic mediating function if it thereby contributes to a demystifying understanding of undemocratic practices and relations. If it can be shown that the relations and conflicts proper to the division of labor bear crucially on the kinds of structural change I have associated with contemporary political impasse, then reflective understanding of the workings of the division of labor may lead to overcoming that impasse.

In thus treating the intellectual problem of democratic philosophy as being about the intersection of knowledge and power as embodied in the division of labor, I am also suggesting that the mediational aims of such philosophy place it in a political as well as interpretive relation not only to structural change but to social conflicts and movements. As mediation, such philosophy finds itself one of many specialized practices in which privileged position within the division of labor does not preclude the influence of democratic movements. Indeed, since, as I argue further below, the division of labor is itself a target of social movements as well as tacit political interventions, philosophy finds itself within a complex of conflicts that make democratic initiatives possible, difficult, and often ambiguous.

Part Two

Philosophy and the Division of Labor

Chapter 4

Making Philosophical Use of the Idea of the Division of Labor

A critique of the division of labor provides a philosophical reflection that steers between traditional theory and contemporary rejections of philosophical reflection on rationality. This critical project provides a way conceptually to find commonality among the different strands of the intellectual tendency I have associated with democratic philosophy.

I refer to this kind of theory as critique to emphasize the idea of a distinctively philosophical reflection concerned with distinctive intellectual problems, above all those concerning the validity of claims about rationality and its conditions. Reflection of this kind is not theory in the traditional sense, if that implies a purely contemplative stance, an autonomous and self-grounding method, or a foundational relation to other intellectual undertakings. Viewed as a practice and understood as engaged in various mediations, this theory, further, is not an exclusively conceptual undertaking but communicates with and acts upon other practices and the reflective relations to rationality in which they stand.

The term "critique" signals that this reflection has a constitutive aspect and so presents both knowing and what is known as involving constructive activity. Critique need not follow a subjectivist understanding of the objects of knowledge, though it tends in this direction so long as it adheres to epistemological aims. So far as epistemology is a matter of establishing guarantees against skepticism through arguments that seek a distinctively philosophical necessity, critique as I mean it here is not epistemology. Reflective clarification of validity claims does not require guarantees, particularly when the kind of suspicion of reason that is at issue concerns not the reality of knowledge but its relation to domination. Critical reflection is needed, however, precisely because there are in fact close associations between power and knowledge, and working out an understanding of democratic possibilities requires appropriate analysis and criticism of the relations and processes that foster these associations.

Preoccupation with guarantees traps epistemology in the circle of its own subjectivity. A reflection that does not presume to establish such necessities is free to argue in materialist terms. It can place the subjective and the active features of knowledge within a context that is in various ways independent of mental and linguistic processes. If such a materialist critique seeks to clarify rational validities, it must concern itself with kinds of universality that are not so closely associated with philosophical necessity as this has frequently preoccupied epistemologists. Whether and to what extent intellectually relevant notions of universality are related to practical universality is one of the issues about normative reflection I explore in the following discussion.

Critique and the Division of Labor

The division of labor provides an organizing perspective with which we can understand philosophical reflection as itself proceeding within history. It allows us to retain a sense of philosophical reflection's historical location while providing a term with which to think about issues of universal significance. Thus it provides a term with which to pursue in a reflective way philosophical mediation, and to do so in a way that makes issues of power explicit. Further, though essentially a critical idea that posits a specific overcoming of the division of labor, this idea also contributes to a way of thinking about the intellectual mediations appropriate to a highly differentiated and knowledge-reliant society. Thus it offers material for reflection on democratic politics.

As the most general way of characterizing the differentiation of social practices in societies organized in relations of conflict and domination, the division of labor is the most general way of thinking about philosophy as a socially located practice. Below I explain how my use of the idea of the division of labor follows theorists like Hegel and Marx, who use it to think about features of modernity conceived in an evolutionary relation to earlier societies. For now it is enough to emphasize that such a usage moves beyond the economic associations of the term to a characterization of differentiation and coordination of social activities in general, and does so while remaining sensitive to ways modern society seems characterized by specific developments in this coordination and differentiation, both as it thereby contrasts with earlier societies and as it seems to culminate tendencies set in motion within those societies.

Before saying more about the idea itself, let us consider further the kind of philosophy to which it is to contribute. I have already touched upon the shift from epistemology-centered philosophy and the requirement that reflection still attend to issues of rationality, though these are now posed explicitly in social terms. The emphasis on social being results from the need to avoid traditional mystifications associated with the oscillation between conceptions of autonomous reason on the one hand and skeptical relativism on the other. In more positive terms, such a materialist orientation will yield attention to the objective conditions as well as objective powers of rationality and so to its social context and historical evolution. A materialist approach allows us to think about the issue of historicity. In particular it allows us to think about historically variable relations to objects, their forms, stability, place in practical activity, and so on.

Adapting the idea of the division of labor to the reflective strategies of historical critique, then, means exploring a nonidealist approach to a conception of social constitution. To speak of a critique of the division of labor is to speak of a critique of knowledge carried out in social terms. Following Kant, this means an account of knowledge in terms of the conditions of its possibility. It also means treating the world that is known as being itself a synthesis in which subjective as well as objective factors have a part. Thus I pursue aspects of a conception in which specific knowledge claims (e.g., about the evolution of prices) presuppose structural relations between kinds of knowing (e.g., economics) and kinds of social relations and practices (e.g., those of market society). On this conception, these structural relations make knowledge possible in part by virtue of the ways social reality is constructed as knowable. This is a constitutive conception because a historical account can be given of the knowability of these social relations and practices. With more specific references to the constitutive theories of Kant and Hegel, I show how such a constitutive conception attempts to avoid idealism by avoiding a conceptualist reductionism when thinking about the intersection of subjectivity and objectivity.

My claim now is that a constitutive approach helps us think about the coherence of social objects and objectivity, and does so in a way that treats them both as result and as involving some kind of interaction of objectivity with experiencing subjects. Forms of knowledge and experience can be reconstructed in relation to objects that themselves are constructed in ways that make them open to experience and knowable. With the division of labor I want to pursue such a reconstructive strategy, but without idealizing synthesis, that is, without subjecting reconstruction to conceptual necessities of existing forms of knowledge. This project confronts various difficulties, for example, regarding the kind of justification of knowledge claims it can provide. But thinking along these lines also vindicates a more socially effective role for knowledge than idealism can sustain, since it allows us to think of the effects of cognitive mediation. Philosophical reflection of this sort cannot and need not aspire to address all issues of validity on which it touches. Rather, such reflection aims to advance the discussion of universal validity in the specific context of the intersection of modern knowledge and power.

For now, we need only to recognize that an emphasis on universality stands in uncertain relation to the kinds of argumentation traditionally devoted to validating rational claims. I have already alluded to traditional strategies in which universality is secured through arguments regarding the necessity of these claims. It is for this purpose that foundationalist or transcendental arguments have been developed. Necessity is required to refute skepticism, but if our aim instead is to find a kind of justification that is content to refute justifiable doubts, then necessity will not be required of our argument. If we seek to show why a given conception of rationality has the force claimed for it, we need to show why it is suited for the tasks facing it and why it is better than rival conceptions. Most of all, we need to show why this conception represents an adequate response to historical doubts, in particular those concerning knowledge-power and invidious cultural relativism.

The aim, then, is the articulation of a historically relevant universality for the conception of rationality in question. Lacking traditional philosophical strategies for guarantees or proofs, the argument cannot achieve traditional standards of necessity. But it can find a relevant conception of universality in a philosophical idea of the division of labor if this idea is adequate for handling the practical and critical tasks at hand. In Chapter 5, I discuss how an appropriate conception of the division of labor provides the required universality. This argument explores philosophical issues proper to intellectual mediation by connecting themes of conceptual universality to those of practical processes in which such universality figures within intellectual and specifically philosophical communication. We need a practically effective reflection that respects the conditioning of social awareness while asserting the potential of reflectively guided practice. This requires precisely the idea of the division of labor. The division of labor contributes to a historical ontology in which the conditioning of consciousness is compatible with an account of the possibility of certain kinds of reflexivity about social being and historical possibility.

A critical approach allows us to think about the universality of rational claims in terms of the historically shaped susceptibility of objects to the knowledge of historical subjects. The demand that philosophy not retreat from the insights of critical philosophy has been observed in recent years with an increasingly social conception of knowledge and the experiences associated with it. One cannot say that an adequate philosophical successor to Hegel's attempt to avoid a subjectivist outcome for critical thought has emerged. I do not claim here to advance this discussion directly, though it is important to make clear where we stand with these more general conceptual issues. We must develop ideas that are consistent with some appropriate notions of historical synthesis and that avoid metaphysical reliance on ideas of subjectivity or objectivity.

The idea of a synthesis with which we think of the practical basis for historically variable forms of subjectivity and objectivity contributes to a kind of historical reflection, which in turn can contribute to a historical and social kind of self-consciousness. This self-consciousness is a theme inherent in the critical project, as witness the place of the account of the synthetic unity of apperception in Kant and in the attempts of his successors to develop a more satisfactory theory. One virtue of the division of labor is that it allows for an account of certain kinds of historical reflection without positing a transcendental or transhistorical subject. Indeed, I will make use of language theory to elaborate on the argument by Habermas that a communications approach enables us to avoid the metaphysics of the traditional "philosophy of the subject."

Philosophy in the Critical Tradition: The Contrast with Kant

A brief contrast with Kant's practice of critique may sharpen the themes I have just introduced: a constitutive theory that takes the form of a critique of the division of labor, reflection on validity issues in universalistic terms without attempting to achieve necessary truths, and inserting such reflection within the practice of democratic philosophical mediation. In its philosophical use, the idea of the division of labor presents a way of historicizing and concretizing the Kantian or critical legacy in reflection on knowledge. That is, with this idea we can pursue the idea of experience as emerging from a process of synthesis in whose terms specific relations between subjectivity and objectivity emerge.

Kant's project of critique and of constitutive theory emerged as a response to skepticism. Kant proposes a critique of reason, not of social activity, as is the case with the critique of the division of labor. His concern is with the conditions for a knowledge that is to be vindicated, not with knowledge he agrees may be problematic at least in certain respects. The parallels between Kant and a critique focusing on the division of labor, then, are limited. But some comparison between the two conceptions may be instructive, and not only for expository purposes. If sound, the critique of the division of labor should eventually allow for a critical perspective on Kant even as it has drawn from him.

With his transcendental strategy Kant tried to answer skeptical challenges to the claims of intellectuals. It is not entirely anachronistic to treat his theory as being about the claims of intellectuals rather than exclusively as a response to the issue of knowledge as such, since Kant drew from his philosophy to endorse those very revolutionary politics that would become the focus of contemporary and subsequent critics of politically ambitious intellectuals. At the same time, so far as we can treat his theory as being concerned with intellectuals, we must do so by way of his claims about the relation of their concepts to the structure of the world and thus about intellectuals in their role as scientists.

By providing an account of the fit between a knowable world and theory, Kant sought to overcome the subjectivism and the skepticism of modern empiricism as developed by Hume. With the synthetic a priori knowledge of philosophical theory, Kant believed he could answer contemporary challenges to Enlightenment. That is, necessary truths about the relations of thought to knowable reality could refute doubts regarding the defensibility of contingent truths asserted by empirical science.

These necessary truths were to establish a homology between conceptual relations and structures of the knowable world. The way Kant tried to secure this homology—his theory of the constitutive activity of the transcendental subject, which assumes not just a homology but a kind of identity—opens his own position to the charge of subjectivism (and, ultimately, of skepticism), for example, by Hegel. But this is not the point to pursue here. Rather, we should note the implications of Kant's account for a conception of intellectuals.

The necessity argument provides a kind of credential. It makes a strong claim for the cognitive power of intellectuals and buttresses their social authority by casting their practical relation to the world in a relatively weak or passive light: they reproduce in thought real relations, hence are not making practical initiatives by virtue of their specifically cognitive claims. Though not a point that concerns Kant directly, this bears on a tacitly social understanding of intellectuals provided by his thought.

There is a political force to Kant's theoretical arguments, even if it does not enter directly into his philosophical discussion. The necessity his argument is to secure against skepticism provides a guarantee about the reliability of scientific work. It is a strong argument for the social promise of those who follow the Enlightenment even though it does not address social uses of knowledge directly. Part of the social implication lies in the objectivity of knowledge; intellectuals develop knowledge that portrays existing objective relations. Although this knowledge has no moral force, it does possess a kind of authority.

This point can be brought into relief by considering the nature of Kant's claim from the perspective of a more historical and interpretive sense of the cognitive achievements of science. From such a perspective, Kant's transcendental standpoint is one version of an overly close relation being drawn between the conceptual achievement of science and the structure of reality. The subsequent demise of narrowly representational accounts of knowledge raises the question of the interpretations constructed by intellectuals in a way that Kant did not face. If one does not draw skeptical conclusions from such accounts, that is, if one does not doubt either the reality of knowledge or the possibility of philosophical reflection on it, then one moves toward consideration of intellectual mediation.

From this perspective, Kant is dogmatic or at least insufficiently reflective, not so much about the reality of science as about scientists and the role of science in society. One could reply that this criticism distorts Kant's own project, which was precisely about the reality of science in the face of Humean skepticism. But Kant's concern with the social promise of Enlightenment indicates a respect in which the standing of intellectuals was at stake for him (see Kant 1983).

Kant is in effect defending the cognitive claims and social authority, so far as this depends upon those claims, of intellectuals when he does battle with skepticism. Viewed in this light, a striking feature of his critical approach is the way it vindicates knowledge claims by ignoring the specific cultural activity of intellectual specialists. That is, Kant's critical reconstruction directly links the conceptual structures of science with the real structures of the known world, the structures of the objects of experience. These are connected by way of transcendental operations that precede any historically situated exploration or theorization on the part of intellectuals. By connecting the structures of cognition to the structures of the objective world, Kant hopes to refute skepticism.

It is only by such strategy that Kant can secure the theoretical argument he needs in order to deal with the skepticism he finds compelling. That is, only in this way can he provide a theoretical argument for the necessity of modern forms of knowing. Without securing necessary truths about the conditions of knowledge, he leaves open the way to skeptical doubt. But the strategy for such truths unavoidably obscures the social being of intellectuals and the process of their knowledge construction. So the strategy of a constitutive theory that reconstructs the formative processes of the world through a conception designed to establish the applicability of scientific concepts here makes its point against skepticism by idealizing the process of knowing. It saves knowledge by eliminating the knowers.

From the standpoint of reflection on the division of labor this is a telling deficiency. Philosophers vindicate intellectuals and the basis of their social authority through an account that abstracts from the social process of knowing. From within the idealist tradition, this is not, of course, an aspect of Kant that preoccupies later thinkers. For Hegel, the significant issue is the subjectivism in Kant's treatment of the world more generally. Nonetheless Hegel's criticism is of interest, since it leads him to introduce a notion of social activity into the idea of a constitution of reality that is keyed to the terms of theoretical knowledge.

Before turning to Hegel, let me offer a few other brief observations on Kant's standpoint. Kant's tacit account of the authority of intellectuals as deriving from an identity between the structure of their concepts and the structure of the world undercuts any very sustained account of the role of enlightenment in history or of the relation between theory and practice. This is reflected in the relative thinness of his philosophy of history and his failure to find a concrete way to connect the demands of practical reason with the pronouncements of theory. But another way to articulate these difficulties is in terms of the idea of historicity I used earlier. I am thinking of historicity as having to do with determinate relations to past and future as organized in the practices and experiences of the present.

Neither the process of knowledge nor known objectivity is conceived as historical process by Kant. No doubt his reduction of the process in which knowledge is generated to a politically and ideologically neutral movement from error to truth has partly to do with his adoption of natural science as the model of knowledge. Apart from the limitations imposed by basing his reflections on the conceptual structure of Newtonian physics, Kant's account suffers from the assumption that the experiences and operations of one set of intellectuals could suffice for reflection on theory and the achievements of intellectuals more generally. By concentrating on the work of physicists rather than, say, political economists, Kant can more easily fix upon a reified conception of known objectivity and a static model of the cognitive process. And by focusing on just one set of intellectuals he can, obviously, miss the philosophical significance of the notion of the division of labor that is just then coming into prominence.

The point is not to dwell on what may seem anachronistic criticisms of Kant but to notice that by focusing selectively on one feature of the developing intellectual division of labor, he manages to construct a model that allows him to think of intellectuals in completely asocial terms. The specific properties of physical science, as he understands it, allow for the identification of conceptual and real orders and thus for the effacement of the social dimensions of knowledge. And it also allows for the effacement of the historical dimensions of knowledge, not just by adopting a certain account of physics but by abstracting away from other available models of intellectual work whose combination would have posed for him varieties of knowledge as well as the dynamics of cognitive development in relation to quite different contexts. This would have provided alternative senses of relations of knowing subjectivity and known objectivity (as this marks the contrast between physics and political economy) and alternative senses of theory and practice (as the disciplinary contrast coincides with contrasting relations to politics, money, and the military).

By thinking of knowledge from a single model and constructing a philosophical account in terms of the necessity of homologous or representational relations, Kant misses features of knowledge that are crucial from the standpoint of the division of labor: its sociality, its diversity, and its historicity, which, as I shall show, touches upon the fact that knowledge is not only always a social process but, as the notion of mediation has already reflected, a process that enters into complex relations with nonintellectual practices and so into relation with a variety of practical questions.

By obscuring these features of specialized knowledge, the Kantian approach also obscures the social being of its own activity. It misses the respects in which, as philosophy, it is a specialized mediation. Thus in failing to conceive knowledge in terms of various practices within the division of labor, it fails to see its own activity too as part of that division of labor. Just as this failure obscures the social claims to authority of the scientist, it obscures the social claims to authority and influence on the part of the philosopher. It pretends that the issue of power is a special concern of a distinct domain, that of politics, and so presupposes differentiations that a more historically minded critique must reconstruct and question.

Hegel

Hegel's Approach to Constitutive Theory

As part of his strategy for overcoming difficulties with Kant's approach to knowledge, Hegel introduces themes of the division of labor into modern philosophy.

For Hegel, a weakness in Kant's approach to synthesis is that it restricts its account of the construction of the objects of experience to the forms of their knowability, where this knowability is itself restricted to a certain kind of knowledge, the reifying and quantifying thinking Hegel calls the "Understanding" (1991b, 80–107). By being restricted to these formal properties, the activity of synthesis remains subjective; that is, it does not really penetrate the objects themselves and leaves the knowing subject cut off from a world Kant conceives as persisting independent of knowledge (the thing in itself). Hegel's objective idealism results from his attempt to think of synthesis as objective, which is to say, as involving activity that is material as well as formal. This is "subjective," but not simply a matter of thinking understood as the application of concepts to independent, subjectively received material. Here thought itself is in the world by being embodied. The mediation of form and content involves in Hegel's account a notion of constituted objects whose knowability, unlike that achieved by the understanding, is ultimately affirmed in a process of self-knowing that results from a process in which the subject-object of knowledge has been constructed along with the evolution of knowledge itself (see the preface to the *Phenomenology*). Synthesis here is objective, not objectivistic, since it involves factors that are independent of individual subjectivities but that figure within a rationality of embodied activity.

The mediation of form and content is thus joined with a developmental logic in which all forms of otherness to thought are overcome and philosophical knowledge can be a kind of self-knowledge. The premise Hegel makes is that his philosophy can show that activity generates a progressive universality, a process in which everything in some way comes within the net of rationality. One can challenge this philosophy internally, that is, by claiming that this premise is never justified, as Hegel insists that it must be, with his dialectical argumentation, which overcomes internally generated incompleteness and contradictions. In making such a challenge, one can from within Hegel's argument make a point that seems evident enough to those who excuse themselves from this exercise. That is, Hegel's idealism seems not really to escape the charge of an idealizing subjectivism so far as it treats all objectivity as somehow rationalizable, or, to put the point differently, so far as it fails to acknowledge adequately the independence and priority of nature to the human species.

For the present argument, this criticism has to be made in a somewhat different way. The problem of idealism's residual subjectivism needs to be seen in terms of the mystification of intellectuals. Claims about knowability have to be brought back to claims about the methods developed by intellectuals, and claims about universality have to be confronted by the particularisms proper to the division of labor.

For this purpose, it is useful to recall that Hegel's account of historical objective synthesis proceeds by integrating into philosophical reflection forms of social activity, including labor, that traditionally remain beyond the pale of philosophical reflection. This aspect of his strategy is inseparable from the attempt to overcome subjectivism, and it seemingly raises the question of the social relation between the various objectifiers and the philosophers who enact the process of collectively valid self-reflection. Hegel's self-conception is personally modest but professionally rather ambitious. Though the individual thinker can take little credit for carrying out a reflection that is the completion of a wider historical process, to philosophers is attributed a reflective capacity that allows them to make claims valid for all on the basis of their rather isolated enterprise. In particular, no act of acknowledgment or confirmation on the part of the objectifiers is required, because philosophical method is self-enclosed. To be sure, it is for Hegel a matter of exoteric knowledge, in principle open to all, but the condition for entering the discourse of universality is to adopt the rules of the philosophers' activity, that is, to become a philosopher and make no essential reference to any of the other activities in which—by hypothesis—one might be contributing to the possibility of philosophical insight.

The absolutizing claims for philosophical reflection, then, decontextualize the philosophical practice, which is so insistent about intellectual contextualization. Thus, though Hegel introduces the theme of the division of labor into philosophical discussion, he is unable to think of his own practice in its terms. But before I discuss the problem of Hegel's treatment of philosophical practice, let us consider more explicitly how his social conception functions philosophically.

As I have noted, Hegel's conception of *Geist*, or Absolute Spirit, can be seen as a historical and social reworking of Kant's conception of transcendental synthesis. Because of its use of the idea of the division of labor, it can also be assessed from the standpoint of its contribution to overcoming the problems with the Kantian conception I identified when approaching Kant's philosophy as a moment in the history of the philosophy of modern knowledge-politics. For Hegel, major difficulties with Kant's account are its subjectivism and its skepticism. Though Kant seeks to vindicate the knowledge claims of science, by treating knowable objects as objects of experience only, that is, as objects only for us, he denies us knowledge of the world as it is in itself (see Hegel, the introduction to the *Phenomenology*). From the standpoint of the critique of the division of labor, we in turn have attributed to Kant a problematic treatment of the relation of intellectuals to the world by way of his conception of synthesis, in which the concepts of the understanding are at once the constructive principles of the objects of experience. From this account flowed a conception of the necessity of theoretical knowledge and a corresponding authority for intellectuals.

For Hegel, an irony plaguing Kant's vindication of knowledge is the persisting gap between theoretical and practical reason, so far as the former is construed as empirical science and the latter as morality. This is a problem of which Kant himself is aware, so far as it involves the impossibility of knowing that practical reason can or has been employed and the empirical probability that moral action will be defeated by the course of the existing world (Kant 1956). This internal theoretical deficiency of Kant's philosophy does not prevent his conception from figuring within the mediating practices of modern philosophy. Nonetheless, from the standpoint of the critique of the division of labor, the ideological quality of this mediation represents a defect and introduces a distinctive split between theory and practice.

Hegel's alternative to Kant is of interest here, then, because it does introduce the division of labor into reflection over synthesis that constructs the world and that figures in the possibility of knowledge. Rather than treat "world making" as the activity of a disembodied transcendental subject, Hegel speaks of an objectification that proceeds within historically evolving practices (Hegel 1977, e.g., the discussion of "Spirit," 263–363). He relies explicitly on political economy, both in developing the idea of objectification itself and in drawing from modern accounts of the increasing differentiation and interdependence of specialized activities as these contribute to qualitative changes in humanity's relation to nature (Hegel 1991a, e.g., the discussion of the "System of Needs," 227–39). This provides modern detail to Hegel's more general conception of the history of the state as a process of increasing differentiation in which individuals emerge as independent and reflective subjects who live and work in institutions that in turn exhibit specialization and interdependency on an unprecedented scale.

Hegel's account of the constitution of the world is inseparable from his treatment of its knowability. He conceives both historically, with evolving forms of knowledge corresponding to evolving objectifications. This theme reaches its furthest development in Hegel's claims about Absolute Spirit. Philosophy, religion, and art all provide to humanity knowledge about its historical makeup.

Within this account Hegel treats specific kinds of intellectual functions as they are bound up with specific social arrangements. Particularly in his account of the state we find a variety of specialized roles (e.g., various civil servants, judges, legislators, but also leaders of corporate bodies, journalists, lawyers) (Hegel 1991a, 240–59, 270–74). Within his argument, these roles embody various aspects of practical reason and so provide a way reason is reconstructed socially. Philosophical reason grasps this rationality in part by grasping the appropriate relation between specific kinds of knowing and acting in relation to specific object domains, hence specific synthetic achievements. Similarly, it reconstructs specific alienations tied up with loss of synthetic basis for experienced objectivities and capacities (e.g., in the *Phenomenology's* treatment of Rome, modern wit, and modern culture generally) (see Hegel 1977, 294–321, "The World of Self-Alienated Spirit; Culture and Its Realm of Actuality"). Reason as coordinating reflection is connected to the most general conditions of the possibility of specific rationalities, for example, economic, moral, technical, and the corresponding objects and social relations.

According to Hegel, philosophical reason comprehends specific rationalities and places their claims in determinate social locations. In effect philosophy meets the requirements of a normative reflection on knowledge-politics by showing how modern specialized knowledges figure within a world that has itself been shown to be knowable and at least implicitly reasonable. In this way Hegel provides reflection for liberalism as conceived earlier in the discussion, that is, as a politics closely associated with modern forms of knowing and with modern forms of reflection on knowing. Hegel thus can be taken as advancing the claim that only an idealism can make the liberal case regarding modern rationality and modern institutions. We can only show that science and technology are potentially part of a reasonable world and that modern institutions are part of a knowable and potentially reasonable world if we think of the world as itself unified by an inherent rational potential.

Historical Constitution and Reflection on Knowledge

Hegel changes considerably the terms of constitutive theory by employing a conception of historically evolving differential complexes of social practices. Nonetheless, his argument remains tied to the epistemological preoccupations of modern philosophy. By seeing how Hegel offers his own alternative to Descartes's and Kant's response to skepticism, we can see why his conceptual framework must contain his social conception within the terms of the problem of the relation between subjectivity and objectivity. This commitment will come into conflict with the social side of his reconstruction.

When outlining his dialectical method in the introduction to the *Phenomenology of Spirit*, Hegel (1977, 47) argues that we cannot validate our ability to know independent of the pursuit of knowledge itself. He means to reject both Cartesian and Kantian approaches to the problem of knowledge, but this does not mean that he entirely abandons the epistemological project. In fact, Hegel adheres to the modern project of refuting skepticism, despite his rethinking of what this project involves. We have already noticed traces of this adherence in his complaint against Kant about that philosopher's failure to overcome skepticism. And although his own dialectical approach is explicitly presented as an alternative to Cartesian foundationalism or Kantian transcendentalism, echoes of these earlier strategies may be heard in Hegel's argumentation. He rethinks skepticism as a series of challenges that, when met, advance the comprehension of knowledge, and he treats this advance itself as a progressive identification of ever more comprehensive conditions for the possibility of knowledge and freedom. Through the necessity of this argument, the reality of knowledge is to be established against reasonable doubt.

It bears remarking that Hegel's reflection on knowledge is a theory concerned with mediation. The *Logic* depicts thought as thinking itself; thus the *Logic* is an account of concepts that generate and resolve problems. This occurs in a process of mediation whereby thought is a dynamic organized by oppositions that require a mediation they themselves provide by virtue of the relations that hold between these oppositions. Concepts can "think themselves" because they are crystallizations of thought activity. Thought activity in turn is not for Hegel disembodied reflection but is inherent in activity as such. The rationality of any social activity is thought activity, and the objectivity of even the most abstract thought is a matter of the self-embodiment of thought as such. As a result, we can think of conceptual mediations as matters not entirely separate from social mediations, even if we do not immediately identify the two kinds of mediation. The conceptual structure of the *Logic* is not simply applied to social content in the

Philosophy of Right, but the conceptualizations of the latter are possible because of the relations demonstrated in the former, and thus the social mediations of the latter presuppose and embody mediations of the former.

To appreciate the significance of the theme of mediation here, we need to recall that Hegel's dialectic of knowledge is at the same time a dialectic of activity. The unification of the knowing subject and the known object is linked to a dialectic of subjectivity and objectivity within an identity theory whose characteristic notion of synthesis is worked out through a variety of mediating processes that are themselves mediated by the necessary dynamics of *Geist* as such. From the standpoint from which social mediation appears irreducible, the striking difficulty with Hegel's approach to knowledge is that its strategy for refuting skepticism involves an identity theory whose metaphysical unity tends to undercut the mediations on which it relies. Social mediations are reconstructed as conceptual mediations whose compromised objectivity cannot be sustained in the face of a conception of metaphysical unity mandated by epistemological considerations.

My claim about Hegel, then, is that two objectionable features of his theory are instructively related. Though he makes fruitful use of the idea of mediation, in the end his is an idealist mediation that functions within a totality that in significant respects undercuts mediation altogether by treating the differentiations and oppositions in which mediation works as fundamentally unreal. This compromised version of mediation is inseparable from the idealism it serves. And both are features of a philosophy that organizes its unprecedented effort to incorporate historical content as an argument for the reality of knowledge.

Hegel is confronted with a paradox that Kant had already constructed when he abandoned intellectual intuition as the basis for epistemological validation. The necessities that are to validate the epistemological claim and refute skepticism never are entirely mastered by the reflecting subject, whose insight is fundamental. That this is a paradox haunting even philosophies of immediacy is an argument Derrida has made repeatedly (e.g., in Derrida 1978). The point is that Hegel's account of mediation takes Kant's transcendentalism another step away from classic epistemology's illusion that knowledge could be validated against doubt within the philosophical subject's own reflective experience. In the place of Kant's transcendentalism, Hegel proposes a different kind of reflection on the conditions of possible knowledge. This new strategy reconstructs the relation of knowing subjectivity and known objectivity by way of various social and historical practices.

The dynamic interrelation of ideas corresponds to a dynamic of social practices. Now philosophical reflection traces conceptual relations that can be seen in certain crucial respects to be identical with relations characterizing historical activity. Thought mediations coincide with mediations with the world of humanity's evolving daily experience. Hegel's effort to satisfy the demands of epistemology is doomed because any alternative to intuitive certainty will seem dogmatic to those who adhere strictly to the epistemological quest. On the other hand, his introduction of historical material into the epistemological quest has distorting effects on that material. The corresponding idealization of history is itself a falsification.

This familiar general point about Hegel needs to be stated more specifically in relation to the theme of mediation. I have noted in general terms that the idealization of the terms of mediation undermines mediation as such. Now let me make this point more directly in relation to themes proper to the social understanding of knowledge.

The epistemological project is to result in the advance of knowledge achieving self-knowledge. Humanity/*Geist* unifies experience through activity: as "substance becomes subject," the oppositions of subject and object—first humanity versus nature, then socialized humanity versus its own alienated products—are overcome, and the unity of the world is affirmed. But it is affirmed explicitly and rigorously only in the philosopher's theory. Humanity/*Geist* is the subject whose self-knowledge coincides with apprehension of the mediated identity of things. But the self-understanding of most humanity is partial and indirect, even as history approaches the synthetic unification that makes the philosopher's theoretical affirmation possible and true. Quite in contrast with the immanent insight of the Cartesian subject, Hegel's subjects have limited and indirect insight made possible by an immanence that characterizes the logic of historical and social mediation as reconstructed by philosophical theory.

Hegel's reworking of Kant's critical project introduces conceptual and historical mediation as features of a dynamic approach to thought and reality. With his notion of *Geist*, or spirit, Hegel thinks he can break with the dualisms and reductionisms of the tradition. More specifically, he thinks he can avoid the subjectivist features of Kant's philosophy and thereby avoid its concessions to skepticism. Hegel's

conception of differentiated yet unifying activities departs in important ways from the tradition by introducing historical content into
philosophy and rethinking concepts in terms of conceptual mediations. But he maintains a traditional notion of independent philosophical theory and the modern aims of an epistemological reflection that
can refute skepticism through arguments possessing a distinctively
philosophical necessity. The identity theory, crystallized in the idea of
Geist, stands in tension with the theme of mediation. I take this theory
to reflect Hegel's abiding link to the epistemological tradition and have
suggested that the tension between it and an account that preserves
the specifics of mediation results from the impossible, and ideological,
features of the epistemological project.

With the idea of *Geist* Hegel casts social and historical being in terms
of a collective subject. By doing so he can carry out the epistemological
project, since his treatment of this subject's knowing itself provides a
way to overcome otherness in cognition as well as in being and to avoid
skepticism and subjectivism. For purposes of the present discussion
there are two noteworthy difficulties with this conception. One concerns the relation between *Geist*, a collective subject whose internal
necessities in the last analysis govern the process as a whole, and the
individual subjects and empirical collectivities whose action and experience is said to be so governed. This is really a complex of problems,
including such diverse issues as the meaning of individual action and
the place of philosophical theory. If this first difficulty has to do with
mediation between the whole and parts, the second concerns the
relations between the parts themselves, relations that in my perspective are also a question of mediation. How are we to understand
mediations between social practices, including those of intellectuals? I
have already asserted that Hegel's epistemologically motivated identity theory undercuts these mediations. It remains only to relate
Hegel's argument to themes of liberal knowledge-politics and to return
to the specific issue of philosophical mediation.

Hegel and Philosophical Mediation

We can approach Hegel's relation to themes of intellectual and specifically philosophical mediation by way of the relation in his work between the two sets of difficulties mentioned above. Specifically, let us
consider the way mediation between practices responds to the problem

of the relation between specific practices and the totality, or the development of *Geist* understood philosophically.

The world as understood in terms of the theory of *Geist* diverges from the world of nontheoretical experience. This divergence concerns the relation between the present period and the past, in which past struggles and achievements are drained of the meaning they held for contemporary participants and are reconstructed in terms of humanity's goals as defined in the present. Not only is the understanding of those whose agency is treated as the actual formative historical process discounted (or, more accurately, functionally recast in terms of historical necessities as perceived in retrospect), but their aspirations and sufferings are written off to the necessities of a process they could never grasp. There is a latent reductionism and objectivism in this approach. The divergence I have in mind can also be approached in terms of the world contemporaneous with philosophically rigorous understanding and thus achievement of the stage in which Spirit's goals become "for themselves." I focus on this latter issue, since I take the former to be intractable and in any event not subject to the solution Hegel offers for the latter.

It should be clear that Hegel has to offer some solution. His focus on freedom and knowledge requires that he be able to square the one-sided and partial views and motivations of agents not only with the working of the world as he casts it theoretically but also with the claim that in this world all are free. In this respect, his dilemma is a variant of the problem of liberal universalism. We can treat this as the problem of the relation between the world as reconstructed in theory and the world of everyday experience, where the former involves normative as well as explanatory claims about the agency exhibited in the latter.

Conceived as a problem of the generalization of world historical insight, the diffusion throughout society of the philosopher's insight on behalf of the whole, this becomes for Hegel a matter of complex mediations in which experts, including philosophers, play various specialized roles. Reviewing his account as a whole would require rethinking the entire *Philosophy of Right*. I will instead make a few general claims about Hegel's strategy in order to make plausible the claim that this feature of the way he develops the theme of mediation can be understood along the lines sketched earlier in discussing epistemology and liberalism. Hegel's account provides a validation of knowledge-politics in general and of the power of intellectuals in particular.

The problem, again, has to do with the generalization of those insights that Hegel equates with a historically forged self-knowledge of humanity but that exist in explicit form only in the theory of the philosopher. For Hegel the general possession of appropriate social comprehension is not a matter of the diffusion of theoretical knowledge, but rather of the effective possession by everyone of differentially articulated but universally valid insight. Such a general possession of social understanding appears required by Hegel's dictum that in the modern world, in contrast to the past, *everyone* is free (see the introduction to Hegel 1956).

Viewed as a matter of universalistic political consciousness, a variety of mediations involve institutions in which intellectuals play vital roles and through which appropriate social insight is cultivated and diffused. For example, in Hegel's discussion of what he calls the corporation, this institution mediates between modern self-interest and the interest of the whole by articulating a group interest based on shared conditions of economic activity. Such corporations rely upon intellectuals as officials, representatives, and so on. The corporations provide the link between the middle classes and the parliament, so those who represent the corporations within the government also return to these organizations in an educational role. Political discussion that takes place in corporations, as in the legislature itself, is primarily educational, a means by which the general population, assisted by appropriately trained specialists, learns to think in the appropriate terms about matters of general social importance.

Representatives are not only educators, since they are to convey particular standpoints and experiences to the universally directed state institutions. Nevertheless, "public opinion is to be despised as much as it is to be respected" (Hegel 1991a, 355). The point is not so much that Hegel is not a democrat as that he does not really see this as a matter of power relations. There is no genuine conflict of interests, though there may be dramatic struggles. There is no real domination in the rational state, though there is hierarchy. Reason itself levels out these divisions in favor of rational differentiation. And this differentiation is sustained by specialists whose reasoning has to do with various interpretations, instruction, reporting, and so on.

My claim is that Hegel's epistemologically conditioned theory results in political mediation being organized by ontological necessities inherent in his account of objective reason. The mediations between intellectuals and nonintellectuals are not themselves cast as genuine interactions but play out a rational necessity inscribed in the theory of the spiritual whole or the state. The reduction of the give-and-take of politics to an educational model itself gives way to a reduction of interaction to the workings of a necessity to which agency conforms.

This tendency in Hegel's account is confirmed by the eclipse of the analysis of a specifically interactive rationality (see Habermas 1973, "Labor and Interaction: Remarks on Hegel's Jena *Philosophy of Mind*"), as well as by the absence of an account of the mediational role of philosophers. For a philosopher of activity, the treatment of theorists as socially passive might not seem a paradox. But Hegel requires reflective insight into the world for politics itself. It is not the job of philosophers to approach the world in a future-oriented way, yet political leaders must grasp elements of philosophical insight to pursue appropriate policies. Hegel's own readiness to take positions on matters of contemporary political debate reflects a sensitivity to the practical functions of modern abstractions, a sensitivity that makes his discussion of specialist mediation of genuine political and historical interest. On the other hand, his theoretical rejection of any political role for philosophical insight reflects his commitment to an epistemological approach to rationality, a commitment that paradoxically validates the claims of modern intellectual insight while obscuring its political and social reality. In the end, to the extent that political leaders are intellectuals whose expertise is validated by philosophical theory, they assume the same expressive or passive relation to rational necessity as the philosophers.

While the result of these features of Hegel's thought is a failure to carry through with an adequate account of intellectual mediation, it is also in effect the provision of an account of knowledge-politics. Hegel validates expert insight even if he does not provide an adequate social account of its possibility. In these respects he follows the path of earlier liberals, despite his philosophical innovations. While the theory of *Geist* seems to anticipate an account of the division of labor so far as it portrays differentiation and unification of practices, it fails to sustain an account of the social interrelations that make such a division itself a complex of practices united by practices. Thus Hegel contributes to an ideological understanding of the modern division of labor and provides a justification for the authority of intellectuals, an understanding of intellectuals within a politics of knowledge.

Hegel's way of weaving together reflection on knowledge with historical theory remains too close to the aims and strategies of epistemology and is insufficiently concerned with a social understanding of knowledge that would include an understanding of the relation between knowledge and power. We still need an adequate social and historical way to think of the social mediations Hegel introduces into philosophy, in particular in relation to reflection on rationality and society that allows us to respect the actual weight of social interaction and avoids reducing mediations to the reflection of an alleged deeper necessity. Specifically with regard to philosophy, we need a conception that grasps its social reality in relation to its intellectual tasks, that thus treats philosophical practice as responsive and receptive to its context as well as active and constructive in its relations to other practices. We need to see philosophy itself as a mediating activity, and doing so involves treating intellectual practices generally in a critical light.

Marx

Marx as Philosopher

I turn here to Marx on the assumption that his break with Hegel produced a fruitful approach to critique in the sense I have already outlined, that is, a philosophical reflection on rationality by way of a philosophical reflection on the division of labor. With his radicalization of reflection on the division of labor, Marx introduces an idea of social constitution that locates synthesis in a differential complex of social practices rather than in the activity of a global subject. While this approach involves historical reflection on rationality, it is not a reflection that follows the mandate of modern epistemology. Since Marx is not concerned to refute skepticism, he can dispense with Hegel's global subject. Of course, he also has reasons specific to social theory for rejecting such a subject, but these are not entirely independent of philosophical issues, since they bear both on the critique of ideological universalisms (in favor of class analysis) and on the pursuit of genuine universality associated with historical possibilities of supplanting class society and the exploitation, domination, and alienation that go with it in its capitalist form.

The relation of this practical universalism to universalistic claims of theory remains an open question so far as Marx's own work goes. His comments on knowledge are important and influential, but fragmentary and in some respects contradictory. In discussing Marx, therefore, my aim is not so much to characterize features of a position he worked out explicitly as to trace features of a critical philosophical conception at work in much of his nonphilosophical work.[1] In characterizing what I take to be some of Marx's contributions to philosophy understood as the critique of the division of labor, I refer to features of his work that were not solely or primarily matters of philosophical concern to him. If my account of Marx seems one-sided, that is due to the fact I am emphasizing one aspect of a much more complex project.

I am suggesting, then, that Marx's "Critique of Political Economy" is also a critique in a philosophical sense, a reconstruction of a certain kind of knowledge and rationality from the standpoint of the conditions that make it possible. *Capital* is a philosophical work in providing a reflection on the rationality of political economy understood, in the language I am using, as an intellectual practice. It seems fair to attribute concern with intellectual practices to Marx, since he is interested not only in the conceptual productions of political economists but also in the social relations into which these intellectuals enter by virtue of the specific kinds of knowledge they fashion. Marx is a philosopher, then, in part because he is a theorist of intellectual mediation who is interested in the historical conditions and effects of specific kinds of knowledge whose cognitive achievements cannot be understood independent of their ideological functions.

To speak of Marx as working in the critical tradition is in part to say that for him society is constructed in a complex of social practices that can be reconstructed structurally and narratively. Breaking with Hegel's teleological conception of history includes, as I have noted, rejection of the idea that society as a whole can be understood as a subject. Marx retains Hegel's theme of objectification but historicizes it by applying it to practices, including knowledge practices, without conceiving them as guided by a subject/object dialectic. Both production and objectivity are conceived historically by Marx: as the social and technical features of production evolve, the experience of objects, of objective necessity, and of practical possibility also evolves.

Marx's constitutive theory is materialist in thus breaking with Hegel's conception of social construction as organized by necessities proper to the knowing subject. Marx is not a reductive materialist if that would mean reducing away practice in some kind of objectivist account. Agency is irreducible, but experience is shaped in various and varying ways by physiological, environmental, and social necessities that escape consciousness in important respects. By the same token, these necessities evolve historically as practical achievements, possibilities, and conflicts evolve. In this light we can virtually equate the irreducibility of agency with that of historicity, that is, with evolving relations to past and future within existing practices. Evolving forms of objectification coincide with changing senses of necessity, possibility, and reflective social awareness. Marx's account of commodity fetishism provides the classic statement of his conceptualization of these themes (1976, 163–77).

With these general considerations in mind, we can turn to Marx's reflection on knowledge. A specifically modern knowledge like political economy is bound to specifically modern practices. This is not only in the general sense that there can be no economic theory without a market economy, but also in the sense that concepts and methods of thought used by political economy have their historical basis in the social practices of modern exchange and production.[2] Modern knowledge presupposes modern practices, and in turn makes those practices possible so far as reflective insight is needed to advance the workings of the modern economy. By reconstructing the relation between economic thought abstractions and the social relations organized by commodity exchange, Marx explores the historical conditions that make possible a historical form of knowledge.

In this way his constitutive approach to society contributes to a constitutive reflection on specific kinds of knowledge, to an argument for the cognitive achievements of political economy: Marx's account shows why these knowledge claims can be sustained. On the other hand, as a framework of historical constitution conceived in terms of specific social relations and their associated conflicts and struggles, his account also seeks to establish limits on the knowledge political economy can achieve. Its object is limited historically, since its abstractions lose their cognitive fruitfulness outside commodified relations, but this kind of thinking is limited within its own historical setting as well. Its abstractions reify contextually dependent and contingent relations and enshrine a sense of necessity that is both real and open to political challenge (see Lukács 1971, chap. 4). Marx's materialism contextualizes thought and contests claims for its absoluteness and neutrality, but it also establishes ways thinking is socially effective.

From this perspective, knowledge both provides a partial representation of the world and figures in the reproduction of a specific world. Political economists add a latently political dimension to their activity by asserting for their knowledge an objectivity independent of power relations. In capturing this dimension of political economy, Marx is linking the cognitive assertions of specific intellectuals to debates over the understanding of knowledge within modern society. This is one reason the philosophical dimension of critique is directly involved in specific problems of social theory.

The involvement of this critical philosophy within a social theory that is itself contesting other kinds of theory shows that philosophy here is historical in its argumentative materials. The identification and challenge to historical necessities is not itself based on arguments claiming some kind of philosophical necessity but is bound up with the historical and empirical arguments for the alternative social analysis. Philosophical contextualization does not here involve a systematic theory, though, as I argue below, it fits within a synthetic conception of modern society and its historical possibilities.

Marx does not himself present what I am calling his philosophical argument as philosophical, and he does not discuss the relation between critique as bearing on political economy and critique within an explicit democratic philosophy of the sort I have in mind. Nonetheless he does provide the conceptual elements I have reviewed, and he contributes to the conception of the division of labor that I present as central to an explicit democratic philosophy. One point worth making here is that his avoidance of philosophical necessity does not preclude a concern with what I take to be proper to a historical philosophical reflection, namely, the establishment of a framework by which historical claims to universality may be contextualized and assessed. That is, the kind of philosophy I am attributing to Marx may not require philosophical necessity, but it does need some historical idea of universality in terms of which it can frame its criticisms and pose its democratic goals.

We see elements of such an idea in the themes by which Marx thinks capitalism can be supplanted by a classless society, namely, the objective possibilities of advanced industrial production conjoined with the social aspirations of the proletariat, the "universal class."[3] These claims are sometimes dismissed as echoes of Hegelian metaphysics, since they can be interpreted in terms of a collective subject retrieving its historically alienated objectifications. At this point I want only to point out that the idea of new kinds of historical universality does not depend on that metaphysics, and that one can pose it as a historical hypothesis open to practical testing. Such an approach is consistent with the reading of Marx I have sketched here, and can be developed in terms of the division of labor.

So Marx provides an account of the possibility of certain kinds of knowledge while trying to locate the limitations of such knowledge. In the first instance, this critique has to do with political economy, though it involves more general claims about liberal thought and modern philosophy. At the same time, Marx's own intellectual project, his critique, has to be grasped in a way that is consistent with his argument about political economy and modern philosophy. In particular, it has to be grasped in a way that keeps the historical issue of the division of labor in view. In all these respects, Marx is concerned with reflection on rationality as intellectual activity and attempts to think about the conditions for such rationality by referring the constitutive principles of the world in which it makes its cognitive achievements.

This reading of Marx might seem to imply that he pursued social theory for philosophical reasons. The point, rather, is that for Marx social theory has a philosophical moment because we cannot achieve an adequately critical understanding of society without remaining critical regarding our forms of understanding. This is not only because we face opposing ways of thinking but also because conflict between forms of thinking is inseparable from wider social conflicts. Ways of thinking are practically involved in the social world that is to be understood.

Critique, Ideology, and Knowledge-Power

In portraying Marx as a philosopher, I am attributing to him a reflection on rationality that breaks with the epistemological attempt to refute skepticism without breaking with philosophy's traditional concern about challenges to knowledge claims. Following Hegel, Marx refuses to see arguments for or against skeptical doubts as an all-or-nothing game. He wants to sustain doubts about certain kinds of knowledge without rejecting that knowledge altogether. But in following Hegel's attempt to think dialectically about specific historical knowledge claims, Marx does not pursue an absolute philosophical standpoint.

His argument neither seeks to guarantee knowledge against doubt, subjectivism, or irrationalism, nor does it promote a purely philosophical theory or method. His reflection is philosophical in the critical sense because it approaches issues of validity from the standpoint of the conditions of the possibility of knowledge. But it is historical by focusing on specific kinds of knowledge using specific historical arguments. Insofar as it raises doubts about knowledge, his argument does not follow traditional lines of suspicion. And so far as he seeks to validate knowledge, he does not do so to refute these traditional forms of suspicion. Rather, in both doubting and validating knowledge, Marx's argument is concerned with the limits and achievement of cognitive validity as they intersect with power relations.

This characterization of Marx is defensible in view of his reworking of philosophy's challenges to knowledge claims. The challenges to classical political economy and then to vulgar political economy emphasize the relation between intellectual claims and the pursuit of class interests. Ideological shaping of conceptualization develops as the practically grounded process of thinking leads to cognitive distortions. For Marx, practical interests may in some cases contribute to genuine insight, as he thinks they do in the scientific phase of political economy. Later, as class conflict can no longer be ignored, political economy's relation to class interests contributes to distortion. In both cases, intellectual work serves class power. The philosophical critique of political economy, on the one hand, allows us to see both how knowledge is possible and how it intersects with power in ways that limit the application and temper the understanding of genuine knowledge and, on the other, allows us to identify ideological distortion in cognitive disguise.

The complicated relation between intellectual claims and the object of knowledge, on Marx's conception, bears notice here. Political economy can be scientific because its concepts and claims allow us to reconstruct the world in thought (see Marx 1973, introduction). So there is the element of a realism or representational view here. At the same time, this is a "conceptual appropriation" that is practically conditioned and open to rethinking and criticism. Thought abstractions are made possible by social abstractions, as I have noted above, but their formal homologies should not lead us to ignore the respects in which, as abstractions, these thoughts are selective and practically conditioned. The conceptual abstractions proper to the theory of value, for example, are rooted in the social abstractions of exchange, but they also provide a selective understanding of the world that is being promoted by political economists. Dividing things into use values and exchange values is both true to the world of the modern market and one-sided. Promoting this analysis contributes to social understandings and practices that contribute to the workings of specific and contingent systems of power.

Both in their genuine knowledge and in their ideology, then, political economists engage in social practices that have practical effects. Though Marx does not in so many words speak of knowledge as a mediating practice carried out by intellectuals, he in fact contributes to an account of such practice. In the cases of knowledge and ideology alike, his concern with intellectual constructions figures in the study of what is done with such constructions. Political economists provide social understanding to those who directly pursue individual and class interests in economic and political contexts (see, e.g., Marx 1976, 174–75). In part they do this by drawing from the experiences and by articulating the standpoints and concerns of those who are more directly engaged in economic and political conflicts.

By claiming that Marx is a philosopher of knowledge-power, I am arguing that he is interested in knowledge as knowledge: the intersection of cognition and power is not conceived by him in a way that reduces knowledge claims to effective functions of social interests. But cognitive achievements are not separable from the historical relations in which they have functions. And if we must preserve the distinctively conceptual achievements of knowledge as knowledge, we cannot reconstruct the force of these achievements without seeing them as social actions. Similarly, ideological distortion is not simply a conceptual error or willful mystification but something that figures within specific kinds of intellectual practices where practical functions lead to contradictory results when measured by the culture of abstract knowledge in which they arise.

To characterize Marx as a theorist of knowledge-power, then, is to see his work as contributing to a conception of ideology that is specifically tied to intellectual practices proper to the modern period. That is, it is to see one kind of ideology as internally related to abstract knowledge as cultivated and functioning in modern society. So far as ideology distorts reality in ways that serve class interests, in the setting of intellectual practices it involves distortions that function in close association with knowledge that is employed with practical effects. What is problematic from a cognitive standpoint is also contestable from a practical standpoint.

Of course, other things can be said about ideology as conceived by Marx. One additional feature that bears on my immediate concerns has to do with the utopian element of much ideology, a feature that is highlighted in the treatment of religion as ideology (see Marx, "Critique of Hegel's *Philosophy of Right*: Introduction"). Though the dominant trends in modern intellectual practices assert knowledge that displaces normative with factual or technical considerations, the political features of the processes in which these practices figure typically make for the retention of some tie to liberal utopianism. Marx's relation to the utopian tradition is ambivalent, since he and Engels explicitly prefer a scientific to an abstract utopian criticism of society (a stance that can be interpreted in either a Hegelian or positivist spirit), yet they orient themselves to a radical rethinking of modern ideals along the lines of counterfactual possibilities. For now I shall simply note that the treatment of ideology as knowledge-power leaves the relation to utopian contents unresolved. I believe this will prove to be an issue in thinking through the normative commitments of the kind of critique I am attributing to Marx both with regard to aspects of cognitive validity and with regard to democratic politics.

I am not claiming that Marx provides anything like a systematic approach to philosophy in the sense of a critique of the division of labor, but that he is in effect advancing the kind of reflection I have characterized as the critique of the division of labor. In Chapter 5, I consider the features of such a standpoint in more detail. The aim of the discussion of Marx to this point has been to introduce a sense of reflection on the division of labor as reflection in the critical tradition. One objective has been to fill out the idea of postepistemological reflection on rationality as reflection on intellectual practices. In reworking traditional themes in this direction, Marx moves from traditional notions of theory as these bear on his own activity. To pursue philosophical reflection in social terms requires that one's own reflection be so treated. If one rejects a decontextualizing account of the knowledge on which one reflects, and remains consistent with such a rejection in one's sense of the theory and method by which contextualization is to be carried out, then one must also avoid tacit dehistoricizing and decontextualizing assumptions when it comes to one's own work.

Marx and Democratic Mediation

Traditional approaches to theory and method have allowed philosophers both to treat in nonsocial terms the reason on which they reflect and to treat their own activity as outside social conditions and constraints. Consistently treating abstract knowledge as social practice requires that this reflection be able to frame itself as social practice and to organize its practical self-understanding accordingly. I have used the idea of the critique of the division of labor to interpret a tendency among contemporary intellectual practices that itself has emerged within the practices of modern knowledge-politics. As a way of reflecting on rationality, this critique is a social event within a network of intellectual mediations. It in no way stands above the complex of intellectual practices engaged in the contemporary web of power relations. Like any philosophical position, it makes claims about the force of its specific insights, and like any political position, it makes claims about the value of its specific aims and strategies. I take such intellectual and political claims to involve this critique in assertions of certain kinds of historical universality and assume that the value of this critique can be shown only if these kinds of universality can be sustained argumentatively. As the argument of the book as a whole advances, I am trying to bring out elements of this kind of argumentation. In referring to Marx here, I am concerned with how he contributes to rendering such a philosophical reflection in appropriately social terms.

Marx occasionally discusses his work in social terms. For example, in the *Communist Manifesto* he discusses the historical origins and relations of communist intellectuals (Marx and Engels 1978, 481). In the introduction to the *Grundrisse*, he discusses the historical conditions for one of his key abstractions, that of abstract labor. Engels, too, takes up the historical conditions for the materialist understanding of history in *Anti-Dühring*, where he refers to the rising of French workers as exemplary political developments in the context of industrialization and associated intellectual debates (Engels 1969, 36).

These kinds of discussion dispute claims to the autonomy or independence of the theorist. On the other hand, they also emphasize the constructive and active features of intellectual activity by treating it as an activity that responds to specific social and intellectual conditions. The theme of the productive quality of intellectual work—as the making of a conceptual object—leads to the further theme of the specific communicative or interactive relations into which intellectuals' practice introduces them. Both of these themes, the specific constructive features of intellectual work and the interactive relations in which they function, are crucial to any account of intellectual mediation.

Beyond the social and historical terms in which Marx offers reflection on his own work, there is another respect in which his pursuit of the critique of the division of labor keeps this kind of philosophy historically anchored. This has to do with the argumentative qualities of this specific kind of philosophy. Marx pursues various kinds of reflection in his philosophical activity: the constitutive account provides reasons why a certain kind of knowledge is possible even as it establishes limits on its applicability and limitations on its perspective. On this basis, Marx can challenge specific knowledge claims as ideological, as contributing to knowledge-power. His reflection is structural, but it is also narrative, so far as it casts conservative intellectuals and their social allies as participants in an unresolved drama that leads into the present. An additional moment of Marx's intellectual activity that I want to emphasize here concerns the way this narrative perspective informs activity undertaken in the present. Most immediately, this has to do with the knowledge Marx is trying to develop and defend. The critique of political economy is at once a challenge to prevailing economic theory and an alternative analysis of the modern economy in its political and cultural relations. And the constitutive and narrative challenges made concerning political economy are part of the argument against political economy and in favor of this alternative.

So Marx's argument for his own position includes the kind of critical assessment of the prevailing view I have been discussing. That is to say, he does not simply try to refute, much less ignore, political economy, but takes it seriously in an ambitious and unprecedented way. He wants to change the terms of the discussion and so provides a constitutive and critical account of these terms as they exist within political economy. Marx does not precisely argue with political economists, though there are many specific points on which he takes issue. But the way he develops his critical approach represents a kind of argumentative relation to political economists that takes the value of their knowledge as a point of reference. Marx's critique, then, locates his own activity within history by providing a distinctive way of proceeding from the existing argumentation. He locates himself historically in this respect by taking a specific argument as his own point of departure.

The philosophical side of Marx's argument allows for a certain distance from the prevailing discourse, but it is a distance that allows him a particular engagement with that discourse. Critique establishes the historicity of that discourse and so establishes the historicity of the argumentation in which Marx is engaged. Even if he changes the terms of the debate, he engages political economists argumentatively and in fact does so by identifying levels of their own activity, assertions they are making beyond the scope of specific arguments. Critique allows for a confrontation with political economy on its tacit as well as explicit levels and so makes possible a confrontation of an intellectual mediation in the full range of its mediating activities.

Critique as I am attributing it to Marx, then, allows for argumentative engagement with existing intellectual practices not only on the level of specific intellectual claims but on other levels in which mediating activity takes place. Far from pretending to transcend history by offering a constitutive account of knowledge in general or by claiming to have achieved a historical perspective whose absoluteness allows theory to supersede debate, Marx pursues a critique that is engaged with opponents despite its claims to a higher universality.

So far I have argued that there are two ways Marx historicizes his own work. One has to do with various ways of contextualizing the intellectual and practical activity in which he is engaged. The other has to do with the nature of the argumentation he undertakes. Both features of his discussion have a historicizing function appropriate to the ideal of democratic mediation, but they hardly provide a sufficiently developed account of democratic philosophical mediation. Indeed, one may argue that there is much in Marx that conflicts with the account fashioned here. The aim has not been to find an account that can accommodate all of Marx's claims, nor has it been to find a complete conception or sustained practice of democratic philosophy in his work. Rather, I have been seeking elements of a model of the kind of philosophical reflection presented in this study as critique of the division of labor. So there is no need to make inflated claims about Marx or to deny the gaps and contradictions in his work. It may in fact be useful to highlight some of the features of his work that are in tension with the kind of philosophical practice I have been considering. Doing so is important for a democratic rethinking of Marx in the light of the politics of the twentieth century, especially in the wake of the closure of a certain kind of socialist practice. Such a rethinking is beyond the scope of my discussion, but reference to some relevant themes will help bring out requirements facing democratic philosophy.

I have characterized Marx's philosophical activity as embedded in his engagement with political economy. Reflection on the rationality of political economists is part of the development of a more adequate understanding of production and its relation to historical possibility. Coming to terms with political economy requires coming to terms with the intellectual mediation of which it is a part, and doing both is necessary for the politics that would draw out and act upon these historical possibilities. I have noted that the way Marx tries to make concrete historical sense of political economy involves situating his own intellectual activity historically. Though the self-reflection on his own intellectual activity that is advanced by his critique is for the most part undeveloped, it is a necessary part of the work of establishing an adequate political orientation. This necessity is made evident by the challenges mounted against the political economists and their allied intellectuals (including liberal and epistemologically oriented philosophers): modern society puts intellectuals in a complex of mediating relations proper to the workings of power, and intellectuals who would challenge features of that power must be clear about their social functions as well as their intellectual claims.

The kind of critical self-awareness of intellectual activity his own work advances is often sidestepped by Marx in his own comments on knowledge. His quasi-positivist comments about method, his occasional readiness to treat the development of knowledge and society in terms of a progressive natural history, and his frequent condemnations of philosophy *tout court* all cut against the kind of philosophical commitment I have painted (see, e.g., Marx 1976, 90 and 101–3). These tendencies in his thought are worth noting for the respects in which they allow him to mimic the decontextualization of knowledge that characterizes precisely the position regarding knowledge-power to which he is opposed. Perhaps these contradictions can be attributed in part to the occasional nature of such comments and in part to Marx's never having worked out his philosophical commitments in any sustained, much less systematic, way. But they can perhaps also be attributed to the limitations in Marx's reflection on politics. The trace of positivism in Marx is inseparable from a weakness in political reflection if the connection I am tracing between critical philosophical reflection and democratic politics in fact holds.

Challenges to Marx as a political thinker take many forms. He is sometimes treated as reducing politics (and everything else) to economics; he is accused of having too narrow an understanding of the liberal state, of having too little a place for postcapitalist politics; and he is challenged for missing what is qualitatively distinctive about political action and experience. There are respects in which all of these criticisms can be sustained, though the critical project Marx develops is probably the strongest argument against economic reductionism available. And I have been arguing that his approach to intellectual practice opens up novel directions for political criticism and for self-reflection by would-be critical intellectuals. From the standpoint of the critique of the division of labor, the crucial problem that Marx does not face is that of a politics that confronts the whole range of ways intellectuals function in mediating power relations.

Marx historicizes intellectual activity by bringing it into relation to the evolution of production and the conflicts over it. While he thus breaks with illusions of autonomous theory, he risks oversimplifying issues of power and politics by restricting his focus on conflict to production. His own account of the division of labor is richer than this, since it incorporates other power relations and corresponding conflicts (and corresponding contexts of intellectual mediation), for example, relations of gender and nationality. Marx's strategy for materializing reflection on knowledge runs the risk of opposing philosophical absolutism to an exclusive focus on production. His avoidance of economic reductionism does not suffice to avoid thinking not only of the stakes and conditions of politics as being in production but of politics itself in terms of the instrumentally organized practices prevailing in the sphere of production. If we think of production itself as having a variable position within the division of labor, then we can avoid so close or exclusive a relation between power issues and production and broaden our sense of the contexts in which intellectual mediation bears on issues of power. It is to such a conception I now turn in discussing more directly the division of labor as a philosophical idea.

Chapter 5

The Division of Labor and Its Critique

With the discussion of Marx, I have noted some ways the idea of the division of labor provides a philosophical alternative to traditional reflection on rationality. Marx does not explicitly develop such a philosophical use of this idea, nor do I claim to do more than present some of its features in this essay. In part this is because the conceptual issues inherent in my thesis present a complexity and difficulty to which I cannot hope to respond here. In part it is also because the concept of philosophy concerned with the division of labor has to do with mediations that involve the effort of many philosophers. In this connection, it is worth repeating the contention that the project of the critique of the division of labor is implicit in the work of many contemporary thinkers who do not identify their concern in so many words.

General Features of the Idea of the Division of Labor

In its philosophical use, the idea of the division of labor is a way of thinking about the formation of society through the differentiation and coordination of social practices. Among the distinguishing features of this idea of social constitution is the way it treats historical forms of knowledge as being made possible by virtue of features of other social practices that in turn are sustained by the practical effects of knowledge practices themselves. Thus the division of labor provides a way of thinking about knowledge in social terms. The division of labor can figure in the analytical, critical, and constructive moments of philosophical reflection and provides a way for philosophers to bear in mind the social position and functions of their own activity.

Though the division of labor has broad application as a philosophical idea, it plays a special role in reflection on modern society and modern knowledge in part because the division of labor becomes an increasingly explicit issue in modern thought and social practice. From a philosophical standpoint this special bearing on modern conditions follows from the fact that formally organized systems of knowledge come to play an increasingly important role in social life, and social life itself becomes increasingly organized in the terms of such knowledge. If knowledge has always been social, in modern conditions the articulation of specialized intellectual practices becomes especially prevalent, and practical issues of the mediating role of intellectuals become especially pointed.

The differentiations and coordinations of the division of labor can be conceived in various ways, some of which I have already cited. In very general terms, we can speak of the division between town and country or the division of labor within the family; in the modern world we can place the detailed division of labor within specific enterprises beside the social division of labor coordinated by the market and then locate these divisions within the division between economic, political, and cultural activities. Cutting across all of these is the division between intellectual and manual labor, a distinction that is especially important for the present discussion. The intellectual/manual distinction is imprecise, but serves to mark out the general trend toward the cultivation of expertise and the expansion of what I have called intellectual practices. As such it plays a central role in a more general feature of the division of labor as such, the specialization of persons.

Specialization of persons means something more than the participation by individuals in highly differentiated practices. It has to do with the cultivation of capacities and identities that fit individuals narrowly into quite specific social locations as defined by these differentiations. The intellectual/manual split is one way of identifying features of this specialization, but it also touches upon the emergence of intellectual practices that have for their object the analysis, cultivation, and even therapeutic mitigation of specialization in individuals.

The theme of the specialization of persons and of intellectual practices concerned with details of specialization touches upon another general feature of the division of labor, its contribution to the respects in which social life is disengaged from the dynamics of nature. Economic evolution, particularly with the emergence of complex and increasingly global market systems and the evolution of industrial powers, removes issues of production and consumption from immediately natural conditions. The individual's relation to material goods is mediated by social systems and forms of production that increasingly operate independently of natural rhythms. From the standpoint of the specialization of individuals, this institutional and structural evolution corresponds to increasing reliance on specialized mediations in processes of personality formation. Individuals are increasingly subject to complex and often intentionally organized interventions at the levels of affect, perception, and motivation, as well as belief and judgment. My contrast is not between a natural and a socialized individual, but between historical forms of individuality in which there is a tendential increase in the immediacy and complexity of interventions and adaptations.

In this regard, we can mention the possibility that the idea of the division of labor will help in thinking about qualitatively different ways human society experiences its relation to nature. For Hegel, the division of labor figures in the emergence of Spirit's independence from Nature. The need for a materialist alternative to this reflective negation of nature has grown in importance with the ecological crisis. For now, let me simply suggest that the relation to historicity suggested by thinking in terms of the division of labor may be relevant to the needed ecological conception.

The theme of specialization bears upon another distinguishing feature of the idea of the division of labor as I use it. Specialization results in specific distributions of capacities that in turn are matters of relations to social power more generally. The division of labor is a differentiation that has to do with organization of power, inequality, and therefore conflict.

Specialization of individuals is the way persons live the differentiations and coordinations of the division of labor, and these in turn organize power relations. With this claim, I am not saying that power relations are all functions of divisions of labor, nor am I saying that the division of labor can be reduced through functionalist analysis to a process that meets the requirements of various kinds of power. Rather, I am associating the division of labor with the reproduction of various kinds of power as well as treating it as the medium of a distinctive kind of power. So far as it contributes to reflection on rationality, the division of labor is to help clarify what I have called knowledge-power.

My programmatic claim here is that this idea will prove fruitful for thinking about the workings of knowledge-power from the standpoint of specific associations of knowledge and power linked to the exercise of expertise as such as well as to the functioning of other specific power relations. As I have noted, Marx's argument about knowledge-power concerns the ideological functions of political economy. Here knowledge-power is tied to the reproduction of class relations. Feminist and minority critics have argued for linkages between forms of knowledge and expertise and the reproduction of sexist and racist power relations.

This linkage of the division of labor with the reproduction of various kinds of power relations may seem virtually tautologous, since such power relations can exist socially only in the organization of the various practices whose most general level of organization can be conceived in terms of the division of labor. In this regard it is important to remember that the objective of the division of labor as a philosophical idea has to do with rethinking intellectual practices. The force, then, of linking these power relations to the division of labor lies in part in the implications that follow for the analysis and criticism of intellectual practices. The point here, however, is that with the idea of the division of labor we may have a way of thinking about specific linkages between expertise and power and may do so in a way that bears on a democratic project.

To speak here of power relations, and to do so in relation to expertise, is implicitly to suggest that the division of labor can be conceived as a framework of social interaction or communication. The relations and processes proper to such interaction are themselves in question, but now I note only their bearing on themes of power, conflict, and criticism. This antagonistic aspect of the relations of the division of labor in turn prompts the question of the historicity of the division of labor. I have been claiming that developing this idea philosophically provides us with a framework for thinking about rationality in historical terms.

The nature of this historical perspective depends upon the respects in which the various power relations and antagonisms associated with the division of labor are themselves historical.

As posed here, the division of labor is not natural. Arising within the evolution of human societies (in the transition to civilizations from communal orders), it figures within the process by which societies have challenged the subordination of their existence to natural forces. If the division of labor has emerged within human evolution, might it not also be superseded? Radical democratic criticism, which emerged in the nineteenth century and has had so torturous a history in the twentieth, is committed to the proposition that there is some important sense in which the division of labor can in fact be overcome.

Scarcity

The division of labor is not just differentiation, specialization, and coordination, it is as well all of these within relations of power, inequality, and conflict. Collectively, these constitute the defining feature of the division of labor that I designate scarcity. Without this concept we cannot develop a sense of what is at issue in the debate about the historical significance of the division of labor, let alone talk of overcoming the division of labor.

Scarcity Versus Shortage

Scarcity is often cited in justifications of the division of labor: scarcity of resources, scarcity of labor, and scarcity of time. The point I am most concerned to develop, however, is at odds with any contention, based on objective shortages, that scarcity justifies power relations. Scarcity should not be identified with the shortage of goods; nor does it function solely as an idea within justifications of power that make claims about the unavoidable social consequences of such shortages. Rather, scarcity can fruitfully be conceived as a particular historical way of experiencing shortages and of organizing them within power relations.

With the idea of scarcity we think of what is common to the different ways historical societies organize the shortage of desired goods. In these societies shortage is organized in relations of inequality so that what appears as the inevitable absence of desired goods for some coexists with the inevitable relative abundance of goods and time freed from labor for others. To use Marx's term, scarcity is a feature of societies that produce surplus. Rather than an objective lack or a shortage measured by the quantity of experienced wants, scarcity is a shortage proper to the inequalities and power relations of societies that produce surplus but have not eliminated shortage or created ways of organizing shortage so as to avoid domination and systematic inequality.

To say that scarcity is not inevitable is to assert that under certain conditions shortage could be experienced without informing such relations. It is to suggest that under appropriate conditions, a society could confront shortage as a problem for politics. Such politics would have to be democratic if the inequalities and dominations associated with scarcity were to be avoided. Since shortage in some form seems unavoidable, the replacement of scarcity by politically organized shortage becomes a key theme for a democratic politics concerned with challenging the division of labor.

By connecting the differentiations and coordinations of activity proper to the division of labor with scarcity, I mean to suggest that to the extent that the division of labor has become an issue in recent politics, scarcity itself has been made problematic. How we might decide whether the conditions in which scarcity has become problematic are ones in which it could also be overcome is a theme to which I turn later. First it is necessary to develop the link I am claiming between the division of labor and scarcity and to make plausible the inference that challenges to the division of labor are also challenges to scarcity.

In introducing the division of labor as the most general way of speaking of power relations, I touched on the issue of its distinctiveness as a kind of power and on the question of its relation to other kinds of power. Conceiving power relations specific to this feature of society and claiming that it in some way integrates other kinds of power raises the danger of reductionism or reliance on a totalizing account of power. In fact, the virtue of thinking in terms of the division of labor is precisely that it allows us to think of ways different power relations intersect without thinking of them as being reduced to a single dynamic or form of conflict. Nonetheless, associating scarcity with the division of labor may seem only to increase the danger of reductionism by relying tacitly on an underlying economic account of power. To confront this concern, it helps to recognize that scarcity is not solely a matter of relations to things.

Scarcity of Powers

The scarcity most directly organized by the division of labor is not that of material goods but of effective social capacities. The distribution of practical powers organized by specialization makes social power exercised through historically formed agency a scarce good. Here the power to do things is inseparable from power relations with other persons. Specific power relations, notably those of class, gender, and race, shape the division of labor and thus a particular regime of scarce agency. The power relation that seems to characterize the division of labor as such, that of expertise, is made an issue in all these other types of relation and conflict. Far from assimilating other issues of power, analysis of the division of labor thus provides terms for seeing how various kinds of power are pursued, reproduced, and challenged.

Challenging the division of labor as such, then, is linked conceptually to challenging the scarcity of agency. That is, to make an issue of the division of labor, rather than to contest a specific division of labor, is to question the means by which societies involve power exercised through the hierarchical formation and distribution of capacities. To eliminate the scarcity of agency would be to end the relation between the distribution of capacities and the various systematically reproduced networks of power relations. Or, to draw the parallel with the abolition of the division of labor, to eliminate the scarcity of agency would be to make the distribution of capacities a matter of conscious political choice, and necessarily a matter of democratic choice. The absence of the corresponding political means for doing this implies that scarcity of agency also becomes, at least when the division of labor has been made problematic, a scarcity of politics.

Scarcity of Politics

To speak of scarcity regarding politics here is to speak of a shortage of political choice regarding the cultivation and distribution of agency. It is to challenge the social processes by which agency has been formed. I have already presented reasons to argue that quasi-political processes have increasingly been directed at agency; I characterized this as one of the historical trends that make the division of labor an issue today. Scarce politics characterizes a historical process in which action on agency is an important evolving feature of social life. Scarcity in this context bears on qualities of agency, not just its distribution. It bears on the prospects of an evolving political culture in which more democracy would challenge scarcity in general and not just restrictions on political agency in particular.

Historically the issue of scarce politics is not new. It has been a persistent theme associated with the role of the market in modern societies, and it has been a theme associated with the role of the state more generally. Clearly the idea that the division of labor should be supplanted by politics is an extension of the challenge to the market as the means by which social capacities and practical opportunities are distributed. Without implying an end to markets, in this regard the abolition of the division of labor and of scarcity means the replacement of economics by politics. We may also use the replacement of economics by politics as a metaphor in the wider discussions of agency opened by challenges to scarcity.

Economies of Agency

In speaking of politics replacing economics, I mean that conscious decision replaces processes guided by objective necessities proper to existing institutional frameworks. The process is more complicated than this opposition suggests, because this is a necessity that is interpreted and acted upon by experts who carry out various mediations in the economy and the state and their intersection. In fact, interpreting and acting upon social necessities is the work pursued in various positions within the division of labor and so within the forms and distribution of agency itself. Locating these mediations is an important task for those who question the apparent objective necessity of market economies. Recognizing that even this most reified of all social institutions depends upon mediations of this sort may justify our using the idea of an economy as a metaphor characterizing more generally those social frameworks that shape and distribute agency in nonpolitical ways. The point of doing so is that we can then think of the challenge to the division of labor as such on the model of replacing economics by politics and can see the specifically market form of economy as but one of a succession of economies of agency.

Though use of this metaphor may again raise the specter of reductionism, like the idea of the division of labor it helps to analyze, the idea of an economy of agency actually helps us to conceive a differential association of frameworks of scarcity and power. We can think of divisions of labor as involving various economies of agency, whose principles of distribution organize various forms of power relations. With the economic metaphor, we can emphasize the way these relations possess the appearance of objective necessity of one sort or another (cosmological, theological, political, traditional, as well as economic) and yet involve the specialized interventions of various experts who thereby not only embody the division of labor but do so in ways that reproduce it.

Let me summarize the claims that have been developed in this discussion of the idea of scarcity within the division of labor. With the idea of scarcity I have associated the shortages proper to the division of labor with power relations and socially organized inequalities. With the idea of scarcity of agency, I have shown that shortage proper to power can be understood in terms of conflictual relations to various dimensions of capacity and practical opportunity. With the idea of scarcity of politics, I have connected the issue of agency in general with the issue of the reflective and purposeful shaping of agency as this becomes thinkable in the modern period. With the idea of economies of agency, I have placed this question of politics against various ways in which the division of labor has functioned to organize power relations characterized by historically shaped objective necessities. And in these contexts I see expert mediations addressing the reproduction of the division of labor as such.

Reference to scarcity thus allows us to conceive the division of labor as an economy of powers or as a complex of such economies. Within such economies intellectual expertise plays a variety of special roles. We can approach a discussion of these by considering how the division of labor is itself a framework of social interpretation and communication. In seeing this we can see how philosophical reflection on the division of labor assumes the form of a critique.

Before turning to this theme more directly, let me emphasize that in saying that the division of labor is not natural, I am not suggesting that scarcity and the struggle for existence are simply matters of historical convention, the willful act of power, or that they could be eliminated regardless of levels of technical and cultural development. Rather, I mean to say that there is no automatic relation between social productivity and the existence of scarcity, and that it is conceivable that under certain circumstances a society organized by relations of scarcity, that is, within a struggle for existence, could reorganize itself in ways that eliminated scarcity (even if that did not eliminate the failure to satisfy all wants). Doing so would involve a transformation of the nature and scope of politics.

One result of such an overcoming of scarcity might be a qualitative change in society's relation to nature. The fact that we can consider this possibility follows from the way the division of labor offers a perspective on historical societies as a whole. This perspective complements the way it provides a means of drawing contrasts between different historical societies. Though remaining itself a historical idea, the division of labor thus offers a certain transhistorical perspective. The issue of a qualitative change in society's relation to nature would thus be only one of many issues that might be raised about historical being and its bearing on rationality as understood and practiced heretofore. But the reflexivity proper to such issues is possible only within the division of labor itself. Is it plausible to claim that such reflexivity, with its interrelated theoretical and political aspects, has become possible in concrete terms because of the contemporary evolution of the division of labor?

Historical Reflection and the Division of Labor

Comparative Historical Themes

In exploring aspects of the idea of the division of labor, I am trying to bring out ways this idea can figure in philosophical reflection on rationality. For this purpose it is necessary to say more about how this is a historical idea that nonetheless possesses a scope relevant to philosophical concerns. In particular, even though I am not seeking arguments that establish necessary truths about reason, for this reflection to be philosophical and critical it must be adequate to a certain level of universality. Clearly, the idea of the division of labor aspires to a very high level of generality. What kind of universality is this? To what extent is it transhistorical? How can it be consistent for such a high level of generality to be asserted by thinking that not only acknowledges its own historical character (its being located within history, drawing from historical materials, etc.) but seeks to avoid the ideological misuse of universalistic claims as it considers intellectual practices, including itself, in social context?

In the remarks that follow here I do not attempt a philosophical justification of this idea, even in the respects that such a justification is consistent with the conception of philosophy with which I am working. I return to the theme of justification in Part Four. Just now I am, rather, concerned with characterizing the historical character of the idea, both as it is used to think about history and as it seeks to make such reflections consistent with a historical understanding of its own project.

First, let us consider the perspective on history this idea affords. The division of labor is a transhistorical idea so far as it allows us to compare social organization across thousands of years of human experience. It is not transhistorical in the sense either of claiming to apply to all societies or in the sense of projecting unavoidable conditions for future societies. It embraces all historical societies so far as these involve states, writing, urban administration, and the organization of production by classes. It does not embrace societies not organized in the relations of scarcity outlined in the preceding section. The scope of this idea embraces those societies which involve the power relations specific to the division of labor, namely, those between specialists employing writing and reflective abstractions (e.g., scribes, priests, clerks, accountants, teachers, managers, and professionals) and those made dependent upon them. Historically, these relations have not operated in isolation but have contributed to the organization of a variety of other forms of power (e.g., those proper to class, gender, and race or ethnicity). Thus a general theoretical claim I am making about the division of labor is that it allows a reflective unification of power relations that is sensitive both to the specifics of what has come to be called knowledge-power and to the different kinds of power that have become the focus of social movements.

Thinking of power relations at this high level of generality allows for comparative analysis and raises issues about historical evolution. Evolution need not be conceived teleologically. With his idea of the "civilizing process," for example, Norbert Elias (1978) identifies general tendencies that characterize the division of labor: increasing productive capacity, larger-scale and more complex organization, increasing social regulation of impulses to immediate violence and in general the "normalization" of relations, and the more extensive development and application of reflective abstraction. Such a conception by no means necessarily implies a linear development toward democracy or self-knowledge or other ways history has been conceived teleologically. In his argument Elias seems to follow Hegel and Marx when they attribute a kind of social immediacy to early societies. Speaking in terms of social substance and natural forms of social life, these thinkers associate relatively undifferentiated social relations with a relatively immediate identification with society as a whole. The emergence of the division of labor, and of history with it, involves a differentiation of social being that leads to a more mediated, less direct relation to the whole. We can view this process systemically as the emergence of increasing complexity. As such we can see some of the ways uses of abstraction become necessary, hence the rise of specialized intellectual functions.

Nonetheless, there is a sense in which critical use of the division of labor for critical and philosophical purposes may seem to rely on teleological thinking. This has to do with the possibility of achieving the kind of reflexive relation to the division of labor that such theorization asserts. The issue arises because this philosophical use of the division of labor cannot rely on philosophy of history. Is the division of labor to be seen, as Hegel argues, as an inevitable feature of social life and, under very special circumstances, compatible with realization of the liberal values of justice and universal cultivation of individuality? On this view, the idea of the division of labor is subordinated theoretically to conceptions that establish how such differentiation can be compatible with universal freedom and, in Hegel's case, community. Thus Hegel subordinates the historical analysis of the division of labor to the evolution of *Geist*.

There are two sorts of claims here. One has to do with the compatibility of the division of labor with the universalism of ethical life. If, however, one emphasizes the power relations and inequalities associated with the division of labor, then it does not appear compatible with ethical relations. Marx, for example, argues that institutions that are genuinely universalistic require the abolition of the division of labor as such (Marx and Engels 1970, 52–53). I have made a similar point in linking democracy with the need to challenge scarcity.

But regardless of one's specific view of the promise of the division of labor, its role in philosophical argument is affected by rejection of the teleological framework of a philosophy of history like Hegel's. The need to make the ethical case for one's use of the division of labor is one matter. The need to decide how it figures in one's broader historical reflection is another. Because of the centrality it accords to scarcity, the critique of the division of labor then becomes central to democratic philosophy's thinking about historical change.

Must we assume the possibility of abolishing the division of labor in order to use this idea for the kind of historical reflection we are discussing? One might think so if the issue of the division of labor were to play a substitute role for teleological claims of the philosophy of history. Though not a latent purpose of previous history, the overcoming of scarcity and of the division of labor would then provide a human turning point from which certain kinds of power relations and conflicts would become visible in a way they were not previously. One might attempt a less ambitious claim, however, and assert that retrospective and contemporary reflection on the division of labor and its attendant issues becomes possible not so much when the division of labor can be abolished as when it as a matter of historical fact has been made problematic.

At issue here is a plausible account of how we can achieve a certain transhistorical (not ahistorical) perspective from within history. The division of labor seems to allow us elements of such a perspective, but we may wonder if it does not involve a modernist anachronism. Such doubts cannot be refuted by philosophical argument, but they can be tested by historical reconstruction. As I have noted, skeptical doubt in the abstract has no more theoretical claim than philosophical speculation in the abstract. Showing why the perspective of the division of labor is possible in the present is thus independent of showing that thinking in terms of the division of labor allows us to reconstruct history in comparative and evolutionary terms. And establishing this theoretical and analytical sweep for the idea is separate from showing that it bears importantly on politics in the present, either analytically or normatively.

Themes that are internally related within the philosophy of history thus assume a relative independence from the standpoint of the critique of the division of labor. Why, one might then ask, even link the politics of the division of labor with historical reflection? One does so, in part, to sort out the issues that get run together in the historicist argument against Enlightenment, an argument that mirrors features of traditional philosophy, including the philosophy of history. By sorting out these issues we both address the immediate issues and comment on thinking about historicity.

Whatever its value for reflection on previous history, the standpoint of the division of labor makes specific critical claims regarding contemporary power relations. For clarification about the availability of the idea of the division of labor for thinking about previous history, it may be sufficient to speak of the division of labor being made a problem in the present, even if it cannot be overcome. But for using this idea in thinking critically about contemporary knowledge-power, it may seem necessary to claim that the division of labor can in fact be overcome. Otherwise, we remain within a division of labor that, by hypothesis, distorts our cognitive claims. We can put the requirement less strictly: criticism presupposes that we can adopt the standpoint of the supersession of the division of labor as a real historical possibility. Does not using the division of labor as a critical philosophical idea presuppose that scarcity can in truth be overcome? Is this not implied by treating the division of labor as a matter of power exercised over capacities, including those proper to intellectual work? The critical standpoint of the division of labor is to be one that eludes the distortions of knowledge-power and hence occupies a reflective distance from at least some of the distortions proper to the division of labor. If overcoming scarcity is a utopian illusion, is not the critique of the division of labor similarly illusory?

It is not obvious that there are general principles that can resolve this question, but it has to be taken seriously. Either ruling out or ruling in this kind of critique on such general considerations represents a tacit return to epistemological argumentation or the claims of independent philosophical theory. What has to be taken seriously is the possibility that particularisms of perspective result in critical claims missing their mark and do so in ways that implement aspects of knowledge-power. The general perspective with which I proceed is somewhat hypothetical. Further elements of it are advanced in Part Four, where I take up the respects in which the kind of argument this book represents can be seen as providing a justification of reflective claims about rationality. My hypothesis is that we can plausibly speak of abolishing scarcity so far as key conditions for the possibility of doing so are present. The possibility of such an abolition cannot be theoretically demonstrated any more than its actuality can be. These are in part political issues. But I proceed on the assumption, for now, that the respects in which the division of labor has become problematic are tied to conditions that make overcoming the division of labor possible, if not probable.

In concluding this discussion I want to point out that since the conflict proper to scarcity involves not just conflict over specific things but conflict over social positions, capacities, and recognition, as well as over the cultural definition of all these goods, scarcity has a potentially reflexive dimension. Indeed, scarcity becomes a central interpretive idea in the justification of class relations. Within the liberal theories of political power of Hobbes, Locke, and Hegel, assumptions about scarcity figure crucially in the justification of power in general and of the powers specific to the division of labor in particular. And just as scarcity figures as an interpretive idea within class societies, it can in turn become a contested idea that raises fundamental questions about the practices and values of such societies. In doing so, it may bring the division of labor into question. In such contexts the question of ways in which the division of labor itself sustains scarcity can be raised.

Recent Developments

I will sketch aspects of this reflexivity in the course of discussing some of the historical circumstances that give rise to it. While I assume the claim just made, that scarcity and the struggle for existence are central to historical divisions of labor, the discussion that follows aims in turn to support the plausibility of this assumption. By seeing how the division of labor as a framework of scarcity becomes problematic within the evolution of the division of labor itself, we see how a transhistorical perspective that illuminates issues of rationality emerges within history. What needs to be made plausible, then, is how a critique of the division of labor becomes possible (and, one may add, necessary) within the evolution of the division of labor itself.

In considering the reasons for thinking we stand at present in a uniquely reflexive relation to the division of labor, I refer (a) to ways our period involves significant changes in the division of labor, (b) to ways these changes are accompanied by conflicts that tacitly challenge the division of labor, and (c) to ways these conflicts thus bring into question the necessity and legitimacy of society being based on scarcity. What results is intended to be a sufficiently transhistorical perspective on intellectual practices to inform a philosophical reflection.

(a) In both the general and the more specific forms of the division of labor listed above, there have been important developments in recent years. The relations internal to families have evolved alongside the increased role of women in paid jobs. The nature, scope, and interrelations of educated and semiskilled and unskilled labor have also changed for various economic, political, and technical reasons. Ecological and cultural considerations have even had some impact on debates and policies regarding the evolution of cities in relation to their rural settings. And if there have been corresponding changes in the character and organization of work within the economic sphere, there have also been significant changes in the specifically modern division between this sphere and those of politics and economics. I have already referred to the mutual penetration of these spheres and have alluded to the ways this figures in the evolution of practices concerned with the shaping of various facets of agency. The increase of practices that are concerned with motivation, shaping and stabilization of identity, cultivation of capacities, and so on, arguably represents a practically reflexive relation to the division of labor itself. Another way the division of labor has attained the status of a quasi-political problem has to do with the rapid internationalization of the differentiation of tasks. While this has stirred policy debates of various sorts, it has also illustrated the uncertainty of the power and function of nation-states in relation to multinational corporations.

(b) The respects in which the contemporary evolution of the division of labor includes a reflexive aspect are inseparable from the rise of conflicts over the division of labor, and these conflicts in turn contribute to the still incomplete process of making these questions political. Various social movements, for example, feminism, minority movements, ecology, and critics of various uses of science and technology, have challenged aspects of the evolving division of labor. Their challenges have in turn furthered that evolution by prompting institutional reform. These challenges range from demands for wider access to positions within the existing division of labor to rejections of features of the division of labor as such. They include issues about the ways existing practices reproduce power relations and about ways the construction of agency contributes to the same effect.

Feminist politics, for example, goes beyond specific policies and laws to question both the gender-coded division of activities in society and the quality and presuppositions of many of the specialized activities within this division. Professions and intellectual disciplines have been criticized not just for excluding women but for propagating patriarchal myths and sexist practices within the understandings and procedures of their various specializations. What traditionally have been accepted as objective truths and necessities have come to be reinterpreted as historical practices organizing contingent differentiations of power. Women's and minority movements have refuted appeals to various alleged natural and social necessities as grounds for maintaining hierarchical and discriminatory practices, just as ecologists have sought to refute appeals to economic and technical necessity as grounds for maintaining environmentally destructive practices. As appeal to such necessities loses its force, policies can less plausibly flow from applications of the claimed expertise of specialists and require instead new political understandings.

I take up other illustrations for these claims when I turn to how, by raising the issue of scarcity, they raise the issue of the necessity of the division of labor as such.

(c) Now I want to see if it is possible to argue that in making the division of labor an issue, social movements have raised questions not just about a specific division of labor but about the division of labor in general. If they have, then their struggles have achieved the coincidence in the present of a contemporary issue with an issue about historical being more generally and thus have found in the present questions that yield a transhistorical perspective. If we accept the close linkage I have asserted between the division of labor and scarcity, then finding that the social movements are questioning scarcity provides some reason to think that their challenges to the division of labor have features that contribute to this more general relation to conditions of history.

There is little doubt that scarcity does come up in the aspirations of social movements, though whether it comes up precisely in the sense I have been using it here is less clear. Challenges to the acceptability of poverty in various forms (hunger, homelessness, lack of medical care) increasingly evoke the claim that such conditions are avoidable in contemporary industrialized societies. Ecological challenges to economic growth also frequently argue that such growth bears no relation to necessary production for meeting genuine needs. Within the labor movement, demands for a shorter work week suggest further doubts about the necessity of greater production to meet human needs. While it is rare for such challenges directly to confront the issue of scarcity as a structural principle, it seems plausible to think they are putting this issue on the table for debate.

It is plausible in part because other demands by these movements point in the same direction. In many of the critiques of the ideologies of power exercised along gender, race, and class lines, challenges to the rationales for domination and inequality focus on appeals to objective necessities that figure in tacit and sometimes explicit arguments about scarcity. Sometimes these are direct arguments about differentials within the division of labor, as when disparities in pay, in availability of jobs, in access to education, and so on, are explained on the basis of objective properties of economies. Challenging the claims of experts regarding necessities inherent in social systems (whether or not these are taken as conveyors of natural necessities as well, e.g., sociobiology) has become a major form of ideology critique.

It is plausible to say that these criticisms challenge scarcity as a structural principle, because in them the objective basis in scarcity for various inequalities is denied and instead portrayed as the false appearance of power relations that can in principle be replaced by more democratic relations. In effect, these criticisms claim that various appeals to scarcity rely on constructs of power rather than objective conditions to which plausible appeal can be made in justifying power. Consequently, they imply that those spheres in which scarcity has been said to be an objective barrier to change must now become zones of political debate.

These criticisms frequently accompany direct challenges to the division of labor as well, for example, in claims about gender- or race-encoded distributions of occupations and corresponding development of capacities. And it is important to see that the challenges to the division of labor that have been made in recent years are not only concerned with uncovering patterns of inequality or with disputing the rationales given for them by intellectuals. In identifying the reality and disputing the legitimacy of differentiations organized by scarcity, critics have increasingly stressed the constitutive role of intellectual practices in sustaining these social patterns. Questioning intellectual rationales goes over to identifying functional roles of intellectual work in reproducing the division of labor.

Critics raise issues about the intellectual practices in which these rationales for the inequalities bred of scarcity are constructed and about the practices in which they are acted upon in various consequential ways (e.g., in specific social sciences, in education, in psychological counseling). Such practices now come to be seen as contributing to the latently political construction of that scarcity which characterizes the division of labor as such, namely, the scarcity of positions of determinative agency (choice and planning) within the differentiation of tasks. "Determinative agency" here includes the idea of an agency that acts in the formation of other subordinated agencies.

Critique and the Division of Labor

I have now reviewed the outlines of what I am calling the philosophical idea of the division of labor. As a term of philosophical reflection, the division of labor is the focus of critique or constitutive reflection. It provides a way of thinking about the intersection of knowledge and social construction. It provides a reflection on rationality tempered by the constitutive reflection of Kant, Hegel, and Marx. Like Kant's critiques of reason or Marx's critique of political economy, this critical project concerns itself with the conditions that make certain kinds of knowledge possible. Like Hegel's reconstruction of the historical interplay of cognitive subjectivity and constructed objectivity, or Marx's historical reconstruction of the objects of political economy, this critical project links the reconstruction of kinds of knowledge to the historical reconstruction of what is known and thus treats both knowledge and known as historically bounded. Like Marx's critique of political economy, this critical project uncovers a close connection between the historicity of knowledge and known and political issues within the world of the critical project itself. The historicity of the division of labor and the historicity of the practices specific to the modern division of labor and to its distinctive knowledge-politics are, for this critical project, inseparable from politics.

In a very general way, I have shown this linkage between historicity and politics as a matter concerning scarcity. Thinking about abolishing scarcity becomes a way of thinking about the conditions of a consistent democracy. Critique in this sense is inseparable from social criticism and from the adoption of a critical political perspective, that of a radical democracy. I have claimed that the historical possibility of the critique of the division of labor, viewed as a philosophical project, depends upon the possibility of this wider democratic criticism. Thus a specific intellectual practice depends upon a wider social constellation, and the criticism that is part of that critique depends upon practical criticism initiated beyond the intellectual sphere.

This linkage between various kinds of social criticism, that is, elements of democratic politics, and the intellectual project of critique bears upon an ambiguity in the term "critique of the division of labor." Unlike critique in Kant's and Marx's hands, this critique seems aimed at society rather than specific forms of knowledge. With the comparisons I have drawn above with the sources of the idea of a critique of the division of labor, I have intended to reflect my more general argument that critique of knowledge has to be social critique and that social critique today cannot avoid a focus on specialized knowledge. This kind of critique disrupts the opposition between knowledge and objects known that Kant accepted and that was progressively undermined by Hegel and Marx, but finds in neither a satisfactory elaboration. In fact, a key intellectual problem of a critique of the division of labor thus becomes how to think about this relation. This problem is related to the issue of how to think about the relation between intellectual critique and other forms of social criticism of the division of labor. In other words, we now are faced with conceptual issues proper to thinking about the claims regarding knowledge within the division of labor as well as about claims regarding the challenge to the division of labor. These are issues that include, prominently, the conceptualization of intellectual mediation.

Another way of putting this issue is to say that the idea of the critique of the division of labor as presented so far involves thinking of intellectual practices as fitting within a larger complex of communicative and interpretive relations. In Chapter 6, I turn to issues bearing on this problem. To say that philosophical reflection on the division of labor should take the form of critique implies that the division of labor is itself a framework of social understanding, a historical organization of rationality. More specifically, it is to think of the division of labor as a communications framework whose various positions stand in practical relations informed by general interpretive orientations to society and nature. The hypothesis is that we can understand these practical relations and the corresponding interpretive orientations in terms of inequality, power, and conflict, that is, as sustaining regimes of scarcity of powers. That is not to say that these communicative positions and interpretive orientations can simply be functionalized to the characteristic power relations of the division of labor, but that these power relations must inform our reflection on the intellectual mediations that take place within such historical frameworks.

Turning more closely to the communicative and interpretive aspects of the division of labor should further thinking about those aspects of critique that bear on politics. Criticism involves counterfactual normative commitments that I have linked to the possibility of overcoming the division of labor, of superseding scarcity. We do not yet have adequate terms in which to present what this might mean concretely, but developing an analytical relation to the division of labor should advance this normative concern as well.

My conclusion in the previous chapter was that we can still follow Marx's alienation strategy in a general sense even if we give up the possibility of conceiving community as the negation of the modern economic system as a whole. We can follow Marx's strategy as one of finding democratic political possibilities latent in existing social practices that organize relations of domination. But this requires a shift from economic practices to political ones. Because we will now confront distinctively political practices, one of the ambiguities in Marx's approach to alienation becomes more of an explicit problem. As I noted above, it was never clear how socialized labor under capitalism prefigured a democratic community. It was never clear how what I have called the social synthesis through labor contained in alienated form the possibility of the mutuality proper to democratic politics. While at the very least one must acknowledge that Marx left this problem unresolved, it seems that if there are the elements of a solution in his approach, these must involve linking the process of labor to social struggles over its organization and control. That is, it must treat labor as itself the site of conflicts that are incipiently political. My aim in reviewing this point is to introduce the claim that the respects in which contemporary political alienation prefigures the possibility of community are ones that can only be grasped by conceiving this alienation in relation to the struggles that challenge it. Thus, if I speak of a social synthesis here, it is one that for my purposes should be seen as the locus of conflicting political initiatives. So, rather than try to show that community is latent in existing forms of alienation, we need to give reasons for thinking that community is a possible outcome of existing conflicts over alienation. This is the strategy I follow in the next chapter. That is, I introduce an idea of alienation and argue that the conflicts over it can be seen as posing the issue of community in a somewhat novel historical way.

Chapter 6

Thinking Philosophically with the Idea of the Division of Labor

Reflection on Reason Through Reflection on Intellectual Practices

Drawing from ideas of social constitution, the idea of the division of labor helps us treat the politics of philosophy as an activity and awareness that is at once constituted and constituting in ways of direct interest to democratic reflection. As I have noted, the idea of the division of labor introduces a distinctive approach to philosophical reflexivity. Rather than some version of the traditional project of the rational subject's self-reflection, reflexivity here involves intellectuals critically rethinking intellectual work in terms of its specific functions within the larger differentiation of practices in society. Philosophy itself figures among the various specialized intellectual practices that must be reconstructed as part of the work of making reflective sense of the specialized cognitive achievements that have long held the attention of modern philosophers. Though part of a widespread tendency explicitly to think about rationality in a way that challenges the assumptions of the epistemological tradition, thinking in terms of the division of labor does not imply dispensing with normative issues about rationality. Later I argue that the critique of the division of labor bears on justifying a democratic political ethic and, more generally, bears on efforts to think about rational norms in historical ways. But that is not to claim that by itself philosophical use of the idea of the division of labor resolves all the outstanding issues proper to a non-foundationalist theory of rationality.

At issue, instead, is a democratic self-understanding for intellectuals, in which universalist claims for abstract knowledge are confronted by the historical relations of power in which they have been made. We can distinguish two aspects of philosophical reflection on intellectual work as pursued by the critique of the division of labor. One is concerned with the intellectual reconstruction of such practices, and the other is concerned with the practical implications of such a reconstruction. In both aspects what I am calling the critique of the division of labor is a way of thinking what is common to a range of critical arguments that have developed in recent philosophy.

Democratic Reconstruction

Under "democratic reconstruction" I include various attempts to think about intellectual work in social terms and to do so with philosophical ends in mind. Perhaps the most influential examples of such projects are Foucault's analysis of various forms of knowledge-power (e.g., Foucault 1977, 1980) and Habermas's critique of technocracy (e.g., Habermas 1970, 1984, 1987b). Other recent thinkers who bring to bear a social conception of intellectual argument in their work but for whom a sustained social analysis is not a primary concern include Charles Taylor (1989) and Alasdair MacIntyre (1981). More generally, various trends in recent discussions have raised issues about knowledge in society, for example, professional ethics, feminist discussions of science, historical analyses of scientific rationality, minority challenges to Eurocentrism, debates over cultural criticism, and ecology (see, e.g., Harding 1986; Feyerabend 1988; Asante 1987; Gorz 1980).

I do not mean to claim that all of this literature is concerned with the critique of the division of labor as I understand it, but that within the different strands of these discussions one can find work that contributes to the general intellectual project I have in mind. Nor do I mean to claim that these contributions represent a single or consistent perspective, but rather that they contribute to a debate whose significance lies in making sense of specialized intellectual work as it functions in relations of inequality and hierarchy, that is, in regimes of scarcity. Viewed as scattered contributions to this project, they can be seen as developing a distinctive relation to the historical understanding of intellectual work as well as to politics.

Democratic Narrative in Transhistorical Perspective

Analytical and Normative Standpoint Provided by the Division of Labor

In speaking of historical understanding, I have in mind a kind of transhistorical narrative perspective opened up by the problem of the division of labor. This narrative perspective allows us to think of the present in broad historical terms that inform a practical outlook. By speaking of narrative, then, I mean that the present can be positioned within the general evolutionary trends of human history and can be informed by plausible universalistic values, namely, those of a democratic ethic. While the narrative, as a story of potential democratic agency, presupposes the ethic, the ethic in turn depends upon the evolution of the story as carried out in politics. I return to this theme of the dependence of the ethic on politics when I discuss the historical justification of the discourse ethic.

General features of the narrative perspective have already been mentioned: the evolution of historical societies with scarcity and surplus, the shifting relations to inner and outer nature mediated by changing systems of social relations, and the increasingly reflexive relation to the division of labor and scarcity of agency and politics in our day. The need for such a narrative seems evident for philosophical criticism that breaks with metaphysics. The orientation to conditions and problems provided by a narrative informs the issues and procedures of reflection without prejudging the outcome of specific arguments. The narrative perspective I am proposing should help us to see what otherwise quite different thinkers have in common, and it may suggest ways to address difficulties their work has encountered. Let me briefly illustrate what I have in mind, both regarding how various specific projects contribute to and are illuminated by the critique of the division of labor.

Placing Recent Work in the Narrative

Foucault's analysis of knowledge-power provides an approach to the social sciences and professions that allows us to think in constitutive terms about historical forms of agency and cognitive necessity. His development of the idea of discourse contributes to a sense of the way intellectuals have exercised powers that shape the sense and activity of various forms of subjectivity. His is perhaps the most obvious and profound contribution to reconstructive strategies regarding intellectuals within the division of labor, but his own account of knowledge and power does not establish a clear or consistent relation to political criticism, in part because of ambiguities about the potential relation of succeeding regimes of power.

The division of labor provides a way of contextualizing Foucault's analysis in a historically conceived universalism that avoids theoretical and political relativism. If the breadth of this narrative perspective allows us to establish a critical relation to the present and thus to move to a higher level of generality than Foucault provides, without adopting the transcendentalism or philosophy of history he wishes to avoid, it also offers a contrast to the perspective of the other major contemporary theorist of knowledge and power. Habermas's communications theory has made possible a complex and differentiating challenge to positivistic thought and technocratic practice, but its account of rationality has been challenged for its abstract and ahistorical qualities. But its abstractions have specific merits when turned to the historical problem of criticizing the division of labor. Moreover, the formation of a democratic political culture provides us with a context for overcoming the abstract utopianism often associated with this ethic.

Sources of the Self by Charles Taylor is one more example of an important recent philosophical work informed by the narrative perspective of the division of labor. Taylor draws explicitly on Foucault in contextualizing seventeenth-century thinkers like Locke within the rise of disciplinary practices, but he fails to offer a way of thinking contextually about philosophy itself as a social practice. Taylor's arguments about Locke's notion of the self and its relation to the world are meant, however, to place philosophical reflection within a larger evolution of moral understanding. I do not mean to suggest that mere mention of the division of labor provides the needed account but that the idea of philosophical mediation within the division of labor understood as a communications framework is promising for a consistently realized account of philosophy as social practice.

Reconstructing Intellectual Mediation

Conceiving intellectual work within a narrative about the division of labor requires appropriate social terms with which to analyze such work. Drawing from social theoretical uses of language theory will help place intellectual work within society in a way that meets the needs of a conception of intellectual mediation. I took up this idea in Part One and developed a preliminary conception of philosophical mediation. I should note that some of the thinkers from whom I draw have worked with variants of this theme. Both Habermas and Foucault address this theme in their attempts to think of alternatives to traditional expectations about intellectuals. Habermas uses the idea of mediation in speaking of the tasks of a philosophy that avoids traditional illusions of the master science and instead concerns itself with mediating between expert cultures and the lifeworld, as well as between the specialized value spheres (see Habermas 1990, "Philosophy as Stand-in and Interpreter"). Foucault (1980b, "Truth and Power") offers a related idea when speaking of the specific intellectual who for him has come to replace the "universal intellectual" typified in recent times by Sartre. I discuss these normative ideas later when I turn to the issue of democratic practice for intellectuals.

Let us turn to some general features of the idea of intellectual mediation for which we need analytical concepts. Consider first those features which follow from trying to find an alternative to images of autonomous reason. Mediation implies context dependency with regard to a preexisting discussion and an anticipated audience, to general social conditions, and to preexisting intellectual materials. To speak of mediation suggests certain relevant aspects of this context: contending social and intellectual forces within which issues of mediation arise, and differing levels of abstraction and social discussion between which mediating practice must move. In short, mediation takes place within a relational complex of capacities and power relations. The terms required for conceiving such contextual features of intellectual practice must, of course, not obscure the specific qualities of intellectual discussion. So the second set of features of mediation for which we need analytical concepts involves the means by which valid results are sought, debated, achieved, and reworked in practices of various sorts.

The idea of mediation, then, treats intellectual work as social practice whose specifically intellectual features are to be reconstructed both as social response and as social action. Mediation is a term that covers philosophers mediating between sciences and public culture, writers of fiction, critics, teachers, journalists, but also scientists, engineers, city planners, and so on. Not all mediation is a matter of expertise, but expertise mediates so long as it figures within a social framework.

A framework that can accommodate functions on these various levels has taken shape in language theory as developed by Habermas, Bakhtin, and Foucault. I turn to these thinkers to develop terms appropriate to balancing contextualization with respect for the specifics of intellectual work, in the sense of its relation both to knowledge and to the validity claims contained therein. The required framework must articulate the productive accomplishments of intellectual work as well as conceive its social embodiment. A communications approach preserves the specifically cognitive appropriation of subject matters while maintaining their relation to active social processes.

Uses of Language Theory for Reconstructing Intellectual Mediation

The aim, then, is to assemble enough elements of a communications approach to develop a sense of the intellectual strategies proper to the critique of the division of labor conceived as philosophy. Toward that end I draw from three thinkers who have creatively drawn on a variety of disciplines in thinking about historically located and active qualities of culture and politics. The value of their work for this conception provides some support for my contention that the critique of the division of labor represents a trend in recent intellectual activity. A "trend" is not a theory, but philosophical reflection neither requires nor should aim at a tightly constructed theory, but rather should seek a range and coherence proper to its explicit mediating roles.

Habermas

Habermas's communication theory, though not developed with explicit reference to the issue of the division of labor, is a rich source of concepts for thinking about intellectual mediation. Some of the relevant features of his work come to light in examination of it as a philosophical alternative to traditional subject/object metaphysics, a tradition Habermas (1987a) refers to alternatively as the "philosophy of the subject" or the "philosophy of consciousness." With both terms he emphasizes reliance on a founding or organizing subject, whether explicit, as in Descartes, Kant, Hegel, and Husserl, or tacit, as in objectivist thinkers like Hobbes or the positivists. Without adopting agency as a metaphysical principle, Habermas wants to avoid strategies that reduce it away. He seeks to achieve this aim with a philosophical reconstruction of agency that draws from such specific empirical sciences as linguistics, psychology, anthropology, and sociology. The resulting conception is to be empirically testable, even historical in certain respects. But though it does not claim the necessity traditional philosophers have claimed for their most general conceptions of human agency, it does assert a universality by identifying features of experience and action that apply to humans generally. The resulting communications conception has the additional advantage of avoiding the monological and monadic treatment of subjects typically developed in the tradition.

I touch on features of Habermas's argumentation only so far as they bear directly on the present argument. The extent to which he sustains an empirical approach is a matter of dispute, since there are clear similarities to the transcendental tradition in his account. These issues bear most directly on my concerns when I turn to the normative dimensions of the communications conception. Later I take up the respects in which these can be treated in historical terms.

In Habermas's use of the term, intellectual reconstruction starts from the standpoint of agents and makes sense of the capacities regarding which they have an intuitive, if not infallible or complete, understanding. For example, linguistics reconstructs rules of grammar with the aid of native speakers, or anthropologists reconstruct beliefs and customs relying on conversations with participants (Habermas 1990, "Reconstruction and Interpretation in the Social Sciences"). There is a phenomenological dimension to this approach so far as it takes the experience of agents as a touchstone. But it is not entirely a matter of introspectively grounded description, since there is a distinctive moment of abstraction and reliance on forms of testing that are not exhausted by appeal to the witness of subjects. This denial of absolute authority to subjective experience is consistent with the challenge to the philosophy of consciousness. On the other hand, it is important to remark that Habermas, like Bakhtin and Foucault, retains the experience of agents as a fundamental point of departure for his abstraction.

In Habermas's argument, this dimension of his thought is marked by his use of the idea of the lifeworld, the phenomenological idea of the intuitively available, prereflective sphere of meaning from which all intellectual abstractions take their point of departure. In contrast to those who take traditional subjective approaches, Habermas conceives experience as essentially social. It is social because it is organized by meanings that are facets of language, and language is essentially interaction. Building on speech-act theory, Habermas conceives language in performative terms, but the performance simultaneously involves a receiver as well as a sender of messages.[1] Language use is a matter of making claims that have to be accepted or rejected for communication to take place. The dimension of agency is preserved by conceiving this making and ruling on claims as a matter of validity. The primacy of validity claims coincides with the irreducibility of agency and reliance on the lifeworld as the point of departure. We should notice that the irreducibly normative feature of communication extends to theoretical reflection on language use, that is, to the making sense of ordinary action and experience by experts.

The emphasis on communication, or symbolic interaction, serves a variety of purposes in Habermas's work. In addition to providing a social alternative to traditional subject-centered reflection on rationality, this emphasis allows him to develop a conception of politics that is an alternative to the instrumental conceptions that prevail in modern thought. Habermas seeks a conceptualization that will take him beyond the conceptual limitations not only of traditional liberalism but also of much Marxism and twentieth-century technocratic thought. Thus he seeks to provide a surer basis for the critique of instrumental reason advanced by Horkheimer, Adorno, and Marcuse. On the most general conceptual level, this involves a sustained exploration of that which distinguishes relations between subjects and objects, subjects and subjects, and subjects and themselves. A summary discussion of these distinctions is all that is required here.

A persisting theme in Habermas's writing is the contrast between action and thought directed to other subjects capable of responding symbolically and action and thought directed to objects which are open to certain kinds of impersonal knowledge and over which we typically seek instrumental control. The contrast between potential interlocutors and objects of instrumental action is drawn in terms of types of action and experience, types of knowledge and reasoning, and aspects of our language use. Though a stable feature of Habermas's work over the years, this contrast has been increasingly developed in its linguistic dimensions and for its bearing on debates over Enlightenment. A related contrast that has received multiple uses and less sustained development concerns relations to self. In Habermas's early work on knowledge and human interests (Habermas 1971), self-relations figured in his account of ideology critique and "emancipatory science." In more recent work they figure in those dimensions of speech acts that involve claims about intentions, but they also appear in remarks about aesthetic experience (see Jay 1985). In any event, these contrasts provide Habermas a way of making in practical and linguistic terms distinctions that resemble those drawn by Kant between theoretical, practical, and aesthetic rationality.

Couched in terms of the interactive aspect of language, Habermas's conception of rationality focuses on the offering and recognition of claims to validity. Linguistic understanding here is itself a matter of judgment regarding claims offered by a speaker, and so reasoning is built into the process of communication. At the same time, reasoning itself is reconstructed in terms of interaction. Speech acts involve claims bearing on the different orientations to objects, forms of action and experience, and types of reasoning summarized above. In Habermas's terms, there are claims regarding objective states of affairs (claims to truth), claims regarding the validity of relations between subjects (claims to normative correctness), and claims regarding subjective intentions (claims to truthfulness). The relation between Habermas's general reflections on language and reason and his critical account of contemporary intellectual practices depends largely on how he uses his conception of these various validity claims.

While these distinctions have transhistorical application, they also inform analysis of contingent historical change and articulate terms of contemporary political conflict. Crucial in both respects is a notion with which Habermas's sympathies with and divergences from the philosophy of history are expressed. In keeping with the irreducibility of agency, Habermas uses the idea of learning to characterize lines of development that are made possible by the active relation to validity claims that sustains the various dimensions of language use. Individual biography is characterized by different kinds of learning that can be reconstructed in terms of capacities in which relations to claims about objects, others, and self organize activity. Similarly, social change can be reconstructed in terms of shared learning, for example, in technical advance, institutional change, and cultural practice. The claim is not that historical change follows a logic of learning but that it can be reconstructed and assessed with the terms of such a logic.

It is in this way that Habermas develops his reflections on modernity and the processes of rationalization that, following Weber, he thinks characterize the modern world. Rationalization is a matter not of the inevitability of modern forms of science, technology, religious change, and institutional development of markets and constitutional regimes, but rather of the kinds of learning that takes place in these developments. This learning includes forms of explicit and abstract elaboration of general linguistic capacities and the development of an increasingly reflective relation to rational and linguistic powers. Such learning is embodied in the evolution of specialized intellectual practices.

Habermas's general account of rationality makes for a complicated treatment of the intellectual and cultural differentiations that contribute to the modern division of labor. On the one hand, he offers a way of making sense of the specific cognitive abstractions and achievements of the modern sciences, though the relation between his differentiated account of rationality and the differentiations among the sciences is not always clear. The distinction between objectivizing abstraction directed at nature and interpretive abstraction directed at other subjects allows for a correlation between his general scheme of validity claims and the contrast between the natural and human sciences. On these two levels Habermas appears to be reworking the Neo-Kantian dualism among sciences. But this correlation has difficulties, beginning with the fact that many sciences combine features of both rationalities. It may be that no science represents a pure case of either. This does not represent a serious difficulty for Habermas's scheme, however, since his analytical distinctions may be sound and may be soundly related to different features of language without having to correspond to types of science.

Indeed, the fact that these more general distinctions can be flexibly applied to various sciences underlies an important feature of Habermas's critical use of these distinctions. Being able to contrast different types of rationality provides him with a basis for challenging specific intellectual practices without resorting to irrationalism. For example, without disputing that objectivizing reason can be applied to society, Habermas can challenge postivistically minded social sciences for overextending the application of such reason; at the same time, he can offer alternative directions for social scientific research to take.

His differentiated approach to reason underlies his version of the challenge to instrumental reason and so allows for a critique of technocracy that is hostile neither to modern science nor to features of modern philosophy and methodology. This conception of rationality allows Habermas to criticize the historical differentiations and understandings of intellectual work. It is important to emphasize this, since Habermas's conception of rationality commits him to a version of the much-contested modern differentiation of theoretical, practical, and aesthetic rationalities. Habermas acknowledges these Kantian features of his conception by speaking of the irreducibility of the distinction between modern values spheres, those of science, of ethics, and of art. Despite the fact that a specific science may have interpretive dimensions, or a work of art may incorporate physical theory, or many contemporary ethical debates turn on issues about technology, for Habermas different rationalities are incorporated respectively in accounts of objective states of affairs, interpretations of meaning, and expressions of beauty. Modern reflection on, and even institutionalization of, these distinctions represents for him a kind of learning rooted in our most general rational capacities.

This point is important because it bears both on features of the communications conception of rationality and on the theme of understanding historical differentiations of activity. It is worth noting in this latter regard that the irreducibility of the difference between value spheres is not for Habermas a reason to affirm the necessity of the division of labor, at least as I have been speaking of it. In fact, this set of differences provides for him some of the terms for thinking about the task of a critically minded philosophy. He speaks of the need for philosophy to mediate between these different spheres (Habermas 1990, "Philosophy as Stand-in and Interpreter"). I take this to include reflectively bringing out the actual qualities of rational achievement and contributing to language cutting across disciplinary and institutional boundaries. The political thrust of this concern with mediation becomes clearer when we refer to the other kind of mediation with which Habermas associates it. This is mediating between the practices of experts and the everyday experience of the lifeworld.

I want to make clear certain features of the historical perspective in which Habermas thinks about the desirability of these kinds of mediation. The theme to be emphasized here is that with which Habermas uses his communications framework to think about the effects of the late-twentieth-century capitalist economy, welfare state, and mass culture on the democratic potential of citizens. In speaking of the "colonization of the lifeworld," Habermas (1984, 332–73) characterizes the intrusion of imperatives rooted in structural properties of contemporary economic and political institutions into the capacities of individuals to understand and act politically. In a variety of ways, tradition-dependent possibilities of communicative action directed toward mutual understanding are eroded by economic and bureaucratic imperatives.

"Colonization of the lifeworld" is one way to characterize what I discussed earlier as unacknowledged and alienating politics in the face of contemporary structural change. The fact that Habermas advocates a critical philosophical mediation between value spheres and between expert practices and everyday life as an intellectual response to these trends is a reason to see his work as part of the larger trend I am calling the critique of the division of labor. Habermas sees the promise of critical intellectual activity as depending on the prospects of social movements and has tried over the years to provide various structural accounts of the context in which these conflicts and political initiatives are taking place. These accounts contribute to a narrative perspective on the evolution of rationality in history, and in particular a perspective in which Habermas can avoid what he sees as the one-sidedness of earlier Frankfurt School thinkers regarding the "dialectic of Enlightenment." Adorno and Horkheimer (1972) and Marcuse (1964) sometimes came close to equating modern reason with instrumental reason and to finding the liberating potential of Enlightenment turning into a totalitarian nightmare. Habermas (1987a, 106–30) does not dispute the cogency of many of their analyses, but argues that a communications approach is required to develop an account of rationality that, among other things, can accommodate their own critical insights.

For Habermas, an adequate self-understanding is inseparable from a more consistently carried out social analysis of the workings of

Enlightenment. With his communications approach he hopes to provide terms with which to think about the various aspects of intellectual operations so as to grasp the workings of knowledge and power concretely. By coordinating claims simultaneously asserted regarding objective states of affairs, social relations, and intentions, communicative reconstruction can sort out the various respects in which rationality contributes to insight, mystification, and domination, and it can do so historically. A striking instance of this is Habermas's rethinking of ideology in the context of contemporary technocracy.[2] With his communications approach, he can think about ideology both in the classic sense of interested distortion with utopian content and in the more contemporary sense of technocratic obfuscation of practical questions.

To be sure, Habermas does not concentrate on the reconstruction of intellectual practices as I have been speaking of them. His categorical distinctions allow for arguments that complement such an account, but his interest in challenging positivism and objectivistic thought and later in developing the general conceptual outlines of a communications notion of rationality seems to have left to others the problem of translating these themes into sustained social reconstructions.

The narrative perspective afforded by rationalization (across epochs before modernity as well as defining what is specifically modern) thus contributes to a narrative proper to the critique of the division of labor so far as it traces a process of differentiation and coordination and does so in terms of emergent social capacities. Habermas's communications approach allows him to cast issues about the evolution of rationality in social terms so far as it allows him to speak of conceptual orientations being embodied in specialized practices. The methodological self-consciousness accompanying the elaboration of empirical-analytical and historical-hermeneutical thought in specialized disciplines is a component of the embodiment of such practices. The differentiation is both conceptual and social. This social differentiation is a particular kind of mediation whose various possibilities help allow for the ambiguous role of science and technology in modern society. Specialized disciplines, like the modes of abstraction they employ, can be applied to subject matters and practical uses that are not determined a priori but are socially determined in complicated ways. A case in point is the rise of objectivating social science, or the application of instrumental and strategic thinking to social management.

It is important to emphasize that the methodological and normative side of Habermas's reflection involves cognitive claims about the process of specialization. While the social deployment of these forms of expertise is always open to debate (e.g., over the appropriateness of objectivating thought in areas of social study or over the morality and social benefit of strategic approaches to administration), they are taken to involve what is intrinsically a growth in rationality. In one respect, this has to do with the more explicit and consistent use of abstraction, but more basically, it has to do with the kinds of criticism and consensus formation that specialized intellectual procedure makes possible. Since the focus and application of specialized rationalities is always open to debate, this idea of an advance in rationality is not a reworking of traditional notions of the autonomy of reason, though perhaps it should be seen as recovering something sound in those notions. In any event, expertise typically brings specialized language and methods that allow for reflexive and careful organization of thought and the validation of results. This is an element of the formation of what Habermas calls discourse, the reflective focus on argumentation in which procedures emerge to ensure that outcomes are governed solely by the strongest arguments (Habermas 1990, "Discourse Ethics: Notes on a Program of Philosophical Justification").

Such a conception does not have to claim that the ideal of a discourse is usually, or even ever, achieved. This may be a regulative ideal, though one with real effects. Here I touch on one use of the ideal speech situation, which figures in Habermas's version of the consensus theory of truth and normative correctness. This idealized form of communication is a norm tied to the meaning of the validity of outcomes. That is, it does not imply that all considerations or impulses extraneous to relevant arguments can be excluded, but it does imply that the ideal of such an exclusion is meaningful. It does not imply that such an agreement is possible in all settings or that agreement does not therefore have specific preconditions. It only identifies a necessary condition for the validity of an agreement: that it survive discursive argumentation guided by the norms of the ideal speech situation.

With this ideal developed for thinking about the meaning of achievements of abstract intellectual work, we also confront Habermas's conception of the normative basis for specific contexts of practical reasoning. The ideal speech situation, construed in terms of equality of participation, communicative resources, and unqualified mutual recognition of all involved, provides the conditions for a discursive process whose outcome may be consensus over norms. Norms over which such discursive consensus arises thereby achieve provisional validation. Here I am briefly touching upon the core idea of Habermas's discourse ethic, an idea to which I return more than once in the following discussions.

If we grant that such an ideal is relevant to the norms internal to modern specialized intellectual practice, we may hesitate nonetheless to extend it beyond the realm of expertise. One may wonder if a political application of this ideal is not an illegitimate extension of the morality internal to intellectual life to the ethics of society. But rather than perceive here the overextension of an intellectual's orientation, we might see this ideal as figuring in a way nonintellectuals can discipline intellectuals. This at any rate, is the line of argument I pursue later when trying to historicize Habermas's discourse ethic.

Bakhtin

Although in many respects Bakhtin's ideas can be used to enrich and perhaps concretize features of Habermas's work, it is worth noting at the outset that Bakhtin's work is not concerned primarily with systematic issues about social theory or with technical issues in philosophy. But he pursues his primary interests in language and literature with the conviction that both must be approached as social activities and that reflection on both necessarily involves philosophical considerations. Thus, despite the different focus of his writing, he is in agreement with Habermas over the idea that language in its constitutive features is communicative and that communication involves acts of rational judgment. An aspect of Bakhtin's literary interest that establishes another similarity to Habermas is the distinction he develops between novelists who project a dialogical sense of language and theorists who fashion a monological discourse in what Bakhtin calls an authoritative voice. Speaking or writing as though one had transcended historically located interactions is always an illusion, but the articulation of such monological language can serve to enforce power relations. Bakhtin's analytical framework, then, quite explicitly involves a critical relation to intellectual activity.

Though there are political as well as intellectual similarities between these thinkers, Bakhtin's specific politics is as much a matter of dispute as his general intellectual orientation. Drawing conclusions about him in these respects faces the double difficulty of drawing conclusions about any critically minded thinker in the world of Stalinist and neo-Stalinist Communism. On the one hand, political pressures and constraints on intellectuals mean that all statements have to be weighed with great contextual sensitivity. On the other hand, we students of such thinkers have to consider how our understanding of them is colored by our relations to the political worlds of which they are a part. There is no need to go into how this double difficulty has affected the literature on Bakhtin. But one needs to acknowledge that conclusions about such a thinker must be even more tentative than is usually the case with so original and freewheeling an intellect.

Another issue that has to be acknowledged concerns the relation between Bakhtin and the work of his close collaborators Volosinov and Medvedev (see Clark and Holquist 1984, chap. 6). There is some basis for attributing texts published under their names to Bakhtin, just as there is basis for associating these texts with Bakhtin on the grounds of the close nature of their working relations, especially in view of the social conception of language use they developed together. These issues raise problems on which I do not pretend to cast new light, but I proceed on the assumption that for presenting Bakhtin's views I can legitimately cite so key a text as Volosinov's *Marxism and the Philosophy of Language*. At the same time, I draw from Volosinov or Medvedev on matters where there seems to be significant divergence from texts published under Bakhtin's own name. Even this is an uncertain procedure, since Bakhtin's thought evolved over his long career. And as a thinker whose interest in dialectic comes by way of an appreciation of the multiplicity and frequent conflict of voices to which each of us must respond in developing our own voices, he would be the last to suppress the tensions between views with which he was working.

Dialogical Analysis

In certain respects, reference to Bakhtin allows me to supplement and develop ideas found in Habermas. For Bakhtin, the irreducible dialogical quality of language is captured in language study having the utterance as its first object. Cast in opposition to Saussurian linguistics, the idea of utterance treats language as activity rather than as a formal system (Volosinov 1973). Part of what is meant here is that meaning is contextual, not only a property of the language system. On this view, the meaning of the utterance is inseparable from the interaction, both anticipated and realized, between speaker and hearer. Utterances must be grasped from the standpoints both of their production and reception. So far as they can be taken out of this context and be regarded in isolation, their meaning is reduced drastically. This focus contrasts with language understood as an abstract system of rules. The concern of conventional linguistics with the latter results from reifying an abstraction and giving it priority over language in use.

Bakhtin's conception of language also resembles Habermas's in treating utterances as involving normative judgments. He thinks of utterances as interactions in which judgments are made and assessed and in which such judgment can concern language forms as well as specific assertions. Since for Bakhtin the act of language use is primary, he conceives the meaning of specific utterances as well as the reflexive relation to language forms in a thoroughly historical way. Theoretical reconstruction of meaning and language forms can be a legitimate and fruitful intellectual project, but the distance of both from specific acts of communication involves an abstraction that inevitably drains semantic content and suggests greater permanence than really exists in the organization of language.

Unlike Habermas, however, Bakhtin does not provide a developed account of validity claims with which to think about the specifics of judgment in interaction, and so does not theorize respects in which properties of language and rationality coincide. In any case, judgment implies a normative point of reference, which for Bakhtin may concern a variety of aspects of the dialogical situation, for example, the truth or appropriateness of what is said or the intentions or role of the speaker. In this connection there is a further parallel to Habermas so far as Bakhtin's idea of tacit orientation in all interaction to an idealized third person or ideal listener resembles features of the idealization in Habermas's ideal speech situation. Built into language use is a communicative utopia, never realized but always anticipated.

Another feature of Bakhtin's conception that has a certain utopian quality is his claim that semantic potential exceeds the meaning realized in actual speech and writing. We can return to texts and find meanings we did not see before. Traditions harbor semantic potentials that go unacknowledged for generations. This is not a platonic point, since these potentials are not independently existing ahistorical ideas. Rather it has to do with linguistic possibilities that have to be awakened through new initiatives that are themselves in part responsible for the meanings that are then realized.

So far as there are "forms" in Bakhtin, these are not fixed meanings but types of utterance. With the idea of speech genres, Bakhtin provides a way of bridging between the enduring and the context specific features of language. Genres are units of communication and may vary from a specific kind of comment (an exclamation) to a literary form (e.g., a novel). Judgment in receiving an utterance may concern the genre, for example, its appropriateness, or the adequacy of performance. This illustrates one of the lines along which the reflexive relation to language can be explored.

If genre provides a way of thinking about forms of usage, the idea of voice offers a way to think about positions and dispositions of speakers. If the one identifies a certain constancy in forms of utterance, the other identifies a certain constancy in the agents who employ these forms. Voice allows us to think in dispositional terms appropriate to historically organized societies. Voices can themselves be the objects of communication and judgment, and various reflective or even strategic relations to them can have a profound role in communication. One of Bakhtin's more fruitful analytical ideas is that of double-voicing, in which a speaker can draw upon, mimic, or in some other way rework the voice of another even while asserting a voice of his or her own. The idea of double-voicing is of interest not only for the way it allows us to conceive individual speech as a step in an ongoing social process (in which a new utterance occurs as a situated appropriation of preexisting linguistic materials) but also for the way it emphasizes one aspect of the self-referential dimension of language use. The appropriation of linguistic material in double-voicing, by articulating a new use, is a kind of commentary on that material. Similarly, reception involves an evaluative and therefore commentative relation. This dimension of commentary illustrates the reflexivity in language use, a reflexivity that can extend to the articulation of reflective judgment about an utterance or its presuppositions. The degree to which we can distance ourselves from utterances and their presuppositions is itself a historical matter. Reflection can emerge regarding factors proper to the identification of the division of labor, namely, factors of scarcity in the various dimensions of agency proper to communications relations.

The idea of double-voicing is an extension of features of the utterance. For Bakhtin an utterance is always an interaction. The hearer or reader both registers and comments upon the message of the speaker or writer. In a certain way, hearing has some of the characteristics of speech. Similarly, speech is a kind of hearing, insofar as it always involves the reworking by the speaker of materials encountered in previous communication. Bakhtin develops this theme in the idea of double-voicing, in which speech proceeds as a kind of quotation of previous speech, but quotation filled with commentary that makes it a distinctive utterance. Bakhtin explores various kinds of direct and indirect quotation (direct and indirect discourse) in literary works, but for me this idea has more general application in settings of intellectual practice.

Indeed, for my discussion the interest in Bakhtin's account of language lies in its fruitfulness for thinking about intellectuals, both in ways he himself pursued and in ways his concepts make available to us. Emphasis on the dialogical qualities of language contributes to a critical stance toward much of the practice and self-understanding of many modern intellectuals. Making abstractions primary to specific language events undercuts appreciation of the dialogical quality of language and contributes to a monological understanding and practice of intellectual activity. Missing the dialogical quality of language or underestimating its importance thus contributes to missing the dialogical or social character of specialized intellectual activities and allows for a reflective removal of intellectuals from their social context, raising their rationality above society. This is reflected in what Bakhtin calls the authoritative quality of the monological voice of traditional philosophy.

I consider other features of this critical stance when I turn to the relevant narrative and critical features of Bakhtin's approach. I have already touched upon the possibility of using the idea of the utterance for thinking critically about monologically organized specialist practices. One should, of course, not assume that monological practices are inherently defective even if no utterance is possible outside communicative relations. The methodological suppression of this dimension of language clearly has proven to have been cognitively fruitful in specific intellectual practices, most obviously those of the natural sciences. But reconstructive analysis can explore what goes into this suppression, to examine how it is achieved, to what extent it is partial, to what cognitive and social effects it leads, and so on. It can also explore the functioning of such language in contexts where the monological form is more controversial.

More generally, the idea of the utterance, with its emphasis on the receptive and constructive features of speech and writing, points to a host of questions for social reflection on intellectual practices and specifically on knowledge-power. Thus it offers a way to think about mediating relations between specialists and nonspecialists. The utterances of specialists may be reconstructed from the standpoint of the appropriations they make of popular discourse (e.g., in the social sciences), just as they may be reconstructed from the standpoint of the linguistic proposals they go on tacitly making to others (e.g., psychologists offering language to their clients). The explicit communicative relations between specialists and nonspecialists (e.g., sociological surveys) may be explored for tacit linguistic operations in the construction of knowledge (e.g., those that structure possible answers to surveys) and later in the application of knowledge (e.g., in the language of social scientists as policy consultants).

This sort of reconstruction of utterances has clear application to philosophical mediation. The theme of appropriation and promulgation of linguistic materials applies to the relations between philosophical language and that of other specialties, just as it does to relations between philosophical language and that of nonspecialists. Philosophers both draw from specific scientists and have provided language for scientists to understand and justify their work. Similarly, political thinkers have drawn from popular language, just as they have provided terms that find their way into the discourse of citizens, though perhaps by way of the mediations of other intellectuals.

Some of Bakhtin's other ideas allow for this kind of analysis to be concretized. For example, his development of the theme of genre provides ways of analyzing how utterances are organized as well as ways of thinking about types of content. Monological language can be examined in terms of the various genres in which it is organized, for example, those of scientific theory, philosophical argument, professional analysis, political pronouncement. Genres may be designed for promoting speech contents, for example, those of teaching and publicity. They may be analyzed for the speech positions and opportunities they impose on participants in interaction. Like the intellectual utterance itself, intellectual genres can be explored for their functions in mediation, both between experts and between them and nonspecialists.

If genre refers us to the organization of the content of utterances, voice directs us to speakers and hearers themselves. In the case of monologues, we may explore tacit social identities and corresponding tacit audiences. Like genre, voice can itself be the object of evaluation and appropriation in an utterance, so analyzing voice may involve us in exploring specific ways language use refers back to itself. We can see this in the reconstruction of certain kinds of double-voicing (e.g., speech makers introject the voices of others in their remarks, or philosophers play with the voices of other specialists). Clearly the possibilities for thinking about mediation are rich here too. We can explore ways philosophers draw from and construct elements of voice for specialists and nonspecialists alike, for example, when Kant constructs the impersonal voice of the categorical imperative.

The last idea I cite in this survey of materials Bakhtin offers for reconstructing intellectual mediation stands in a complicated relation to all the themes on which I have touched. Thinking about genre and voice in relation to historical utterances involves us in thinking historically about the semantic content available to specific speakers and hearers. I referred earlier to Bakhtin's idea of the revival of semantic contents in new historical situations. My suggestion is that the suppression, management, and freeing of semantic content is a fruitful theme for reconstructing intellectual mediation. Acting on genres or voices affects what can be said and so too one's relation to inherited linguistic possibilities. Relation to semantic potential thus figures in the social role of intellectual mediators. We can for now perhaps sufficiently appreciate this from examples of specialists who manage semantic potential (e.g., teachers who order appropriate forms of expression, or producers of mass culture who shape acceptable interpretations) or those who elicit such potential (e.g., various kinds of therapists but also intellectuals associated with social movements).

Bakhtin's Narrative Perspective and Democratic Criticism

So far I have shown that Bakhtin provides analytical means that can help in the reconstruction of intellectual mediations proper to modern knowledge-power. To what extent does his more general theoretical reflection contribute to the narrative and critical perspectives I have associated with the critique of the division of labor? One could explore this question by way of Bakhtin's relation to Marxism, but his views here are understandably schematic and vague. The Volosinov books on language and Freud explicitly adopt a historical materialist perspective, but this is by itself of less interest than the fact that the version of historical materialism they develop is nonreductionist, antimechanistic, and ready to draw from non-Marxist sources (Volosinov 1973, 1976). Apart from this lack of dogmatism, the Bakhtin group drew carefully from a variety of contemporary social sciences while having absorbed insights from turn-of-the-century Neo-Kantian and Neo-Hegelian thinkers. And they seem close to Marx in striving to think historically while breaking with idealist philosophy of history and in emphasizing issues of agency while criticizing contemporary subjectivism.

Bakhtin thinks in evolutionary terms in treating modernity as characterized by an extensive development of heteroglossia, the differentiation and interplay of a multiplicity of voices. But he also draws parallels with premodern times, especially the heteroglossia of the late ancient world (Bakhtin 1984a). The idea of heteroglossia figures dialectically in narrative reflection by combining populist overtones with concerns of the devaluing of language as grasping objective conditions in the world. This kind of ambiguity marks Bakhtin off from poststructuralist celebrations of the freeing of the signifier from the signified, despite his parallel challenges to crude representationalism.

In his juxtaposition of the dialogical novel (typified above all by Dostoevsky) with monological theory (where dialectic that has lost its connection to dialogical language comes in for especially pointed criticism), Bakhtin poses questions about modernity in a distinctive way. The opposition between dialogical and monological offers a fruitful variant on the critique of objectivism, positivism, and the fetishism of technological advance, a critique Habermas pursues with his opposition between interaction and instrumentalism. Moreover, as the contrast between the novel and theory suggests, Bakhtin's opposition is explicitly tied to types of intellectual activity even if he does not develop a sustained social reflection. Yet it may seem that, combined with his vagueness on matters of political analysis and criticism, this lack of social reflection results in Bakhtin offering little that is a very definite contribution to a narrative and critical perspective.

Despite the vagueness and abstraction of his work in this regard, Bakhtin does offer suggestive forms of reflection. One influential theme is that of carnival, by which Bakhtin refers, especially in his work on Rabelais, to premodern celebrations in which the existing order is inverted along with its dominant cultural practices (Bakhtin 1984b). This is a concrete assertion of heteroglossia against the powers that routinely recognize only certain voices and genres. If in the modern world the practice of carnival has been marginalized, for Bakhtin it persists in novels and other literary achievements (e.g., Bakhtin 1984a, 106–78. Moreover, Bakhtin seems to associate the impulse to carnival with modern democratic movements. At issue for him is not simply matters of material wealth and political power but the differentiation of high and popular cultures and corresponding forms of one-sided and alienating development. In this light, challenges to monological and authoritative intellectual practices are linked to broad possibilities of democratic culture. It is difficult not to associate Bakhtin's failure to elaborate very explicitly on this idea with the contradiction between Soviet socialism's democratic promise and its Stalinist practice.

To be sure, the idea of carnival is ambiguous from a democratic standpoint. After all, actual carnival could be seen as a compensation and substitute for real challenges to domination, and the abstract inversion carnival represents does not offer a very concrete sense of alternative democratic possibility. At the same time, viewed through the lens of Bakhtin's reading of Rabelais, the carnival theme becomes associated with efforts to overcome the split between high and popular culture in the work of critical intellectuals. On this reading, the normative model is not so much carnival per se as the critical intellectual who uses carnival themes to initiate a different intellectual practice.

One democratizing feature of such a practice lies in what earlier I spoke of as freeing semantic potential. Carnival is a democratic norm so far as it challenges the genres and voices that reproduce scarcity of political capacity. Of course, the freeing of new speech possibilities itself represents an abstract norm that does not ensure democratic practices or outcomes. But the possibility of genuinely universal participation, universal access to socially recognized voice, is surely a precondition of democracy.

Foucault

In counting Foucault as a contributor to the critique of the division of labor, one must acknowledge respects in which social theory becomes problematic for Foucault by virtue of his frontal engagement with themes of knowledge and power. He explicitly rejects systematic theory and persists in an ambiguous relation to the normative claims of criticism in part because of his flirtation with the reduction of knowledge or rationality to power that is often associated with Nietzsche. At the same time, he explicitly adopts a critical standpoint that retains Enlightenment association of insight and freedom. I shall not pursue the unfruitful task of attributing a consistent or sustained relation between Foucault and normative issues of philosophical and political reflection. Foucault's contribution too often seems to consist in his pursuit of insights that were never refined by him so as to fit comfortably with other of his commitments.

These are insights that bear on the kind of skepticism I have claimed is most relevant to philosophical reflection on knowledge today. This skepticism does not deny the reality of knowledge and so would not be satisfied by cognitive guarantees even if they were forthcoming. It rather challenges knowledge by claiming that its effective reality combines cognitive achievement with the imposition of domination. Foucault's work is never simply an effort to deny the claims of Enlightenment, however, because challenges to domination are for him always assertions of liberty, and he takes these very seriously. The political side of this seriousness about a revised strategy of Enlightenment criticism can be seen in his affiliation with the kinds of social movements that in his view make possible criticism articulated by intellectuals like himself (Foucault 1984, "What Is Enlightenment?"). After pursuing some of the ideas with which Foucault contributes to the critique of the division of labor, I return to these themes of his political and narrative perspective.

Language and Power

There is a nominalist quality to Foucault's thinking about language that establishes a certain similarity between his work and Bakhtin's. But his suspicion of intellectual reification is associated with the primacy of events rather than of interactive utterances. Nonetheless, he too treats the social dimension of language as fundamental. His stress on the specificity of the event rather than of the act reflects his interest in the primacy of structural features of action over the coherence of agency. Accordingly the constitution of subjects is for him of central interest. If this, and the fact that subjects emerge within relational complexes, indicate the "structuralist" sympathies of Foucault's work, the fact that these complexes are to be seen in practical terms indicates his uneasiness with ideas of fixed structures.

Emphasis on the event, then, contributes to an emphasis on historicity rather than to an atomism. Like Bakhtin and Habermas, Foucault seeks materials for a consistently historical way of thinking about language and rationality. In his most sustained work on knowledge and power, he develops for this purpose the idea of discursive practices. Conceived in a reflection that Foucault presents as archaeological and genealogical, discursive practices are linguistically organized relational complexes in which what I have been calling intellectual mediation takes place (see, e.g., Foucault 1980a, 18).

Let us first consider something of what it means to call this approach archaeological and genealogical. With these terms, Foucault signals his ambivalent relation to the critical tradition. He follows Kant in seeking the a priori of knowledge by way of an account of the conditions that make knowledge possible (Foucault 1972, 127). But this is a historical a priori having to do with historically specific cognitive practices. Rather than trace the conditions for possible knowledge back to the synthetic accomplishments of a transcendental subject, this critical reflection frequently concerns itself with the emergence of historical forms of subjectivity within the practices it reconstructs.

We might say that Foucault is a radical Kantian in his suspicion of metaphysical concepts, especially that of the subject and the various respects in which it depends on claims about rationality. If he is more radical than Kant by refusing any place for a transcendental subject, he adheres to Kant's reliance on existing forms of knowledge and experience as points of reflective departure. Consequently, though Foucault treats "the subject" as in fact a variety of historically emergent subjectivities, he does not resort to a quasi-positivist reductionism. I note other tensions and ambiguities of this position when I come to the theme of his relation to narrative and political reflection.

The term "archaeology" indicates this effort to provide a constitutive reflection that does not take the subject for granted, that is not, to use Foucault's contrast, "anthropological." The terms in which we are to reconstruct subjects are in important respects prior to those in which agents understand themselves. At the same time, it is important to see that archaeology cannot presume to establish a standpoint above (or below) all agency, since that would imply an ability to transcend history, the last thing Foucault is prepared to admit. For him, reconstruction of intellectual practices is a genealogical enterprise, which, among other things, means that it takes its starting point from a particular historical experience. The historical path of genealogical reflection always departs from assumptions or beliefs that have been made problematic for specific agents (Foucault 1983, 208–27).

The archaeological strategy within the genealogical quest implies more than that subjects will be approached from the conditions that make them possible. This reworking of Kant is paired with an equally equivocal relation to Hegel. The present is to be grasped as historical, and if this means that our historical a priori is to be placed within a process of change, such reflection must resolutely disavow teleological assumptions. Genealogy seeks to avoid treating the past as if it were designed to produce the present, as though it were, to use Hegel's language, historical substance evolving conditions for the emergence of modern subjects. As the term suggests, this claim about historical reflection draws from Nietzsche, to whom Foucault stands in a rather complicated and ambiguous relation. The point against teleology was made by Marx as well (Marx and Engels 1970, 57). But Foucault sometimes seems prepared go well beyond the rejection of teleology to dispense with all conceptions of progressive development in history. His abiding concern with freedom seems to lock him into an ambivalence in this regard, but for now we need only to see that the genealogical emphasis implies a skepticism about claims regarding progress and a methodological determination to avoid corresponding presuppositions in one's reconstructive analyses.

Of course the most important source of such skepticism arises from the historical experience of dominations that emerge from within politics ostensibly committed to freedom. Genealogy as Foucault practices it is concerned with such paradoxes of modern political experience. Archaeological analysis should help us understand how rhetoric about free subjects figures within the construction of new and complex forms of power, both those directly associated with the state and those guided by seemingly more neutral uses of professional expertise. With the idea of discursive practices, Foucault tries to connect modern power to a wide range of modern knowledges.

Discourse as Foucault speaks of it concerns language as it functions within cognitive activities that organize power relations. To say that it is a matter of language is in part to say something about the medium in which power operates. Foucault does not emphasize speech acts or their reception, but he is concerned with actions that take place within communication. He tends to speak of such actions in terms of strategies, and so evokes the ordering of power relations while setting the use of moralized language in a context of premoral operations. To speak of these as premoral operations is to treat them as concerned with effects rather than the achievement of substantive values or the observance of moral norms. It is to see them as concerned with the imposition of specific kinds of order.

One claim associated with the idea of discursive practice, then, is that certain kinds of modern knowledge figure within this kind of strategic action. So far as the social sciences approximate the models fashioned by methodologists and philosophers, they do so within a wider context and with associated operations that have to do with the shaping of social relations. To pursue one aspect of this general line of Foucault's analysis I return to the theme of archaeology. By thinking in terms of discursive practices, Foucault seeks a kind of analysis that allows us to see subjects—indeed, the whole range of characteristics we associate with agency—as emerging and being sustained in specific historical forms by a set of linguistically organized operations. These operations take place in practices that bring specialists and nonspecialists into relation by virtue of cognitively organized activity. One set of examples of this is what Foucault calls normalizing activity (see, e.g., Foucault 1977, 177–94). Here specialists articulate and contribute to the internalization of norms on the part of nonexperts. These nonexperts, the subject matter of a discipline (e.g., psychology, scientific management, advertising), come to be knowable as they come to know themselves and the norms by which they should order their actions.

Here discourses are frameworks within which experts establish effective relations with persons who not only are the "objects" of specialized knowledge but become "subjects" by virtue of their entering the discursive field promoted by the experts. Specialized knowledge codified in theory is thus inseparable from routines of self-knowing that are adopted in practices by which experts integrate nonexperts into regimes of knowledge-power. The social theory of criminology is related to the language imposed on criminals in the process of their incarceration and rehabilitation. Psychiatric theory is related to the language adopted by those undergoing therapy and analysis. In the *History of Sexuality*, vol. 1, Foucault traces the possibility of psychoanalysis to various normalizing practices that make the quest of analytic self-knowledge possible. In this example, it is not just those directly concerned with psychological questions who contribute to the shaping of relevantly knowable subjects; it is also a host of practices with specific aims that contribute jointly to characteristic features of self-experience that modern philosophy takes as an unhistorical point of departure.

The idea of discursive practice provides a way of thinking about what I have been calling intellectual mediation. Here a specific framework of intellectual activity is understood in social terms that relate the cognitive activities of specialists to practical interrelations with those who become the object of their study. This conception of intellectual practice involves the interaction of specialists and nonspecialists where the conceptual features of intellectual work figure in the acquisition of linguistic patterns associated with features of identity, capacity, and motivation. By reconstructing such practices in relation to the terms of modern philosophy, Foucault in effect lays the groundwork for reconstructing mediations between features of specialized intellectual practices, for example, philosophy and psychology.

It is by seeing social knowledge as bound up with the formation of subjects that Foucault contributes to the analysis of knowledge-power. He contributes to the conception of power itself in so doing. In contrast to what he calls the repressive hypothesis, Foucault (1980a, 17–35) proposes a formative conception of power. Speaking of the repressive hypothesis allows Foucault to connect political conceptions of power as repression with psychoanalytical conceptions. It also allows him to connect these conceptions with the language of modern philosophy, by arguing that power is conceived in this hypothesis as a negative instrument of subjects who can be understood in principle without reference to power. Against conceptions that reify power as an instrument or a thing to be possessed by subjects who are essentially power-neutral or to be used by them to block actions by subjects who thus face power as an external threat, Foucault proposes that we conceive power as constitutive and formative. We are in power and power is in us so far as what we are is inseparable from the operations of power through which we assume our capacities, identities, and motivations.

The contrast between such a formative conception of power and power as repression is probably overdrawn by Foucault, but the specifics of his account are of less importance to us than the kind of conception it advances. From the standpoint of the critique of the division of labor, Foucault's conception of discursive practices is attractive for a number of reasons. It allows us to think of important features of the modern differentiation of activities in terms of knowledge-power and does so in a way that challenges the modern philosophical tradition precisely on the point of the misconception it provides of intellectual activity. Furthermore it does so by connecting traditional conceptions of agency with practices in which the workings of knowledge and power contribute to the formation of historically very specific kinds of agency.

Here I am touching on a crucial Foucauldian theme, that of the constitution of subjects. This reflects an aspect of Foucault's critical relation to the modern philosophical tradition: subjects are constituted rather than original and originating. More specific to my concerns is his claim that these historically variable subjects are constituted within forms of knowledge and that modern subjects are inseparable from modern forms of knowledge. Here I touch upon a "structuralist" aspect of Foucault's approach that is worth emphasizing. Unlike Habermas and Bakhtin, he tends to think of subjects in their constituted relations rather than as agents. While Habermas and Bakhtin also insist that subjects are historical and not metaphysical entities, their analyses focus on forms of action rather than on structural position. Foucault, on the other hand, tends not only to downplay action as such but to neglect the normative concerns proper to adopting a critical practical standpoint.

Discourses internalize in agents orientations that involve them in practices organizing their domination. Rather than be externally exercised over or against them, power figures in their own makeup. Normalizing and disciplining routines shape agency of the dominated, articulating and directing normative orientations in which subjects exist as self-subjugating processes. Discourses involve active interaction between experts and citizens through which this internalization is propagated. To use Habermas's term, discourses organize learning processes in which acquired rationality integrates individuals into relations of power.

Though the structural, or relational, quality of Foucault's approach makes agency a function of processes in which agency emerges, Foucault's account does not simply reduce agency away. Despite his occasional resort to scientistic rhetoric, Foucault keeps his distance from positivism both as it tries to eliminate reference to agency and as it fosters illusions about impersonal objectivity. One can refer to his structuralist or quasi-positivist side, but precisely the tension between structure and agency remains effective in his work, and neither is reduced to the other. This can be seen from the genealogical dimension of his reflection, as we will see in a moment. It also can be seen from the fact that for Foucault structural (or relational) analysis always captures a process that is both unstable and characterized by conflict. If agents

are always constituted, the discursive practices involved in their constitution take place always between agents in conflict. For Foucault,
domination exists in opposition to freedom, or at least to resistance
oriented to freedom (Foucault 1983, 225–26).

I explore issues about this feature of Foucault's work as I proceed
with the relation to historicity to which it contributes. My present point
is that this emphasis on the permanence of conflict, within which the
historical character of relationally organized agency is established,
implicitly asserts the permanence or irreducibility of agency. I do not
take this to be a metaphysical claim, but a matter of the kind of
historical analysis and political orientation that Foucault undertakes.

Disruption of All Narratives?

In arguing that Foucault treats agency as irreducible I mean to cast his
concern with discourses of knowledge-power and their formative relation to subjects in a specific light. This relation to agency can be taken
as a way of pursuing a consistently historical reflection, just as it can be
seen as asserting a kind of pragmatist concern. Reflection that takes
agency as problematic here is itself a response to a "problematic situation" in which historical forms of agency have become the focus of
conflict.[3] We can see how this bears on the idea of a critique of the
division of labor by considering the kind of narrative activity Foucault's
own work undertakes.

It may seem strange to speak of Foucault and narrative, since the
critical side of much of his work cuts against narrative as practiced in
traditional philosophy and history alike. So far as there is a sympathy
in Foucault with narrative, it seems to be a matter of the irreducibly
fictive character of his work. Nevertheless, despite Foucault's occasional recourse to just this kind of irony about his own reconstructive
reflection, his narrative discussions contribute to a political orientation
that is very much concerned with the realties of power and conflicts
that might contribute to greater freedom.

That we should take Foucault's narrative discussions seriously is
suggested even by the way they conflict with many of his pronouncements against totalizing theory in general and Marxian analysis in
particular. The works in which Foucault's polemics aimed at Marxism
are most pointed are also those in which he borrows extensively from
Marx's account of modern history to situate the themes of his own
analyses. Thus, for example, he treats the politics of bio-power in

terms of phases of capitalist/working-class conflict stated in rather conventional Marxist terms (Foucault 1980a, 124). One reason this continuing relation to Marx is important is that it indicates Foucault's continuing interest in having a framework in which he can place his analyses so they cast light on the continuing political conflicts of our world. His reliance on Marx in no way undermines his opposition to reductionist conceptions of power or his introduction of analyses of differential and local complexes of power relations. It does bring into question the sense in which his opposition to totalizing theory can be sustained, but this is a problem internal to Marx's work as well.

Nor does his reliance on narrative perspectives in Marx seriously undercut the conception of genealogy with which Foucault tries to sustain the historicity of his own thinking. I have already noted the contrast he draws between archaeology and genealogy. If archaeology problematizes assumptions about subjects and their capacities, genealogy emphasizes that all such reflection turns to history on the basis of experiences in the present. Despite Foucault's use of this Nietzschean term against teleological philosophy of history, it is worth noticing that even Hegel pursues a version of such a genealogy when he treats the philosophy of history itself as possible only on the basis of the achievements and debates of the present (see, e.g., his closing remarks in the preface to the *Phenomenology*, Hegel 1977, 45). The problem of genealogy is posed with greater complexity for Marx because he abandons the linkage of past and present asserted by the philosophy of history. Nonetheless, Marx contributes to a reflection on how the present can inform understanding of the past and does so in a way that contributes directly to the need for such a conception within the critique of the division of labor.

The point of these claims about the prehistory of the idea of genealogy is not just that it is debatable how deeply Foucault breaks from earlier claims about historical thinking or that his work can be seen as contributing to issues facing a critique of the division of labor. It is also that genealogical thinking can be seen as concerned with the quality and possibilities of agency rather than as contributing to a reflective canceling out of the subject. Both the genealogical and the narrative aspects of Foucault's discussions advance his concern with classical modern themes—self-understanding and freedom. This is evident in the way genealogy takes its point of departure from conflicts in the present. Foucault's concern is with discursive practices that come to light by virtue of being made problematic, first by resistance, then by intellectual reconstruction. The idea that reflection takes its cue from popular struggles is a theme Foucault shares with Marx even if his particular emphasis is influenced by the political fortunes of Marxism since Marx. And emphasizing reflection's historical point of departure is not only a way to keep issues of intellectuals and power in view. It is also a way to urge the primacy of the practical over the theoretical, to avoid reifying abstractions. This by now is a familiar theme, since it dovetails with Habermas's retention of the standpoint of the lifeworld and Bakhtin's primacy of dialogical process.

This narrative orientation to liberation raises the possibility of a different notion of intellectual mediation from that associated above with discursive practices construed as imposing domination. Foucault is interested in a normative conception of intellectual mediation in which knowledge would serve the emancipatory aims of social movements (Foucault and Deleuze 1977). He draws a schematic contrast between the universal intellectual (read Marx and Sartre) and the specific intellectual, whose more modest self-conception is tied to the provision of practically useful insights in specific settings of knowledge-power. The force of this distinction is more polemically evocative than analytically satisfying. Though Foucault celebrates the specific intellectual, his own work does not really fit the model. His own philosophical concerns and narrative practice provide a far more sweeping perspective, however partially developed. That is not to say that Foucault thus falls under his own heading of universal intellectual, but to suggest that the distinction is inadequate to accommodate reflection that is rightly suspicious of the ambitions and inflated self-conceptions of intellectuals while not losing sight of the synthetic dimensions of philosophical and democratic thought.

My point is partly that Foucault succeeds more in presenting us with fundamental dilemmas facing would-be critical intellectuals than in offering an adequate political conception. In noting this gap in Foucault's reflection I touch on a reason for the value of a perspective like the critique of the division of labor. This critique offers a more sustained narrative and practical orientation and provides a way to integrate Foucault's insights with those of kindred thinkers.

Assembling the Elements of an Analytical Framework

With my discussion of ideas from Habermas, Bakhtin, and Foucault, I have tried to identify themes that are helpful for developing the philosophical use of the idea of the division of labor, what I have been calling the critique of the division of labor. My aim has been in part to support the claim that the work of such writers can be seen as contributing to such an intellectual project. Despite their differences, these thinkers and many others can be seen as helping us think about the intersections of power and rational capacities at a time in history when the specific shape and distribution of capacities has become a political issue. In the language of the critique of the division of labor, I have described this as a time in which the historically formed scarcity of capacities has been made problematic. In ways that are sometimes complementary but sometimes in conflict, these thinkers contribute to what I have identified as three aspects of this critique. They establish a narrative perspective on rationality and intellectual practice appropriate to political understanding; they pursue the reconstruction of intellectual practices in a way that contributes to demystification of those practices while exploring their actual social effects; and they advance a democratic approach to intellectual mediation that connects a democratic political understanding of knowledge with practical issues about the role of intellectuals in modern society.

The aim of this discussion has thus been twofold. Beside arguing that the critique of the division of labor is a plausible way of interpreting important contemporary work, I have sought to identify specific ideas and arguments with which to sharpen the idea of that project. In what follows I briefly summarize features of the kind of reflection that thus draws on the authors I have discussed. Then, by returning to earlier references to the critique of political economy and the social role of modern philosophy, I illustrate the kind of reflection on specific kinds of intellectual work this approach permits. This discussion provides a transition to a discussion of the bearing of the critique of the division of labor on contemporary issues of knowledge-power.

First, although with the idea of critique I have associated the philosophical use of the idea of the division of labor with the standpoint of constitutive reflection, it is clear that this kind of reflection cannot aspire to traditional models of theory, either in terms of argumentative rigor or conceptual unity and completeness. My use of the idea of narrative signals this, not just because it departs from traditional theoretical form, but also because it reflects the self-consciously practical bearing of such reflection. It cannot easily detach issues of meaning and validity from the quality of the practical relations in which its intellectual activity takes place. What the interrelationships here are remains vague. But at least for now reference to them serves to reiterate that in saying these authors contribute to the critique of the division of labor, I am claiming that they contribute to a different way of thinking about theory and, in the course of this conceptual change, contribute to a different way of doing theory. They invigorate theory by demystifying certain conceptions and practices of it and by exploring concretely how knowledge is effectively important in social experience.

A second point to be made about this kind of theoretical reflection is that, as philosophy, it continues to be concerned with issues of rational validity. As reflection on rationality, the critique of the division of labor resembles traditional philosophy in certain respects. It enters into critical relation to received arguments about knowledge and asserts its own distinctive approach with a view to making sense of genuine rational achievement while accommodating legitimate doubts and counterarguments. But, instead of taking skepticism about knowledge seriously so as to overcome it, this critical reflection takes doubts about the political innocence of knowledge seriously so as to work toward an understanding of rationality proper to democratic politics. Without denying the value of clarifying the nature of cognitive achievements, the critique of the division of labor is not so much concerned with the epistemological validation of the reality of knowledge as it is with the social and political understanding of the legacy of the Enlightenment. It is concerned with the nature of cognitive achievements as it bears on practical possibilities of human freedom and well-being.

A third point regards the use of conceptions of language. The kind of linguistic approach made possible by these theorists allows us to think of the division of labor as a framework of communication and interpretation, and it provides us with terms for thinking about what I later call the communicative infrastructure of a democratic political culture. I shall summarize the relevant ideas in a way that makes more explicit their relation to the critique of the division of labor and specifically to the theme of intellectual mediation.

Narrative

The communications approach for which I am drawing from these thinkers is meant to provide the conceptual materials for specifically philosophical reflection. The discussion of Kant, Hegel, and Marx at the beginning of this chapter revealed some of the requirements facing such thinking. It is to provide constitutive reflection, to make sense of rationality, and to do so in adequate social terms, including those appropriate to intellectual mediation, and it is to avoid various problematic features of the tradition: subjectivism, representationalism (homology of thought with what is being thought about), autonomy of reason, and so on. It is to be able to think of philosophy itself within history, as a social practice whose reflective achievements do not remove it from social involvement. Theory here is in certain respects a matter of narrative.

To speak of narrative is to provide a general contrast with theory in the traditional senses of foundational or transcendental philosophy. The contrast has to do not only with the aim of such theory (providing cognitive guarantees) but also with its means (monological deductive or transcendental arguments, fixed theoretical frameworks). The term "narrative" suggests various respects in which this kind of reflection would depart from traditional theory: it is explicitly concerned with historical forms of activity; it pursues interpretations that establish conceptual links to everyday speech and social interaction and so to practical concerns; and it treats language as itself a historical medium. To speak of philosophy as narrative is to include in philosophy an activity of sense making that bears on historical possibilities; the present is placed in the context of a past and a future conceived in terms of human projects, conflicts, and constraints. Philosophy thus is engaged in making sense of the historical quality of the experience in which it arises.

Of course, the term "narrative" is used in a somewhat figurative sense here, so it is necessary to specify some of the ways this kind of thinking departs from familiar forms of storytelling. Reflection cannot be stated in relation to a telos, and reflection is concerned as much with the limits to agency as it is with its exercise. Constraints upon agents include structural conditions that distort and limit efforts to make sense or communicate understandings. If philosophers are working on this narrative, it is from within the story whose terms they are using and proposing to others; their attempt to construct the narrative does not provide them with a privileged position regarding its movement or relation to a never-to-be-reached conclusion. Narrative here is by no means a story told by an impersonal author or by someone with privileged insight into the future. Certainly there is no legitimate claim to political power rooted in strengths of narrative insight.

So far as the critique of the division of labor involves a narrative dimension, this is to be understood as a facet of the intellectual mediation proper to this kind of philosophy. In such philosophy, narrative itself can only be part of an ongoing debate.

As explicit philosophical mediation, narrative here involves utterances that propose a specific reflective relation to a specific historical context, and does so to various specific audiences. The stories it tells have to do with knowledge and rationality reconceived in social terms so as to question certain mystifications and locate specific functions. This reflection responds to contemporary distrust of abstractions with accounts that explore the ambiguous reality of specialized knowledges by relating them both to the empirical disposition of powers and to claims about possible alternative dispositions.

We can sharpen this discussion by referring to some of the themes I have touched upon in the foregoing discussion of Habermas, Bakhtin, and Foucault. The problem of reason—in particular, that of knowledge-power—becomes explicitly tied to dilemmas of modernity. Rationality, which for many philosophers has been the defining quality of humanity, becomes associated with modern rationalization, the conjoined processes of science, technological development, market economies, formalized legal systems, bureaucratic organization, the erosion of traditional beliefs and ethical codes, modern high art and mass culture, and so on. The problem of reason comes to turn on our ability to negotiate our way through these characteristically modern developments, and so it turns in part on our ability to make sense of these developments. The background to more specific interpretive and critical initiatives remains for these thinkers not only the kinds of Weberian themes just enumerated but also the Hegelian and Marxian themes of alienation, exploitation, and social conflict. But these wider economic and political concerns themselves need to be historicized, qualified, and related to specifics. So we have the general problem of thinking the relation between experience and structural evolution (addressed by Habermas in terms of the colonization of the lifeworld) as well as specific problems of knowledge and power (addressed by Foucault with ideas of normalizing and disciplinary practices).

The problem of reason becomes inseparably connected to language as a medium in which historical forms of rationality are organized and contested. Monological discourse, authoritative voices, and instrumentalizing strategies all must be explored for their historical content. The specific claims and achievements of experts must be set against contingent institutional relations and broad differentiations of cultural value spheres. The extent to which categorical distinctions are either overstated or used to cover specific historical contents becomes a matter of ongoing debate. Thus issues of professional practices, specific differentiations of speech and social practice, and the organization of modern heteroglossia become issues for reflection on reason. Questions of forms of participation, distribution of resources for speech, kinds of recognition offered and withheld all figure in this binding of language issues with questions of rationality.

Because reason becomes historicized by virtue of questions of power, this kind of narrative concern is inseparable from questions of politics. By this I mean as much questions about the nature and possibilities of politics as questions about specific policies or existing organizations of power. The reconstruction of the political dimension of intellectual practices is an issue to which I turn momentarily. In narrative perspective, the question concerns placing official politics in relation to conflicts over other kinds of power operations and finding terms in which to pose the nature of the alternatives.

My claim for the idea of the critique of the division of labor is that it provides a fruitful narrative perspective for making use of these various themes. Various aspects of the idea of scarcity provide ways of thinking about aspects of power operations within intellectual practices and about their role in the reproduction of power more generally. At the same time, the division of labor provides a kind of transhistorical perspective that allows us to balance the historicization of knowledge with normative perspectives that both accommodate cognitive achievements and point to coherent political possibilities from within the paradoxes and dilemmas of modernity. In particular, the critique of the division of labor offers a perspective on a democratic public within which the question of knowledge-power can be explicitly and effectively posed in political terms.

It is premature to claim that I have shown that this somewhat abstract standpoint (scarcity) informs a narrative perspective that can contextualize the great ideological conflicts of recent history without pretending to step beyond them. For example, the issues of late capitalism and the collapse of Communism, and the question whether or in what sense socialism remains a viable ideal, can be approached from this perspective. That is because it allows us to explore democracy as a framing issue without reducing this to a celebration of the liberal forms of democracy practiced in the wealthier nations. The narrative standpoint of the critique of the division of labor allows us to reflect on forms of domination and inequality without immediately assimilating these to economic systems, yet it leaves open the relation between such forms and these systems.

A Communications Approach to Philosophical Reconstruction

Having discussed how the communications approach allows us to conceive the narrative aims of the critique of the division of labor, I now turn to how it allows us to reconstruct intellectual mediations within the world of the division of labor. In its narrative dimension the critique of the division of labor provides a historical self-reflection to intellectuals that includes reference to their own mediating activity. This historical perspective locates specific mediating practices that can be reconstructed in communications terms. I touch on three reconstructive concerns: conceiving rationality in social terms; conceptualizing intellectual mediation, particularly as it involves action upon agency; and thinking about conflict and democratic criticism.

Constituted Agency, Constitutive Practices

In reflecting on how developments of language theory allow for a social conception of rationality, I am pursuing ways of thinking about knowledge-power. By breaking with idealizing conceptions proper to the philosophy of the subject in which the social being of intellectuals disappears in their alleged embodiment of rational necessity, these conceptions contextualize rationality, break with absolutizing claims for it, and deprive intellectuals of an account that both obscures their social being and asserts their social authority. While such a social and historical approach to rationality rejects the sweeping metaphysical claims associated with modern epistemology and thus disputes the expressive or representational relation between reality and reason/intellectuals, it does not therefore minimize the importance of rationality in society. This is not a way of implying that rationality is somehow illusory, either in its normative claims or in its effective role in the world.

On the contrary, it is only by rejecting the inflated and apologetic conceptions of rationality associated with the epistemological tradition that we can begin to appreciate the extensive though variable effectiveness of rationality in history. Only a conception that does not pretend that rationality is somehow the unifying principle of reality can establish how specifically rational achievements have a distinctive force within human experience. While in important ways this means a more modest conception of reason than that of the tradition, it also treats rationality as an object of empirical and historical study, as a factor that can make a variety of differences within the contingent play of human reality. By treating reason as embodied in social practices, it also makes for a more critical conception of intellectuals, one that avoids the characteristic modern oscillation between ambitious, overstated claims for rationality on the one hand and disingenuous statements of self-abnegation on the other.

Such a project is what I have identified with the idea of the critique of the division of labor. Now, considering how the various analytical conceptions I have reviewed in Habermas, Bakhtin, and Foucault contribute to this kind of critique should indicate more concretely how this critique pursues its reflection on rationality.

In conceiving rationality as constitutive of communication, Habermas helps us see both how rationality itself is social and how social reality is in important ways constructed through rational operations figuring within social practices. The social quality of communication depends upon rational claims and their recognition, while the sustaining of and reflection upon these claims depends upon further social communica-tion (in the most ideally reflective way in discursive practices). Effec-tively asserted validity claims play constitutive roles in the patterns of social reality established by social practices. So in these general terms the communications approach provides a role for reason in social consti-tution without resorting to a transcendental constitutive subject.

Bakhtin's analysis of the utterance, with its various ways of treating production and reception, double-voicing and commentary, helps con-cretize operations analyzed in terms of validity claims. It provides a way of thinking about how orientations to different object domains can be internalized (e.g., citizens internalize expert voices about economic necessity and so apprehend their social relations in objectivist terms). Action on voice, understood as a means of interpretive commentary as well as articulation, then can be reconstructed as shaping responses of citizens to contemporary heteroglossia and the conflicts it contains (e.g., media voices shape citizens' interpretations of the demands of movements). Using such conceptions, we can see how linguistic pro-cesses place individuals in distinctive historical relations to self, others, and things.

When cast in terms of intellectual practices, these features of the communications approach can show how embodied rationality figures in social constitution as conceived by the critique of the division of labor. I have shown how Foucault's notions of normalizing and disciplinary practices offer historical conceptions proper to modern knowledge-power. Foucault's own statements about the similarities between features of Habermas's communications framework and his own analyses offers some support for filling in his account of discursive practices with the themes I have been citing from Habermas and Bakhtin (Foucault 1984, "Politics and Ethics"). Normalization involves strategies that shape individual learning so as to promote specific relations to self, others, and objects organized by the corresponding Habermasian validity claims. Similarly, we can think of such practices as employing genres and fashioning and employing voices as conceived by Bakhtin. For example, we could examine professional knowledge-power as involving communications that normalize clients through the articulation of monological voices.

With these features of language theory, we can think about how rationality figures in the construction of a knowable world. This approach historicizes modern Enlightenment without treating modern reason as arbitrary, much less as illusory. Enlightenment is historicized because characteristic rational accomplishments of modern intellectual activity are tied to historical forms of objectivity and experience. At the same time, as I have noted in my references to the narrative perspective of the critique of the division of labor, these historical forms can be examined in terms of historical learning and historical possibilities. Linguistically organized cognitive practices can pursue different possibilities as constrained by conditions of ecology, production, inherited culture, and so on, that is, as constrained by the conditions of historical forms of scarcity.

While the communications framework allows for a relative independence of relations to objects, others, and selves, their coexistence within communicative activity provides a way of bringing them into relation with one another: certain kinds of objects linked to certain kinds of social relations and to certain kinds of selves. Language orients us to the world while at the same time articulating intralinguistic relations and self-reference. On this basis, we can see how the division of labor is itself a framework of interpretation. It organizes the understandings of various kinds of object domains, social relations, and selves while at the same time providing an interpretation of itself as a framework of scarce goods and capacities.

This point can be stated in terms of voices. The division of labor can be reconstructed as a differential complex of voices whose interaction tacitly establishes a relation to the complex, not as a coherent totality but as transcending the individual speaker and position. What result are differentiations proper to kinds of participation, resources, and recognition. We can see this in the double-voicing in which subordinate voices rework utterances of specialists and so allude in their speech to the differential relation to linguistic initiative.

Intellectual Mediation and Social Evolution

In concretizing historical reflection on rationality by couching it in terms of the division of labor, I am saying that embodied rationality has to be conceived in terms of social practices, in particular, specialized intellectual practices. I have already discussed the idea of intellectual mediation in various respects. Now I show how the elements of a communications approach I have assembled allow us to think about such mediations within the division of labor. We need to consider how this approach allows us to think about ways rationality figures in the construction and reproduction of various aspects of scarcity. Doing so would help us see how we can sustain the proposition that the critique of the division of labor provides a way of thinking in a nonreductive way about various kinds of power in relation to genuine cognitive achievements.

In Foucault's conception of normalizing and disciplinary practices we have already encountered a treatment of intellectual mediation. My suggestion is that we can fill in the details and consider variations on such practices by making use of themes from Habermas and Bakhtin. With the conception of the making and assessment of validity claims we can think about details of the practical relations between specialists and nonspecialists so as to see that the organization of power that results contains a moment of rational judgment that is open to subsequent challenge or reiteration. Similarly, with Bakhtin's idea of voice we can think about how specialist mediation introduces a way of speaking and self-relation to those who are being normalized.

Learning and double-voicing are complementary notions that allow us to consider how mediation works in more detail, as an individual internalizes the voicings of the expert through the acceptance of certain validity claims that in turn may introduce a higher level of reflective potential. This may be seen in cases of medicalizing politics in which individuals internalize voicings of experts who construct social interpretations in terms of health. This is a process that goes on in the contemporary politics of health care. That is, the debate over national medical policy includes not only debates over the politics of health but also extensions of the treatment of political issues in medical and health-related terms. Social problems are to some extent treated as health issues, and within health issues are practices that are directly normalizing in their response to social problems (e.g., various kinds of counseling, psychotherapy, social therapy). Those who come to see themselves and their problems in such terms are at the same time increasing certain kinds of reflective capacity even as they are adopting certain positive lines of understanding with accompanying exclusions of interpretive possibilities. In cases like these, learning may proceed within discursive practices that have their strategic aspects (e.g., campaigns for winning acceptance of a certain politics of health) even as they advance normalization using the terms of ethical language (justice, fulfillment).

The respects in which rationality is functioning here are rather complex. We have the rational operations constitutive of the various communicative features of normalization, but this also involves the application of specialized knowledge by those who are involved (e.g., not only medical expertise, but that proper to using mass media) as well as representing features of that knowledge. That is, various kinds of rationality are employed to influence the exercise of various kinds of rationality that are in the process of interpreting various kinds of rationality. Strategies are employed to shape citizens' understanding of the nature and role of specific expertise.

Intellectual mediation functions in a correspondingly complex way. Experts working on citizens' understanding are themselves interpretively reworking materials constructed by other experts. For example, political advisors rework the language cultivated by philosophers for thinking about general social and political principles. Philosophical voices echo in the mediations by which citizens adopt language of rights or responsibilities. At the same time, experts are fashioning interpretations that respond to political pressures of powerful interests or movements by redefining what is politically thinkable, politically reasonable (e.g., with regard to the role of the state in funding or organizing the payment for medical care). These interpretations are offered as political understanding of the possible roles of other experts (in this case those of the medical profession).

Specific themes from the authors cited here contribute to thinking about the operations of these various mediations. For example, Bakhtin's exploration of the monological authoritative voices of modern theory provides a way of reconstructing characteristics of the linguistic practices that are being advanced and integrated at various levels of mediation. Similar use can be made of Habermas's account of technocratic language.

In speaking here of mediations, I am concerned with active shaping by experts of the social practices and understandings of rationality. Though my emphasis at this point is on the linkage of power and rationality in the division of labor, I do not mean to imply that these mediations are matters of manipulation or simple imposition. By hypothesis, mediation here takes place within various contexts of interaction that allow for active and passive resistance, conflict with alternative programs, and so on. I come back to the theme of conflict and resistance in the next section of this discussion. In speaking now of power, I am emphasizing various aspects of inequality and domination.

Power as it figures in intellectual mediation is by no means homogeneous. On the one hand, I am considering how to think about power exercised through specifically intellectual practices. On the other, knowledge-power is implicated in the reproduction of various conflicts that result in scarcity of agency. In addition to power specific to the respects in which relations of knowledge organize scarcity, there are the various kinds of power relations that characterize modern conflicts and have become the focus of modern movements: class, gender, ethnicity/racism. Further, there are the various institutional frameworks of power that embody and reproduce these specific power relations: the state, the economy, education, art, and so on.

With the communications approach to the reconstruction of intellectual mediation, we are not committed to any specific account of the interrelation of these power relations and institutions. With the standpoint of the critique of the division of labor, we are committed to seeing them as depending on (but not as being identical with) the reproduction of the division of labor. Given the reflexive relations to the division of labor characteristic of its modern development, we can see various respects in which specialist activities work directly on features of agency as a factor in the workings of all of these various power relations.

Conflict and Politics

Application of the communications approach to the division of labor allows us to see why the idea of the division of labor can function philosophically. In its modern forms, the division of labor not only is a framework of various kinds of interpretive activities but also organizes reflection upon itself. In the modern period, the division of labor assumes increasing philosophical qualities; that is, it involves increasing reflection on rationality as a function of the increasingly reflexive quality of social action, that is, as a function of increasing action upon agency. What I earlier discussed as unacknowledged and alienating politics figures centrally in this action upon agency and so contributes to the increasing role for a reflective relation to rationality. The growth of unacknowledged politics of agency is at once a growth in knowledge-politics.

Focusing on the issue of knowledge-power allows us to see how specialized mediations figure in the reproduction of various specific kinds of power relations. My account follows the widespread view that modern social rationalization involves a growth in forms and complexity of power. It also, as I have noted, leads to a political impasse centered on the problem of politics as such. But even if exercises of power become more extensive, differentiating, and detailed, this does not mean that they proceed without resistance or that they achieve or can achieve stability.

The communications approach provides terms with which we can think why this is so. The refinement of power operations involves increasing reliance on a multiplicity of social interactions, on solicitations of interpretive agreement or acceptance. If there are more points on which power is exercised, there are also more points at which it can be resisted, redirected, or otherwise frustrated. One might observe, of course, that the growing multiplicity of power operations makes as much for problems of overcomplexity and incoherence as it does for purposeful resistance. Instability by no means implies the potential for better alternatives. The aim here is not to defend any historical or political projections but rather to see how some of the elements of a communications approach to philosophical reflection allow for reconstruction in which conflict and criticism can play a significant role.

Because this approach allows us to see action upon agency as involving the activity of the agent acted upon, it also accommodates resistance and conflict. As with the positive effectiveness of action upon agency, the general features of the communications approach cannot predict specific resistances but provides terms in which they can be interpreted. An advantage of the emphasis on interaction favored by

Habermas and Bakhtin over Foucault's more structural approach can be seen in this context. Foucault wants also to treat knowledge-power relations as inherently conflictual but has to posit a general dialectic of power and liberty, domination and resistance. This is just one of the ways Foucault preserves elements of a conception of the subject that is more traditional than he typically acknowledges.

The division of labor is a complex of differential agencies with correspondingly differentiated voices. An idea like discursive practice may seem to imply a rigid order to this differentiation, but all of the theorists from whom I have drawn treat such communicative relations as potentially unstable, in part because they are inherently conflictual. In view of his debt to structuralist thinking, Foucault may be especially instructive in this regard. For him relations of power are potential contexts of resistance because power and the impulse to liberty exist in reciprocal tension (Foucault 1983). Effective resistance is not a necessary or inevitable result of this tension: Foucault is committed to treating conflicts as emerging from historical complexes of factors. However we understand the conditions that give rise to conflicts, the key point here is that the potential for them is inherent in power as such.

For all three authors, the use of language theory is related to an instability within the world of modern knowledge. Though all three are concerned with specifically modern forms of stabilization, in particular totalizing forms of stabilization, they also reconstruct the medium by which order is imposed as not possessing that objective fixity whose image it so frequently projects. We can see this in the various appeals to validity power must make. If we think in terms of Habermas's conception of reciprocal relations between the makers and receivers of validity claims, we are able to connect power, resistance, and conflict to judgments of rationality. That conflict can be articulated in such terms is what we would expect if we were to think of power itself in terms of such judgments. Doing so is inherent in this kind of communications approach. This is true whether we follow Habermas's use of the theory of validity claims or Foucault's conception of knowledge-power. This point is worth developing for its relevance to conceiving intellectual mediation.

Resistance in general has to be connected with challenges to the division of labor in particular, and this must involve reference to what was earlier called the narrative standpoint of freedom. Resistance can be conceived as conflict within and over communications relations when these figure within the division of labor understood in its self-referential features. Such is the case where knowledge claims intersect with the regulation of social relations; here challenges to knowledge and to power can converge in challenges to specific claims of expertise. Under certain circumstances conflict becomes a challenge to the principle of the division of labor itself. It may do so when specifically communications issues arise, for example, over participation, resources, and recognition within the communicative organization of knowledge and power. Voice, or position within the making and assessing of validity claims, can become a contested issue of scarcity of agency, scarcity of capacities, identity formation, and so on.

Mediation may be contested, it may itself involve conflicts (conflicting mediations), or it may modify itself in response to conflict and resistance. There may be reflexive relations, self-referential relations within agency, or the retrieval of lost potentials, creativity, and imagination. Struggle takes place over identities, semantic contents, and language itself. Ultimately, we see ourselves to be working with a conception of language that encompasses but does not explain an open-endedness involving linguistic creativity linked to artistic and political creativity. Learning in historically progressive ways can be linked to struggle, for example, in the emergence of more universalistic institutions and practices. Crucial here is the evolution of law, an evolution in which we stand at a crucial moment, so far as the regulation of international relations is concerned. In the setting of the demise of the Cold War, conjoined with the various trends that limit the capacities of national organization and identities, new forms of common understanding and conflict resolution must emerge from conflicts and mediations associated with them.

One must acknowledge, at the same time, that the way the communications approach accommodates resistance is itself abstract. None of the theorists cited above is particularly successful in linking historical conditions of action with specific prospects of freedom. In fact, this gap is reflected in the relative independence of the reconstructive aspect of the critique of the division of labor and the narrative effort to establish historical perspectives. Maintaining this gap represents a necessary modesty in the face of complex circumstances and limited understanding. But the narrative effort at perspective building offers an understanding that links reconstruction to its unavoidable counterfactual presuppositions.

The critical standpoint of democratic intellectual mediation raises issues that take us beyond my immediate concern with reproduction of the division of labor through constitutive processes in which intellectual practices have a part. I return later to the theme of democratic mediation in some detail. Clearly, the narrative standpoint of the critique of the division of labor and the challenge to scarcity it includes makes these issues of democratic orientation and the project of democratic mediation inescapable for my argument. At this point, I need to reiterate the aim I have been pursuing in this section, namely, regarding the project of democratic reconstruction, that is, in conceptual reconstruction proper to democratic philosophical mediation. The framework is to provide us with the terms of a philosophical reflection, in which we understand intellectual mediation in communicative terms appropriate to democratic criticism.

From the standpoint of my earlier discussion of constitutive reconstruction, we can treat this analytical framework as providing terms appropriate for the philosophical use of the idea of the division of labor. Aside from allowing for reconstruction of the kinds of differentiation and integration appropriate to social complexes of scarce capacities, this kind of analytical framework allows us to think counterfactually in terms of the challenge to the division of labor, particularly regarding knowledge-power.

As I noted in the discussion of Kant and Hegel, this critical relation to the division of labor means placing intellectuals, including philosophers, in genuinely mediational positions and relations. It challenges theoretical mystification and the autonomizing of reason. The terms I have reviewed in the discussion of Habermas, Bakhtin, and Foucault are to provide a general approach to a constitutive reflection that can treat intellectuals not as passive representatives or reflections of rational necessity, but as constructive mediators. They provide terms for thinking about historicity within the relations of concepts and forms of experience, structures of constructed reality.

This framework is to take us some distance toward clarifying how we can speak of democratic, universalistic reflection within philosophy while surrendering the claims to necessary truths. The communications framework's normative standpoint is crucial in this regard, since it is to help us place claims about knowledge within a discussion in which universalistic claims can be rationally assessed. But for us to advance toward this goal, we need to go further into the way this framework helps us reconstruct knowledge as intellectual mediation.

Democratic Reconstruction

Having discussed ways a communications approach can advance the narrative and reconstructive reflection I am attributing to the critique of the division of labor, I shall now briefly illustrate the possibilities of this philosophical strategy as it bears on themes I have already discussed. Earlier I noted that Marx's critique of political economy is philosophical in the present sense of the term. Now I shall elaborate on this point by showing how the communications approach allows us to restate Marx's argument so far as it concerns intellectual practices. Then I shall illustrate how some of my earlier claims about modern philosophy itself can be explored using the communications framework.

While these are presented only as illustrative discussions, they should clarify what I mean by democratic philosophy in two of its aspects: reflection on embodied reason within intellectual practices and, specifically, reflection on philosophical practice as such. This illustrates the specific kind of reflexiveness I associate with the critique of the division of labor. After these illustrative discussions I turn briefly to the other feature of democratic philosophy I have described in the discussions above, namely, that of democratic mediation. Here I anticipate some of the themes that are developed in Part Four of this study.

Reconstructing the Intellectual Mediations of Political Economy

I have already discussed ways Marx contributes to the critique of the division of labor in general theoretical terms. Now I turn to aspects of his "Critique of Political Economy" to see specific ways his reconstruction of capitalism can be read philosophically, that is, as contributing to the kind of reflection I am associating with the critique of the division of labor. In part the aim is to see how the narrative and reconstructive approaches I have sketched above are illustrated by Marx's work. In part the aim is to see how these approaches allow us to develop philosophical possibilities implicit in work Marx himself treated as an alternative to philosophy. Earlier I discussed ways of characterizing

Marx's relation to traditional philosophy by treating him as a thinker of social constitution whose challenge to intellectuals raises but does not answer important political questions about modern knowledge-power and the division of labor. Having in the meantime discussed general elements of a reconstructive approach to intellectual mediation, I can now characterize ways Marx's critique of political economy involves the kind of reconstructive account of intellectual mediation that I am calling philosophical.

The Kantian reference implicit in Marx's subtitling *Capital* a "Critique of Political Economy" reminds us of his interest not just in a specific intellectual activity but in the conditions that make it possible. Not only is the resulting historical account a contrast to Kant's transcendentalism, it also involves an active relation between the subject and object of knowledge quite different from Kant's. If we regard the political economist as the knowing subject here, we can say that the subject plays a practical role in shaping the social conditions for its historical object of knowledge. As consultant to policy makers, as interpreter of economic phenomena for a wider social audience, and as teacher of other professionals, the economist engages in various intellectual mediations whose effects include contributions to the social patterns cognized in economic thought.

In order to develop this claim about intellectual mediation, it helps first to refer to the historical reconstruction Marx provides of the preconditions of political economic theory. The abstractions in thought proper to political economy, for example, the ideas of economic value, abstract labor, and the associated quantifying and objectivating schemata, are possible because of the abstractions in the social reality of capitalism. These social abstractions are constructed through exchange, which organizes a quantifying abstraction to useful things in a way that both separates economic value from utility and requires individuals to separate their desires from their capacity to pay. This further requires them to organize their qualitative activity, that is, their work, around imperatives codified in money terms. These experiential abstractions, imposed by the logic of commodities, enable individuals to enter into the complex and anonymous relations organized by the exchange economy.[4]

Though drawing from the practical and conceptual aspects of economic activity, the thought abstractions of theory are nonetheless idealizations that do not simply represent or express the practical abstractions that make them possible. For Marx, the thought abstractions make possible a cognitive "appropriation" whose epistemological standing he does not theorize in any systematic way.[5] This activity of appropriation is part of what has to be reconstructed in an account of political economy as an activity of intellectual mediation.

With this general background, I can begin to reconstruct Marx's reflection with the communications approach. Political economists are engaged in various kinds of utterances, each with its distinctive interactive conditions and dynamics. I consider two of these: first, those proper to the political economist as theorist in the strictest sense, that is, as constructing theory addressed to other theorists, and, second, those proper to the political economist as policy advisor, that is, as formulating interpretations addressed to state officials. I concentrate on features of political economy that for Marx allow it to treat historical relations as natural conditions. In particular, I focus my reconstruction on political economic communications as they naturalize the modern economy by conceiving its workings in reified and quantitative terms associated with an objective necessity beyond the control of the individuals acting within the market economy.

The utterances of political economists, whether formulated in such genres as the treatises of Adam Smith and David Ricardo, or in contemporary journal articles, employ validity claims that, on various levels of abstraction, establish the basic terms of economic discourse as well as specific claims about production and distribution. If we limit ourselves to the themes of objectivating abstraction and naturelike necessity, we can say that these theorists assert interpretive claims about their subject matter in a communicative setting in which they draw from preexisting traditions of science and philosophy as well as a preexisting tradition of reflection on production. They take over features of previous utterances as they fashion their own communications. Programmatic claims both establish a relation to an existing intellectual culture and provide a framework for the reception of empirical materials bearing on the argument at hand. Thus there is an interactive relation both to the philosophical and scientific traditions and to the work of those who have dealt more particularly with economic phenomena.

The articulation and use of reifying and quantifying conceptualization asserts the validity of treating social relations in an objectivizing manner. From the standpoint of Marx's critique this treatment translates the social relations between the theorist and economically active individuals into a contemplative relation to objective states of affairs. In promoting the conceptual strategies of political economy, intellectuals eliminate reference to their interpretive relation to their fellow citizens and avoid the possibility of having to defend the practical dimensions of that relation. In general, they abstract away from the historical conditions of propertylessness and dependence that give most individuals little alternative to entering not just the activity of market exchange but the commodification of their own activity.

If we follow Habermas in speaking here of speech acts that organize validity claims about social relations as claims about objective states of affairs, we can see that Marx (and there is little reason to doubt that Habermas would follow him in this) would treat this as presupposing and reproducing the power relations of capitalism. The theorist's utterances promote an interpretation of the world of these relations, an interpretation in which they are for the most part naturalized and drained of social content. If we think of these utterances as circulating with an intellectual conversation among theorists, we can see them organizing a shared voice in which they take up a specific social relation to historical contents that are not identified as such.

If the intellectual genres of political economy involve devices of abstraction and means of reasoning that naturalize the social world, they contribute to a voice that has the monological and latently authoritative qualities Bakhtin associates with modern theory. As I noted in discussing Bakhtin, the idea of monological voice serves dialogical analysis. It is a way of characterizing the social self-presentation of one group of speakers to others. It is also a way of characterizing the way intellectuals take over what is presented to them by other social voices. The increasing scientization of economics discourse does not free it from communicative dependence on other communications for the information and analyses it reworks into political economic argumentation. No rewarming of empiricist rhetoric can eliminate intellectuals' reliance on previous utterances, themselves operating in an interpretive medium. This reliance ranges from preexisting theoretical voices and genres (philosophy, natural science, history) as well as sources of data for specifically economic arguments (government reports, newspapers, business records). It also involves communicative relations to the various social groups within the economy itself, selecting some perspectives as instructive, others as below the threshold of scientific relevance.

Marx sometimes overstates this point by identifying the standpoint of the political economist with that of the capitalist. Apart from indicating that political economic interpretation cannot be above social interests, however, this overstatement has the advantage of emphasizing the real social connection between intellectual experts and primary social agents. The political economist has to take over the voicing and interpretive approaches of economic agents in order to anchor the theory in social experience. At the same time, there is a conceptual transformation consonant with the theoretical project, the effort to think systematically about the economy and its dynamics.

Here, then, are the elements of a conception of intellectual mediation. It involves a complex receptive and assertive relation to multiple interlocutors, organized by certain programmatic validity claims that have the effect of naturalizing specific standpoints and experiences. For Marx, the theoretical rigor of political economy depends in part on the success of its practical involvement. That is, the reflective insight abetted by political economic argumentation contributes to policies that enable the social tendencies depicted by political economy to advance. This takes us to the other kind of intellectual utterance I consider here, that of the political economist to state officials. For Marx, the role of the state in sustaining the modern economy is fundamental. The state guarantees and must modify as required the historical conditions that make a modern market economy possible. One important example of this developed in *Capital* concerns limits on the length of the working day (Marx 1976, chap. 10). Left to themselves capitalists were quite ready to work their laborers to death. Restoring the preindustrial working day was not only a condition for survival and minimal well-being on the part of workers, but also a condition for the stable functioning of the capitalist economy. But individual capitalists cannot and do not take the standpoint of the whole into account either as it affects their class or society as such. Adopting a more general standpoint is a function left to the state, which must, therefore, occasionally curb the interests of individual capitalists to preserve the interests of the class.

In this narrative perspective the mediating role of political economy becomes clear. It contributes to reflection that makes formulation of state policies possible. Though its cognitive claims emphasize the objectivity of the necessities it traces, this naturalizing quality of its reflection is belied by the very historical and political nature of the state actions it helps inform.

Now we have the very general outlines of an account of intellectual mediation in which the cogency of intellectual insight is in part accounted for by the historical construction of its object, to which this intellectual mediation itself contributes. We see here elements of the kind of subject/object relation found in Foucault's notion of discursive practices, so far as the objects of specific social studies are trained by them to adopt basic elements of the behavior that is studied. I believe the anticipation of Foucault by Marx in this regard is extensive. So far as we see the mediating function of the political economist as in part an educational one toward the state officials but also the more general public, we can see a kind of normalizing function. The image of the economic subject fashioned in economic theory provides terms for the training of economic subjects.

As this last point suggests, any attempt to fill out the tacit notion of intellectual mediation in Marx would have to explore a rather complex interplay of intellectual mediations well beyond those specific to political economists. If the political economist contributes to a formation of modern economic (and political) subjects, it is only in conjunction with the mediations carried out by many other mediators, including journalists, politicians, teachers, and so on. In any event, in its practical relation to the state, political economic intellectual practice figures within a complex of practices acting upon modern forms of agency. As such, the contribution of these practices to knowledge-power operates on a variety of levels, from those concerning state policies and economic strategies to those concerning the formation of social perceptions and capacities.

From this discussion we can see that Marx addresses issues that assume great significance in the twentieth century, for example, the relations between technological change and social control, or the formation of certain historical kinds of persons through disciplining in various institutional settings. In claiming this, I do not imply that Marx has already done the kind of work Habermas and Foucault undertake a century later, or that he is immune to the various lines of criticism such theorists direct against him on the basis of their own analyses. In fact, Marx's work is much richer than it is often credited with being, but in pointing to these aspects of his argument I mainly want to emphasize the picture we get there of the complex kinds of mediational practice that sustain the modern economy. The richness of Marx's account is such that a reconstruction of what it touches upon identifies many issues and lines of reflection that go well beyond Marx's own sustained investigations. In particular, we see the specifically modern economy as sustained by practices that organize historical relations to outer and inner nature. This is relevant to my later discussion of mediation and ecology.

In all of this we can see Marx as contributing to the philosophical critique of the division of labor. He reconstructs intellectual practices in a way that connects their cognitive achievements to the historical organization of power relations. He places this within a narrative perspective of social conflict that provides a political orientation on his own theoretical interpretation.

Reconstructing the Intellectual Mediations of Modern Philosophy

With my discussion of Marx, we have an example of philosophical reflection in the form of reflection on embodied reason, intellectual practice, in which the question of knowledge-power is explored in a way to identify the intersection of insight and power. While this is only a sketch, it serves to indicate how the analytical materials I have been discussing can be developed in specific analyses. It also shows that the elements of such an analysis are to be found in Marx. The link to Marx is partly of historical interest, partly of interest to contemporary questions of thinking about power so far as issues of the division of labor and economic relations are concerned.

The other illustrative use of the communications approach I attempt before turning to the promise of the critique of the division of labor in contemporary political criticism is a matter of indicating how we can draw from this conceptual vocabulary in thinking about the claims I have been making about traditional philosophy. In particular, we can see some ways this framework allows us to explore the respects in which modern philosophy has contributed to modern knowledge-politics.

If, as I have argued, Marx's critique of political economy is itself philosophical, this is in part because of the epistemological nature of the modern social culture in which the practices of the capitalist market play so key a role. Having seen how the critique of political economy contributes to concerns about intellectual mediation proper to the critique of the division of labor, we may turn from the mediations of political economy to those of philosophy itself. The point is not that philosophy is more important, more fundamental in some sense, though the abstractness of philosophy reserves for its mediations a unique generality of application. The point is, rather, that the distinctive importance that philosophy does possess becomes visible with this kind of reconstruction. And such a reconstruction may be valuable for orienting attempts to pursue philosophy today.

The aim now is to draw terms from the discussion of the division of labor and the reconstruction of intellectual practices in communications to see what implications follow for thinking about philosophy. If reflection on political economy in such terms is philosophical by virtue of providing a historical approach to reflection on rationality, then this reflection on philosophy itself is doubly philosophical, since, besides reconstructing practices of rationality, it raises questions about appropriate philosophical mediations in the future.

I have emphasized respects in which modern philosophy contributes to modern knowledge-politics. Thus I have related themes of epistemologically centered philosophy to features of modern power relations. Strictly philosophical themes—for example, foundationalist and transcendentalist refutations of skepticism, notions of subjectivity and subject-centered reason, rational argument and theoretical knowledge that is independent of specific interests or values, subject/object ontology and the debates over its problematic dualisms, and so on— have been related to features of liberal political culture. These have included liberalism's confidence in the knowability of the world and in the possibility of making the world reasonable for its human inhabitants, its belief in the authority of secular knowledge and the special role for experts within the political order, and various ways of thinking about political subjects, strategies, and well-being. I have claimed that within technical discussions of knowledge and rationality, philosophers have contributed to the terms in which modern politics is understood. Since politics itself involves the articulation of understandings of the world, this contribution by philosophy to political understanding may be seen as contributing to terms in which the modern world is experienced and discussed.

Thus in various ways philosophers have contributed to the terms with which the modern world is seen in secular, objectivist ways, in which individual selves and interests are articulated, in which strategies and moral issues are couched. In general this social and political understanding functions to articulate and reproduce the modern division of labor, including the hierarchical distribution of scarce human capacities. As a framework of knowledge-power, this understanding has a specifically epistemological dimension. Not only does abstract, methodologically secured, knowledge occupy an unprecedented place in society, but it is accompanied by a reflexivity regarding knowledge itself. Methodical knowledge implies self-reflection of some kind, and corresponding to this is an epistemological dimension to modern political culture. The authority of knowledge claims is connected to claims about their validity and the possibility of justifying such claims. While this relation to justification makes possible specifically modern forms of criticism, it also provides an interpretation and rationale for specifically modern forms of authority and power.

On this view, epistemological philosophy has contributed to an epistemological culture and has, among other things, contributed to the self-understanding of intellectuals, that is, those who function at critical points within regimes of knowledge-power. In drawing this connection between philosophical theory and the social and political understanding of intellectuals, I have identified one of the ways in which philosophers have functioned socially. The provision of this self-understanding is one way the conceptually oriented arguments of philosophers have figured in social practices, or in what I have been calling philosophical mediations.

In the course of previous discussions I have referred to various historical examples in order to clarify these claims and provide them with some measure of plausibility. To support claims about philosophical mediation, I have drawn from historical claims about thinkers as well as from claims about wider political, economic, and cultural developments. I have also tried to make this argument plausible as an interpretation of general trends in contemporary philosophical and political criticism. For the general purposes of the critique of the division of labor, as well as for its specific application to philosophical practices, the strongest arguments will be those that are most concrete historically. In this respect, the argument I am making is not that of a systematic theory but that of an approach to research that has a philosophical dimension. In turning now to the use of the communications framework for thinking about modern philosophical practice, I hope to provide terms in which such research can be fruitfully pursued and so with which the larger philosophical perspective can be validated.

In the Cartesian tradition (which for my purposes includes a thinker so critical of Descartes as Hegel), we can speak of two positive, or constructive, functions of philosophy: (1) providing modern intellectuals with self-understanding and (2) providing them with materials for more specific mediations. At the same time, I want to emphasize the extent to which the social being of philosophers involves them in a complex of receptive relations to other practices. Let us sketch some lines of reconstructive analysis of modern philosophical practice by discussing the uses to which various elements of the communications approach can be put.

So far as it engages in utterances, philosophy is dialogical like any other linguistic activity. It emerges from a context to which it is in some way responding and addresses an audience, whose response it seeks to anticipate in various ways. As composed of utterances (whether books, articles, papers, lectures, debates, conversations, or reviews), philosophical activity employs specific genres and voices within specific contexts of interaction. These utterances have their audiences and are themselves evaluative responses to previous utterances, responses that take over claims, genre elements, voice elements, and so on. As utterances, they make validity claims, both with regard to specific intellectual matters and with regard to the organizing features of their activity.

In his *Meditations*, Descartes makes claims about specific ideas and procedures, but he also in effect makes claims about the appropriate use of language in theoretical argumentation. In particular, he excludes conversation and justifies a monological practice. In so doing, he is offering a view on what will make any intellectual's claims worth taking seriously. The isolation of procedure is also an absolutization: the monological procedure is, or should try to be, self-sufficient so far as its intellectual task is concerned. This implies a certain relation to ideas, one that is objectivizing and desocializing. It projects an orientation to concepts treated as possessing thinglike properties associated with elements of objective states of affairs.

We have here the elements of a self-understanding for intellectuals, linked typically in claims about an impersonal and asocial method. This self-understanding thus corresponds to elements of genre (methodological procedures) and is asserted in the formation of appropriate voices. It is an impersonal voice, and, in Bakhtin's words, it is an authoritative voice so long as its pronouncements are the fruits of the method whose adoption makes for the distinctively disembodied quality of this voice.

In using a communications understanding of utterance, then, we are concerned in part with the active and socially oriented character of the philosopher. Thus we need to be able to reconstruct a philosophical text in terms of the various explicit and implicit validity claims it makes and in terms of the explicit and implicit audiences to which it is addressed. At the same time, we need to be able to reconstruct a philosophical text as a response to a preexisting communicative setting. Descartes addresses various opponents as well as allies and seeks to win over those whose allegiances regarding modern science have yet to be settled. The text responds explicitly and implicitly to previous utterances and speakers and does so in ways that can be reconstructed in the specific shaping it gives to preexisting linguistic materials. Old theoretical language is given new uses, and problems with present usage (e.g., Descartes's way of distinguishing the objective and subjective) will give rise to future modifications.

Emphasis on the various aspects of the transmission as well as the reception dimensions of philosophical communication is crucial in order to establish what is distinctive about a communications reconstruction. All the same, this emphasis should not distract us from the specific synthetic act that formulation of the utterance involves. We should not lose sight of what makes a philosophical utterance philosophical, or what allows a philosophical communication to have a specifically philosophical force. But the assertion of the communications approach is that precisely the distinctively philosophical achievement, Descartes's specific validation of knowledge, for example, has to be seen as a distinctive social communication. From the standpoint of the critique of the division of labor, this includes the construction of a reflexive relation to rational claims in which elucidation and justification play a key part. In the context of modern knowledge-politics, this philosophical synthesis contributes to respects in which the division of labor is reflexive, that is, respects in which the division of labor involves an interpretive relation to the differentiation of activities it organizes.

The link between the philosopher's intellectual achievement and the corresponding communicative function can be developed with Bakhtin's idea of genre. The types of philosophical utterances I listed earlier represent genres, those evolving, rule-organized ways philosophers adopt to accomplish their intellectual aims. Specifically philosophical genres involve specific ways of achieving philosophical aims; that is, they involve norms of argumentation and so standards for measuring intellectual achievement. Employing a specific genre involves a claim to the validity of these norms as well as to the validity of the specific ways a thinker tries to follow them. The dialogical reconstruction of philosophy thus would concern itself with debate at this reflexive level as well as with debate over specific issues.

Hegel's work represents a useful example, since it so often involves connections between the advance of his theoretical claims and criticism of preexisting standards and practices. As with the battles for and against analytic philosophy a century later, in Hegel's argumentation the issue is not only how to answer a specific question but also what is to count as genuine philosophy. In communications terms, the argument is over what kinds of writing and speaking will achieve appropriate philosophical results.

This attempt to link argumentative content to communicative process connects claims about types of utterances or genres with claims about the voices that employ these genres. To speak of voice is to elaborate on the treatment of philosophy as occurring in utterances. If philosophical activity exists in specific social settings, it involves specific historical identities on the part of philosophical speakers and writers. These identities may be very abstract, but they are irreducible so far as even the most depersonalized methodological commitments cannot release uses of language from specific historical embodiment. In considering voice, we are interested not just in who philosophical speakers are but also in who they are drawing from and speaking to. Voices are both conditions and objects of the social mediations carried out in philosophical practice.

With the idea of voice we can approach a feature of modern philosophy that has become an object of recent discussion, namely, its monological character. Deconstructive challenges to reflection drawing on claims about immediate "presence" to evidence or meaning, as well as Apel's and Habermas's challenges to accounts of language that abstract it from its social aspects, have made this a basic theme (Derrida 1976; Apel 1967). We can think of the claims about method advanced by Descartes, Hegel, and Husserl, for example, as doing something more than asserting theoretical claims about the process of knowing. In addition to a variety of general respects in which these claims are social (e.g., being articulated in language, having specific texts and thinkers in mind, aiming at particular audiences, and hoping for a certain reception and advance of these ideas), there are specific social features proper to their philosophical quality. With the idea of voice I refer to the fact that each of these thinkers takes up a mode of speaking and arguing that he modifies in significant ways. To speak of a philosophical voice is to refer not just to specific conventions but to a specific kind of social agency.

With voice, we can see two of the functions I have attributed to philosophical mediation. As a form of agency, voice includes a sense of social position and role. Bakhtin captures an aspect of this when he speaks of modern monological theory as articulating an authoritative (as opposed to a persuasive) voice. By virtue of the kind of statements being made, philosophers are also asserting a social position, a basis for recognition. Voice asserts worthiness to be recognized. Philosophical voice asserts the importance of philosophical considerations, and the formation of philosophical voice provides others with ways of asserting their worthiness of recognition. Clearly this is part of what is at stake in Descartes's conflict with the Church. His arguments are inseparable from the assertion of the legitimacy and importance of certain voices within respectable intellectual culture.

This aspect of philosophical voice is connected to another that will bring out the connection with philosophical mediation. Part of what philosophers are doing when they articulate their ideas is to cultivate their own voices and part of what they do is cultivate voice elements for other intellectuals. Modern philosophers have shaped the terms with which other intellectuals articulate and pursue their specific fields of activity. Applying the idea of voice to these other specific fields allows us to see a philosophically pragmatic dimension in them as well, so far as they assert claims about the relation of their rational capacities to social authority and power. Pragmatic reflexivity occurs throughout an epistemological culture, not just in the activity of philosophical specialists. Philosophical mediation, then, includes the provision of philosophical aspects of the voices exercised by experts in an epistemological culture.

So claims about rationality are claims about possible voices, possible speech acts. If I claim that relevant knowledge is available only through certain methods, I am denying active decisions to those for whom such knowledge is inaccessible. In fashioning features of the voices in which such knowledge is couched, I may be establishing barriers to those who cannot adopt these speech features, and I may be doing so by making validity claims about rationality.

In modern philosophy, the link between monologue and authority is internal. Solitary validation establishes the necessity and universality of the theoretical claim and so establishes its authority for others. In principle, this is not a dogmatic approach, since, in principle, universality characterizes the method as well as the results: any one can confirm such knowledge. But, in practice, few are prepared to do so. This is a practical condition philosophers have always recognized, and in doing so they have at least tacitly recognized the reality of the division of labor and the fact that their work functions within such a differential organization of activity.

So to claim that philosophy has frequently been monological is not to deny its communicative reality but to say something about the ideals of speech and indeed of rationality projected by the forms philosophers have employed. Further, to speak of philosophical monologue is not to ignore the frequent use in philosophical writing of dialogues or other devices for presenting contending views. Rather, the claim about monologue concerns the way argumentation proceeds and is resolved. In philosophical monologue, a solitary voice orchestrates a plurality of positions and concludes the debate with an argumentation that does not require the agreement of others.

Hegel provides a significant example, given his attempt to incorporate all intellectual standpoints and his unusual sensitivity to language. Within Hegel's work we find many of the linguistic devices Bakhtin identifies as proper to the internal dialogics of language, that is, to the ways that, even within a single utterance, relations are made with other speakers, ways of speaking, and elements of language. An author may speak by mobilizing the voice of others, whether through direct or indirect quotation or through "quasi-direct discourse" (Volosinov 1973, part 3; Bakhtin 1981, 319). Here language that is formally that of the author is accented so as to present and comment upon the utterance of another. This can be seen, for example, in Hegel's use of Schelling's rhetoric about the Absolute while asserting the conceptual vacuity of Schelling's idea.[6] These dialogical operations illustrate what Bakhtin calls double-voicing, in which an author develops an utterance with the words of another. In a monological utterance, the traces or echoes of other voices become absorbed into the unitary logic and standpoint of the author.

In its monological constructions philosophy can function as authoritative discourse (Bakhtin 1981, 342). Such language operates as though it were above the ordinary give-and-take of discussion. As the articulation of unshakable necessities, this language assumes mythological status. It is an exaggeration to construe philosophy exclusively in this way, since even in its monological forms it possesses properties Bakhtin identifies with the contrasting idea of persuasive discourse. Historically philosophy has generated arguments precisely in order to win arguments based not on dogmatic appeals to authority but on the strength of reasons. Recognition of this Enlightenment commitment should not obscure the extent to which objectivism has in fact contained a dogmatic and ideological dimension. But this paradoxical feature of modern reason—that it both elicits active consent and appeals to an objective necessity—needs to be acknowledged if we are to connect philosophy's theoretical claims with its social functions. In particular, acknowledgment of the blending of what Bakhtin calls authoritative and persuasive discourses is needed for considering the mediational role philosophers have played between intellectual specialists and between them and the representatives of institutions of power and the public of nonspecialists.

In exploring voice, we are not only concerned to recover social identities that the devices of modern philosophy suppress. We are also concerned to see how these devices contribute to a self-understanding of modern intellectuals more generally and how this understanding contributes to intellectual practices more generally. In its philosophical articulation, intellectual self-understanding involves the language of epistemology, but as discussed here it is not so much a theory or set of ideas or subjective states as it is a complex of ways intellectuals present themselves and their work to themselves and to others. Self-understanding is not separate from self-assertion. We can speak of a representation of intellectual capacities, including the various social powers that are exercised through them. Thus this includes conceptions of the division of labor as well as more specific claims. When a physicist or a newscaster presents claims to habitual audiences, such an intellectual enters into a practical relation despite occupational disclaimers regarding the practical implications of their reports. The fact that no specific practical application is stated or even implied does not mean that there are not specific ranges of activity that are implicitly illuminated or even required by the content, for example, of claims about subatomic energy sources or unemployment trends. The authority of the speaker's voice implies lines of further discussion and possible activity.

Thus we see one way philosophers contribute to the social understanding of intellectuals, that is, to their self-understanding but also to the understanding of intellectuals by nonexperts. I've already noted the self-reflexive dimension of voice. Now I am claiming that the propagation of claims about rationality includes the propagation of specific kinds of intellectual voices, typically ones that are monological and authoritative. Emphasis on the authoritative dimension may seem to preclude genuine reflection. In fact my claim is that reflection here possesses a distinctly pragmatic character, which in part means that it is not explicitly articulated. But this is not necessary for an effective social understanding to be achieved.

In constructing voices and genres for intellectuals, philosophers contribute to the way they understand and present themselves, to the way they organize their activity, and to the way they are apprehended by citizens generally. In all these respects we are touching on what I have been speaking of as philosophical mediation as it bears on modern intellectual mediation. With the idea of mediation we further emphasize the practical side of philosophical argumentation. We programmatically set out to see how philosophers carry out mediating activities within a culture that not only employs abstract knowledge in distinctive ways but connects such knowledge to power relations, so that claims about knowledge are a necessary part of the ways power is justified in society. Philosophical mediation is then seen as offering conceptual claims about knowledge that figure within the ways power is articulated in the wider political framework. This constructive role played by philosophers can be seen as mediational so far as it involves communicative relations, especially with other intellectuals, in which politically relevant features of the expertise of these intellectuals are transmitted.

When we focus specifically on philosophical mediation, we are talking about the practical construction and provision of features of the mediating activity of other intellectuals. In particular, we are talking about those reflexive features of public culture with which the authority of expertise is understood. Philosophical mediation involves conceptual "production" required for a cognitively reflexive culture. This takes the form of the self-understanding of intellectuals, which includes their modes of self-presentation and justification. It also takes the form of articulating features of the ways intellectuals carry out their own mediations, in which the rational achievements of intellectuals are connected with power operations. This includes representation but also the means by which rational mediations are carried out.

A familiar instance of such philosophical mediation can be found in the language about value-free knowledge fashioned by positivist thinkers and taken over by social scientists and policy makers. Democratic criticism by theorists like Habermas (1970) combines a challenge to the positivist understandings of theoretical rationality with an analysis of the place of this understanding within technocratic politics. Such analysis shows how such an understanding treats genuinely political issues as technical questions and, at the same time, masks the extent to which experts are playing a political role. In this example, philosophers play a mediating role by providing other specialists with a social understanding of their work that contributes to the more specific mediations they carry out. Here we see philosophers both giving license to these specific disciplines, showing why they are rigorous, how they may exercise authority, and providing each with key intellectual terms for understanding intellectual procedure and social position, including authority.

In speaking of mediation we are speaking of the respects in which philosophers draw from other practices as well as the respects in which they shape them. Philosophical activity, like all linguistic activity, is receptive as well as constructive and projective. If I emphasize the constructive side of philosophical practice, I do so not in order to dismiss the contextualization that rejects illusions of autonomy but to emphasize the function philosophy plays in the modern division of labor. Here philosophy contributes to the epistemological features of the political culture of knowledge-power. Philosophical mediation plays what is in effect a normalizing role regarding intellectuals and provides them with materials for their normalizing functions in specific contexts. To say this is to emphasize how philosophical mediation here represents a distinctive action upon agency, both on the agency of intellectuals and on the agency of those who are influenced by intellectual practices.

Philosophers contribute to the epistemological features of the culture of modern knowledge-politics by providing ways of understanding authority as well as of justifying it and exercising it. By drawing from Foucault's model, we can think of modern political culture as involving normalizing and disciplinary features that help form modern individuals as citizens of regimes of knowledge-power. The philosophical dimension of this, what we are calling the epistemological dimension of modern political culture, presents a respect in which the modern division of labor is self-reflexive, or self-interpretive. The understanding of authority in philosophical terms is also an understanding of the differentiation and exercise of specialization in modern terms. Standards of rational competence and all the practices that go into constructing and measuring them rely upon general understandings of the claims and justifications of rationality in distinctively modern terms.

Foucault himself, despite his nominal rejection of totalizing claims, presents concepts of modern philosophy, above all that of the subject, as tied to modern subjugation, the relation of the modern citizen to the state. Though he is prepared to argue at this level of abstraction, he does not attribute to philosophy alone the historical imposition of this kind of discursive understanding. His preferred concentration on specific practices allows him to trace ways specific intellectual mediations employ these general philosophical terms in specific discursive practices concentrating on specific social objectives. In this respect his account is congruent with what I am attributing to the critique of the division of labor. That is, in speaking of an epistemologically informed political culture, this critical perspective is not claiming that philosophy is a dominant practice or that philosophers exercise extensive political influence. With the idea of mediating practices we can see how philosophical contents, themselves in important ways the result of specifically philosophical work, are transmitted throughout the political culture by way of a host of more specific expert practices, which have their own peculiar aims and problems. Thus other intellectual mediations, for example, those shaping education, mass entertainment, and the medical system, employ and propagate philosophical terms of self- and world-understanding in ways that shape individuals' understanding of themselves, their capacities and goals, and their relations to various authorities.

In the preceding discussion I have tried to show how we can think of modern philosophical mediation in terms of the articulation and exercise of a distinctively philosophical voice that provides a self-understanding and presentation to intellectuals and contributes to the mediation capacities of other intellectuals. These represent philosophical functions, I have argued, because they involve pragmatic as well as directly conceptual claims about rationality. In particular, they present claims about the social powers associated with the exercise of specialized intellectual/rational capacities. So far as modern philosophical voice is tied to the reproduction of the division of labor, the assertions it makes of connections between rationality and power provide an understanding of the necessity of scarcity.

The claim is not that philosophy as such is a significant exercise of power but that its mediational activity contributes to the terms in which power is exercised by other specialists. Modern liberal theory has contributed to the organization of power by constructing voices and genres that have then been appropriated into more specialized practices. For example, the language of governmental policy makers reworks of voices and genres cultivated by philosophers. Similarly the advisors and consultants enlisted by the state employ a language that is dialogically related to that of the social sciences and to modern philosophical reflections on scientific knowledge and technical rationality. As these examples suggest, philosophical mediation can be seen to figure not just in the direct relations between philosophical language and the utterances of specialists but also indirectly in relations with individuals throughout society.

In the foregoing discussions I have tried to indicate how the communications approach proper to the critique of the division of labor can pursue philosophical reflection on rationality as embodied in intellectual practices. My aim has been to develop what I mean by this kind of philosophical reflection by elaborating on the promise of specific analytical and narrative ideas as these apply to two kinds of modern intellectual practices, political economy and philosophy itself. Through the development of this kind of reconstruction, the role of such practices within the modern division of labor can be established. In doing so we can, I have been arguing, achieve a sense of the contradictory achievements of modern intellectual activity from a perspective appropriate to contemporary political dilemmas.

One of my aims has been to sharpen the idea of the critique of the division of labor. Another has been to support the claim that various important contemporary thinkers can be construed as contributing to this philosophical tendency. In both respects the argument provided is incomplete but, I hope, not insufficiently developed to be a coherent target of criticism. In both respects, too, I have been trying to elaborate on the idea of a democratic philosophy. In Part Four I sharpen the respects in which the kind of reconstructions I have just been discussing contribute to a democratic philosophical mediation. In Part Three I develop a sense of the narrative and reconstructive aims of this kind of philosophy when it faces more directly the kind of political impasse I described in Part One.

Part Three

Postmodernism in Philosophy and Politics

With the idea of democratic philosophical criticism, or the critique of the division of labor, as presented in Part Two, I have spoken for a kind of reflection that contrasts with the prevailing hostility toward philosophical theory. Rather than the revival of traditional theory, however, this kind of reflection conjoins intellectual construction with political discussion. Nonetheless, it may appear to affirm a return to "grand theory" and thus to run counter to the skepticism about theory that is found among critics of knowledge-power, the kind of skepticism that has some warrant in the evolution of modern knowledge-politics. Though now I have outlined an alternative to such skepticism, it may appear that I have simply adopted kinds of thinking rightly challenged by contemporary critics. In particular, I mean those kinds of criticism that often go under the label of postmodernism. I want to challenge this kind of criticism, though not so much to explore its many facets as to tie my claims about the critique of the division of labor more closely to contemporary debates and to develop further the idea of democratic philosophical criticism.

Part Three has two main aims. The first is to argue that at least one version of postmodernist philosophy has far more in common with the tradition it attacks than may first seem to be the case. From the standpoint of the critique of the division of labor, this kind of philosophy contributes to the evolution of modern knowledge-politics in a way that responds to the historical changes to which I have been referring and that figures within the emerging politics of the division of labor. I argue that the idea of postmodernism can just as well be applied to changes within contemporary politics in which postmodern philosophy represents one trend. Postmodernism's relation to epistemology is not just a matter of the rejection of a certain kind of theory but has to do more generally with the epistemological features of liberal political culture.

After making a case for considering postmodern philosophy to be one feature of a postmodern politics, I pursue in the second part of the chapter the philosophical criticism of this politics. In this discussion I try to show that the critique of the division of labor is useful not only for thinking about the social role of philosophy but for thinking about the evolution of contemporary politics. My claim is that contemporary politics calls for philosophical criticism because the relation to power this politics organizes is one in which philosophical claims play an important interpretive role.

I am here concerned with reflecting on political evolution as it is tied up with intellectual mediation, particularly such evolution as addressed by and articulated in specifically philosophical reflection. I connect the rise of postmodern politics to the evolution of reflection on rationality in postmodernist philosophy. The point is not that the politics follows the philosophy but that the politics is partly organized by articulations that are developed directly or explicitly in the philosophy. These articulations and politics are part of a far more complex set of evolving conditions and practices, which I have cited in terms of structural change. I am here referring to historical forms of the understanding rationality as it bears on important political changes.

Part Three, then, is philosophical; it provides a kind of reflection on rationality. I frame this reflection by reference to the materials that are now at hand and that are in a sense to be tested by the discussion itself: claims about the evolution of politics (and the relation to philosophy), about the general significance of the division of labor for reflection, and about the need and potential of a communications approach. I wish to characterize a certain kind of democratic criticism by discussing its preconditions and problems. The setting is a politics in which knowledge and understanding is taken as embodied and engaged in mediations; in which structural changes and historical possibilities make the interrelations of politics, economics, and culture distinctively complex; in which the perspective of the division of labor allows us to see how changes in politics correspond to changes in the economic and to changes that make the scarcities proper to the modern hegemony of the economic increasingly a contestable matter.

This discussion casts further light on what I earlier described as an impasse facing liberalism due to the changing quality of politics (linked to changing social conditions) and to corresponding changes in embodied assumptions and practices of rationality. This account gives us a historical and narrative perspective on contemporary debates over rationality and philosophy. In working out this kind of reflection on rationality, I am exploring this alternative to the postmodernist rejection of philosophical reflection on rationality as such. My account will provide a historical contextualization of the postmodernist argument itself. Consistent with my general approach I present this kind of philosophy as itself an intellectual mediation, a proposed self-understanding for intellectuals. As such it has a political dimension. I argue more generally that postmodernist philosophy should be seen as a facet of postmodernist politics. The idea of such a politics rounds out my narrative perspective on the setting in which the critique of the division of labor has its philosophical and political significance. In exploring aspects of post-modernist politics, particularly those that bear on assumptions and practices for which philosophical interpretations are relevant and pre-supposed, I establish the terms for thinking about democratic philoso-phy in a sense more general than the fashioning of the kind of historical interpretation this discussion provides.

At the end of Part Two I sketched a way of thinking about philosophi-cal mediation consistent with the argument about the division of labor and the introduction of the communications framework. This has been the outcome of the argument: that a critical relation to the philosophi-cal tradition requires reconstruction along the lines of the critique of the division of labor. This is a practice of philosophy that orients itself historically by reconstructing previous philosophy as social practice, as mediating activity.

The description of philosophy as mediation is both a way of charac-terizing past philosophy and of stating the program of a democratic philosophy. It implies that the success of philosophy lies in its contri-bution to rational understandings within political culture. At least, we can state its contemporary value in terms like these. Thus I have presented the terms in which the current project must measure its aims and success, the terms in which it must understand itself. As I proceed with this project, the aim is to pursue the kind of reflection on rationality I have now equated with democratic philosophy. The target of my criticism is not traditional philosophical understanding, though I continue to pursue claims I have made about the political role of such understanding in liberal knowledge-politics. In part, I intend to make good on a general claim I have repeated in various contexts, namely, that to sustain a philosophical relation to rationality requires confront-ing a specific skeptical challenge to the tradition, confronting the theme of knowledge-power. As an attempt to sustain universalistic claims of reason in the face of such skepticism, the critique of the division of labor must offer reconstructions of rationality that recog-nize the links of knowledge and power without surrendering the possibilities of a democratic universalism.

In Part Three I explore what is distinctive about this kind of philosoph-ical reflection. I have characterized its general intellectual commitments and have discussed how it can be exercised when looking at specific intellectual practices like political economy and at modern philosophy itself. These discussions have both offered examples of this kind of critical reflection and helped to contrast it with intellectual practice that accepts either tacitly or explicitly the necessity of the division of labor.

The chapters here continue this confrontation with rival approaches in conjunction with presentation of analyses proper to critique of the division of labor as such. Democratic intellectual work generally finds itself in the position of having to pursue its specific critical projects while confronting alternative conceptions of intellectual work. As I have noted with regard to traditional modern philosophy, these tasks are not entirely separate, since the critique of the division of labor seeks to comprehend as well as refute rival philosophical positions.

Such a combination of polemic and alternative analysis structures Part Three. The general aim of what follows is to explore some of the kinds of philosophical reflection on contemporary politics the critique of the division of labor can provide. Thus the aim is in part to see more clearly what is distinctive about this kind of reflection. I begin the discussion by referring to perhaps the dominant contemporary critical standpoint on the philosophical tradition, that of postmodernism. This is a theme that has arisen already in different contexts, particularly in framing the alternatives between which the critique of the division of labor tries to steer. I have argued that this critique provides a kind of theoretical project of reflection that is excluded by postmodernism's historicist challenge to the tradition. Now as I consider the postmodernist stance more directly, my aim is not mainly to refute a position that values rhetoric over argumentation. Rather, it is to comprehend this view in its historical relation to the tradition it questions. Doing so allows us to see postmodern philosophy in its contribution to contemporary politics. Indeed, I claim that postmodern philosophy is one version of postmodern politics. After making this argument I turn to features of the postmodern political context.

Chapter 7

Postmodern Philosophy in the Division of Labor

Postmodern Philosophical Criticism

Postmodernism has been a point of reference from the beginning of this discussion so far as I have opposed democratic philosophy to contemporary forms of historicism and skepticism. I have characterized the philosophical critique of the division of labor as an alternative critical response to the modern tradition. Now I shall discuss the idea of postmodernism more directly. As I proceed, I hope to establish the political as well as the philosophical significance of postmodern themes. In doing so I attempt, by making relevant contrasts, to sharpen the notion of the critique of the division of labor itself.

Given the frequent and various uses of the term, "postmodernism" needs to be defined with some precision. At the same time, here, as in most discussions, this term reflects an idealization, a gathering together of themes that few individual thinkers embrace or adopt as a basis for identifying themselves as postmodernists. In this respect, speaking of postmodern philosophy resembles speaking of the critique of the division of labor so far as each term posits a tendency in contemporary thought. As an idealization, my usage has value if it helps develop a critical relation to contemporary intellectual trends. I first discuss a philosophical position and later a kind of politics.

In its application to philosophy, postmodernism involves two concerns, one about theory and the other about intellectuals. Regarding theory, postmodern thinkers question the possibility of systematic reflection on the world and on rationality. Taking Rorty and Lyotard as main points of reference, I characterize postmodernism as rejecting "grand narratives" about society and history and all attempts to provide theoretical justifications for the appeals to rationality that typically accompany modern assertions of knowledge, politics, and morality. At the same time, I include in the intellectual associations of postmodernism such themes as the challenge to representation, the emphasis on interpretation and the interplay of the signifiers with which our interpretations are constructed, and, more generally, a sense of the constructed and historical quality of culture. While each of these themes has a history that long antedates talk of postmodernism, they figure importantly in postmodern discussions and indicate the reliance this tendency places on claims about language.

In its resistance to epistemological reflection in philosophy, postmodern criticism implies a contextual claim about modernity and its promise for human progress. Resistance to foundational and transcendental theory is also resistance to understanding the world as systematically knowable from the standpoint of some conception of possible human well-being. Postmodernism's reliance on historicist arguments about rationality coincides with a sense of history itself, though it is a sense that is more negative than positive. Themes of difference, discontinuity, differential change, as well as criticisms of faith in progress, in unifying transformative political projects, and in overarching collective identities, all tend to cast the Enlightenment as one in a series of mythologies rather than a decisive coming to terms with human conditions and possibilities.

Seeing rejection of epistemological reflection as a relation to the Enlightenment and to history as a medium of potentially progressive action points us to the second main feature of postmodern philosophy. The postmodern challenge to modern Enlightenment's program for theory is accompanied by skepticism about the claims of intellectuals, particularly those whose alleged theoretical insights accompany sweeping political programs. Illusions about what theory can do fuel illusions about what intellectuals can do, and the consequences of these illusions can be, and have been, tragic. If we can associate skepticism about theory with retreat from Enlightenment hopes for modern society, we can see postmodern reservations about intellectuals as responding to what are taken to be the consequences of theoretically informed projects for shaping the world. At a time when neoconservative thinkers draw on conceptions of the "new class" to stigmatize political intellectuals with the tragedies of Communism, the exhaustion of welfare statist liberalism, and the failed promise of sixties radicalism (Steinfells 1979), postmodernist thinkers have a considerable pool of political skepticism from which to draw.

In these two characteristics, its rejection of epistemological theory and its challenge to political intellectuals, postmodern philosophy continues one feature of the modern philosophical tradition as I have described it. Like the Enlightenment against which they define themselves, postmodern thinkers develop a reflection on rationality that bears on what I have called political understanding. Moreover, they do so within the orbit of modern knowledge-politics even though their claims about rationality place them at odds with features of this politics.

Postmodern reflection represents the most sustained and influential articulation of the kind of skepticism about rationality I have said must be taken seriously today. This is not skepticism about the reality of knowledge but about the value of its effective reality. It is perhaps misleading to characterize postmodernism in this way so far as its challenges to intellectual work are selective. Beyond challenging philosophy, its targets are the social sciences so far as these inform political projects. And although it may draw from arguments against positivistically conceived social science, its claims, like those of Habermas in this respect, are not so much against the reality or possibility of such social science (however it is to be reconstructed) as against the practices in which it is embodied. Postmodernism draws from the Hegelian and Marxian traditions of seeing specific social sciences as constitutive features of a social process that can and needs to be challenged as such.

So I treat postmodern thought as a challenge to traditional philosophy guided by concerns with knowledge-power. And my argument is that instructive problems with postmodernism can be uncovered by considering various paradoxes that characterize the way it develops its criticism of knowledge-power.

I begin by citing respects in which postmodern criticism revives the themes of the "end of ideology" that became prominently associated in the late 1950s with the work of Daniel Bell (1960). Ideology counts here not in Marx's sense of an interested and distorting understanding but rather in the sense of a global vision of how the world should be, a systematic program developed by intellectuals on the basis of their specialist insight (Gouldner 1976). If this is not Marx's usage of the term, Marx is nonetheless an important point of reference, precisely as the paradigm ideologist. Bell argues that ideology is superseded as the relevance of the competition between capitalism and Communism declines in the face of common technological and organizational tendencies. From his technocratic and later "postindustrial" perspective, this distinction is a legacy of nineteenth-century production and has little relevance in a setting in which information rather than things are the major objects of production and circulation and in which control over cultural capital is more important than control over capital in Marx's sense of the word (Bell 1976a).

After the fall of Communism, these themes can be interpreted in varying ways. Postmodern conceptions antedate these developments but operate in an atmosphere marked by the crisis of Communism and political defeats of the Western Left. Postmodern strictures against totalizing reflection reduce the likelihood of sweeping claims about socialism or capitalism, but these same strictures present such claims as irrelevant. With this reiteration of how postmodern thought backs away from received forms of politics for intellectuals, we need to recognize its connections to various streams of political radicalism. Rorty draws explicitly from feminist debate, while Lyotard's rejection of sweeping narratives alludes to the claims of those who have resisted colonialism and imperialism. More generally, postmodern rethinking of the authority of intellectuals and emphasis on difference provide terms taken up by intellectuals concerned with heretofore neglected voices and submerged identities (e.g., Butler 1990).

In this respect, postmodernism's break with political intellectuals is qualified. Its aim may be mirrored in Foucault's attempt to distinguish between universal and specific intellectuals, an overdrawn distinction inconsistent with Foucault's own practice. Foucault's example points to some of the dilemmas facing those who would supersede ideology without abandoning politics. In particular, these include issues of the quality of such politics, the role in it of intellectuals and intellectual insight, and corresponding issues of power, the public sphere, and political ideals.

So far the political understanding I am associating with postmodern thought appears ambiguous. While in certain respects conservative, in other respects it seems to affiliate itself with radical social movements. Its ambiguity in this respect is matched by an ambiguity regarding political intellectuals. If opposed to those who propose sweeping programs, it does not distance itself either from those whose criticism has sweeping implications or from those whose involvement in the existing workings of things has sweeping and real consequences in the present. Political ambiguities thus accompany ambiguities about the challenge to knowledge in society and so make the relation of post-modernism to modern knowledge-politics uncertain.

Another way to approach this point is by way of postmodern thought's relation to liberalism. There seems to be an echo of the libertarian and individualist themes of liberalism in the postmodern rejection of totalities and emphasis on difference, on a plurality of voices, and on a variety of language games. Generally these variations on negative freedom and pluralism are not in so many words tied to support for modern liberal institutions, though Rorty makes his allegiances explicit in this regard (Rorty 1983). Perhaps one reason many writers tread lightly on these matters is the residual leftism that characterizes much of their writing. In a more strictly intellectual vein, another basis for discomfort is that the target of much postmodern criticism includes the presuppositions of modern liberal thought and politics.

The rejection of epistemology is also a rejection of the metaphysics that accompanies it, especially conceptions of a stable, self-aware subject. Apart from refutations of the arguments that historically constructed this theoretical idea, postmodern thinkers draw from analyses, like Foucault's, that establish its function within the discourses of modern knowledge-power. Earlier, I referred to the ways modern metaphysics could be construed as a political metaphysics for modern knowledge-politics. Not only the subject, but conceptions of lawfully operating social conditions, the stability of instrumental reasoning, and the representational force of thought contribute to a view of the world as open to orderly and progressively effective action. Modern conceptions of the individual, consciousness, and free decision figure more generally in the liberal version of the Enlightenment program that claims the world to be knowable and that society can be made rational.

Surely one can give up specific liberal commitments without abandoning features of the Enlightenment project. That is precisely what characterizes the critique of the division of labor and the effort to rethink the respects in which the social world can be known and made rational, and accordingly to rethink political concerns with individuality, freedom, and decision. But from the standpoint of this critique, such an undertaking literally requires a rethinking, hence the need for systematically oriented reflection if not systematic theory in the traditional sense. Postmodern thought rejects such reflection without entirely abandoning politics. It has its targets and its aspirations, but risks falling into the ideological traps it condemns, because it does not clarify its own relation to the existing world of knowledge-politics.

The problem here concerns the quality of political understanding that such an ambiguous relation to liberalism can provide. It is not simply or so much that postmodern thought does not work out a coherent alternative intellectual position or that its criticism of liberalism seems inconsistent with its own politics. Rather, the difficulty is that on postmodernist grounds it is unclear how seriously to take such features of the postmodern argument. In particular, it is unclear how we are to consider the relation between ideas and politics. On the one hand, postmodern thinkers seem closely tied to idealist assumptions about the dependence of political evolution on the evolution of ideas. On the other, these same thinkers deconstruct the terms in which such connections have been conceived. Perhaps an instructive example in this regard is Derrida, who attributes Heidegger's Nazism to his residual metaphysical allegiances, as though deconstructive challenge to modern epistemology and metaphysics did not make such political explanations highly suspect (Derrida 1989).

The problem, then, is not just that there is likely a latent metaphysics in any postmodernism that does not work out its historical and social commitments, but that this sits poorly with a readiness to stigmatize thinkers for their tacit metaphysical allegiances. The readiness of postmodernists to ferret out latent metaphysical commitments resembles vulgar Marxist criticism that stigmatizes positions by associating them with an objectionable tendency (e.g., "petite bourgeois idealism") and then dismissing them from further consideration. Any such approach is itself objectionable once the problem of knowledge-power is on the agenda, because it is precisely the interconnections of ideas and politics that is thus made an issue.

To sustain the suggestion that the ambiguities or even paradoxes of postmodern thought harbor residual similarities to the idealist tradition, let us consider respects in which postmodern thought resembles positivism. I have already noted that postmodern thinkers tend to restrict their challenges to philosophy and some social sciences and to leave other individual disciplines unquestioned. A hostility toward philosophy combined with an unreflective acceptance of natural science figures in the positivist focus on methodology. Postmodernists, of course, consign positivist methodology (taken as a normative guide to authentic knowledge) to the dust bin of epistemological illusions. But in the absence of an alternative reflection on the achievements of scientific knowledge, they tend to be uncritical of most of the forms of expertise that characterize contemporary society. In taking the "specific intellectual" for granted, they sustain positivist dogmatism. In the present context, this means they leave the bulk of contemporary knowledge-politics unquestioned. We can see this tendency in Lyotard's treatment of disciplines as independent language games, or in Rorty's juxtaposition of illusion-filled philosophy to specifically focused disciplines (Lyotard 1984, 23–27; Rorty 1987). One need not revive foundationalist notions of philosophy to harbor the possibility of critical reflection on specific intellectual practices. But any such critical strategy seems excluded by the postmodern rejection of systematically oriented rethinking of reason.

The similarities to positivism are of course limited. Though in certain respects antiphilosophical, postmodern thought does not reduce philosophy to what positivism took, in contrast to empirical science, to be meaningless, poetry-like mouthings. Characteristic of the postmodern argument is the refutation of the epistemological assumptions of any such contrast. Along with it goes any very sharp distinction between science and literature. Rather than meaningless, philosophy itself at least reflects the sign-using, sense-making disposition of humans, the one quality that comes closest to a human nature for postmodernism. Science itself figures within a host of interpretive activities, endlessly reinterpreted in the rush of human voices.

This aestheticizing drift of postmodern reflection bears on its relation to philosophy. I have characterized this as an antiphilosophical view because it closes off reflection on rationality in the name of avoiding epistemological foundationalism and transcendentalism. Apart from limiting the insights it can develop about those specific kinds of intellectual activity on which postmodern thinkers concentrate, this inhibition on reflection affects what postmodern thinkers can say about their own activity. Though polemics against ideology and the dangers of overambitious intellectuals can assume a lofty tone, they suffer the limitations of their self-described "edifying" character (Rorty 1979, 357–93). They can neither critically assess their own social practice nor sustain a normative orientation. In short, the politics of postmodern reflection is as compromised as its intellectual argumentation.

For thinkers from the tradition it challenges, such inconsistency would represent an embarrassment. For postmodernists, it is a matter of self-conscious irony. Indeed, rather than treat postmodernism as contradictory—a criticism whose force is blunted by postmodernism's ambivalence about rationality—I will adopt this account of it as ironic and explore ways the ironies of postmodernism overflow its self-pronouncements. As such I shall treat it as both philosophical and antiphilosophical, as political and as hostile to politics. But above all I shall show that its ironic relation to knowledge-politics undercuts its professed challenges to knowledge-power.

Criticizing Postmodern Thought

I have already outlined criticisms of postmodern thought. Though in part a means for fixing what is distinctive about the critique of the division of labor as a philosophical tendency, this critical discussion of postmodern thought has been intended also to lead into the discussion of the philosophical criticism of contemporary politics. With this end in mind, I consider the ambivalence of postmodern thought about philosophical reflection. In doing so, I explore why postmodernism's ironies are politically significant. Thus I connect the criticism of postmodern thought to the philosophical aims of the critique of the division of labor.

Foucault's work has already illustrated some of the difficulties attendant on contemporary ambivalence about philosophy. It has so far proven easier to identify mistakes and dangers of traditional reflection than to characterize the kind of reflection that undertakes this criticism. So far as this reflection seeks to justify its claims about knowledge and power by rational argument, it cannot break entirely from the Enlightenment effort to make sense of rationality. Such reflection can make this break only by giving up its own claims to critical rigor. And such an embrace of nihilism surrenders any claim to providing political criticism. While this consequence may not trouble some postmodernists, it should be troubling to those who see a liberal, neoliberal, or even radical point to their examination of knowledge-power.

With regard to postmodern thought as such, the general issue to which I am pointing concerns the respect in which it functions philosophically. I have used the term "thought" rather than "philosophy" in order to respect the ambivalence of this kind of intellectual work regarding its own reflection on normative issues about rationality. If we agree that such issues can fruitfully be cast in social terms, the philosophical aspect of postmodern thought can be seen in its stricture regarding intellectuals. Though mainly negative, its claims are normative and in fact include strictly conceptual as well as social imperatives. But in rejecting certain kinds of theory and certain kinds of political involvements for intellectuals, postmodernists do not make clear sense of their own activity. This failure of reflexivity is an important part of the more general failure to provide a positive normative conception.

It is important to insist that this is a political failure. Postmodernism makes rationality a political question at least so far as its challenges to ideologists goes. This absence of follow-through on its own political arguments justifies comparing postmodernism to those features of contemporary politics discussed early in this book. Like various covertly or indirectly political practices, postmodern thought pursues a political function without adequately presenting itself as political. Like the practices to which I alluded earlier, postmodern thought can itself be considered a distinctive development in politics, and one whose obscurity about its own political character corresponds to a more general trend. Before turning to respects in which postmodern thought is political and to its relation to more general trends in contemporary politics, let us consider this point against the backdrop of what I have been arguing are philosophical qualities of modern political culture.

It has been one of my contentions that modern political culture contains an epistemological dimension. The centrality of knowledge-politics and the cultivation of modern rationality more generally make reflection on rationality an important feature of social and political understanding. Assumptions about rationality, expertise, and the distribution of capacities have an important place in the beliefs and attitudes of modern citizens. It is in this context that modern philosophical mediation assumes its political significance. If, as I argue shortly, postmodern thought can be reconstructed as a kind of philosophical mediation, its ambivalence about philosophy may be an important aspect of its contribution to political culture.

So it is against the background claim that philosophical themes are important parts of the social and political understandings of citizens that the significance of postmodern thought's ironic relation to philosophy is to be considered. In the next section, I approach this from the standpoint of the problem of reconstructing postmodern intellectual mediation using elements of the communications approach I have been discussing. In the rest of this section, I stick with the conceptual weaknesses of postmodern reflection viewed in this light.

Postmodernism's irony regarding philosophy allows us to describe it as an antiphilosophical philosophy. Like positivism, it performs a philosophical function when it argues against philosophy. One may call this a kind of "performative contradiction" (Habermas 1990, 95), since postmodern thought remains philosophical in providing reflection on rationality in making these arguments. The contradiction lies in providing a philosophical function, not in offering the kinds of epistemological arguments it rejects. Nonetheless, there are respects in which postmodern argumentation does resemble the kind of philosophy it rejects. These have to do with the kinds of abstractions it employs and the categorical nature of the arguments that it makes.

On behalf of its historicist challenge to the mystifications of epistemological absolutism, postmodern thinkers operate on a level of abstraction that resembles that of epistemology itself. Against traditional argumentation we find claims about presence, the relations between signifiers, the primacy of writing and difference, and so on. In arguing against illusions of rational or conceptual autonomy, postmodernists make strictly conceptual arguments. One cannot of course in turn reject the use of such arguments on general theoretical grounds. In fact, they introduce important considerations and have the advantages, for example, in the idea of deconstruction, of immanent critique. But the danger is that, left to themselves, the use of such arguments can promote the appearance that, by themselves, they constitute an adequately critical standpoint. In the case of deconstruction, we find the introduction of an internally generated critical method that paradoxically challenges a tradition of attempts to refine autonomous methods.

Whether we emphasize argumentation that remains at traditional levels of philosophical abstraction or arguments that pursue distinctively philosophical methods (however vaguely articulated and freely applied), we confront procedures that remain close in important ways to traditional philosophical practice. While none of this necessarily implies a commitment to traditional dogmas about autonomous reason or the independence of thought, the similarities of such procedures to such traditional idealizations can be seen in the uses to which postmodern insights are put when developing their historical and political implications regarding intellectuals and ideology.

I have already touched upon the ways postmodern critics link use of ideas of subject, or other metaphysical commitments, to politics (e.g., Derrida's suggestion that Heidegger's politics followed from his failure to extricate himself sufficiently from metaphysics). We can call this a kind of categorical argumentation so far as it not only restricts its philosophical criticism to the issues of basic concepts but then also draws out its historical claims by correlating the use of such concepts with specific political commitments and outcomes. We may hear echoes of Husserl's (1970) attempt to connect the European social crisis of the interwar years with a crisis in Western reason, or Heidegger's (1977, "The Question Concerning Technology") more nuanced and ambiguous efforts to connect modern nihilism with the modern technological standpoint.

Finding this latent idealism in postmodern criticism confirms the suspicion that such criticism remains closer to the tradition than it claims. Its kind of analysis can be stigmatized in various ways, as being too abstract, as reflecting a latent idealism, or as lapsing into ahistorical ways of arguing for historicism. The crucial point is that it fails to generate an adequate analytical perspective on knowledge-politics because it fails to think in sufficiently social terms.

Inherent in this antiphilosophical, yet still philosophical dimension of postmodern thought is what we might also call anti-ideological ideology. It is not just that its criticisms of ways of thinking about society are as sweeping as those it rejects or that its repudiation of one kind of intellectual activity tacitly sanctions other kinds (e.g., the latent technocratic trends discussed earlier). The tendency to overstate the role of concepts and of intellectuals reproduces features of the modern mystification of knowledge that figures within the ideological illusions postmodernism is concerned about.

Let me make the point of labeling postmodernism as antiphilosophy philosophy or as anti-ideological ideology as clear as possible. Mine is not a criticism of its being philosophical, since I am claiming philosophical reflection is unavoidable both intellectually and politically under modern conditions. Postmodern thought's obscurity about its own philosophical character does, however, make the kind of philosophical understanding it provides problematic. The kind of abstraction and categorical argumentation in which it engages illustrates this. These qualities of postmodern argumentation are not inherent in philosophy as such, but they indicate respects in which the specifically postmodern criticism of the tradition falls short. Its pursuit of historical analysis remains abstract and largely negative. As a result its philosophical and political conception of its own activity is sufficiently indeterminate to permit conflicting and uncritical uses of its argumentation. This ultimately is what is problematic about the intellectual and practical irony of postmodernism. Like the irony Hegel (1991, 167–84) equates with the decline of abstract morality into its opposite, postmodern irony allows these intellectual practices to organize and advance practical contents to which it remains uncritical and even unaware.

Reconstructing Postmodern Philosophical Mediation

My discussion of postmodernist thought is designed in part to establish contrasts between this intellectual tendency and the tendency I am calling the critique of the division of labor. Though postmodernism responds to real intellectual and political issues, especially those bearing on knowledge and power, it fails to provide the kind of philosophical reflection that a consistently critical relation to contemporary intellectual activity and political life requires. I am trying to indicate ways the critique of the division of labor, though undoubtedly programmatic in important respects, promises to make good where postmodernism fails. Beyond these expository aims, my account of postmodernism seeks also to consider how we might comprehend it when employing the kind of critical reflection offered by the critique of the division of labor. This is not purely for illustrative purposes, since postmodernism has particular significance in the contemporary intellectual and political scene. In trying to treat postmodern thought as intellectual mediation, I am working toward an account of its significance within the wider politics of which it is a significant part.

Philosophy, I have noted, can be understood as mediating activity that contributes to the social and self-understanding of intellectuals and to the means by which other specialists carry out their specific practices. It is as mediating activity in this sense that I will discuss postmodern thought. I have also been arguing for a certain perspective on the context in which contemporary philosophical mediation takes place. Let me begin my discussion of postmodern thought's mediating practice by referring to its contrasting sense of the historical situation.

Postmodernism's philosophical historicism accompanies a certain sense of the historical moment. To a large degree this draws from theories of postindustrial society, though in some cases it is also influenced by more specifically economic arguments regarding the reorganization of international competition and production (Jameson 1991). For many thinkers, the relative decline of industrial production and the rise of the service sector are associated with the philosophical emphasis on signifiers or on the materiality of language instead of meaning and reference (Baudrillard 1988). Economies of information are taken to supplant economies of things.

That such interrelated phenomena as the rise of multinational corporations, the electronics revolution, new forms of international organization of work, and the expansion of service sectors (including those proper to mass culture) have profoundly altered the modern world is beyond dispute. Attempting to provide a balanced assessment of these changes would overflow the limits of this work, though I have posited a very general relation to them in my earlier catalogue of contemporary structural changes. These included the changed standing of social collectives (above all nationality and its relation to nation states), transformation of the modern institutional differentiation of economy, polity, and culture, and the increasingly problematic standing of labor associated with the uncertain standing of economic growth. While this conception of structural change is more abstract than that I have associated with postmodernism, it allows us to refer to issues about expertise and the division of labor that are relevant for thinking about postmodern intellectual mediation.

On the one hand, this historical perspective allows us to raise the question of an appropriate democratic response, particularly as it involves intellectual practices. This is the problem I discuss in Part Four. On the other, it provides a background for considering existing intellectual practices, in particular those of postmodernism. In this regard, it is useful to recall the theme of scarcity, specifically scarcity of agency, since mediations associated with postmodernist practice have frequently to do with action on agency. Postmodern intellectual mediations occur in a context in which the historical formation of agency and its relation to power relations has come into question. Agency has tended to become unstable and fragmented as institutions themselves undergo crises, and in this context various intellectual practices attempt a stabilizing and reproductive function.

Scarcity as discussed here has to do with ways a society organizes shortages in relationships marked by hierarchy and inequality. Scarcity of agency occurs as elements of historically shaped activity—capacities, opportunities, resources, identities, and so on—are distributed in ways that contribute to specific kinds of hierarchy and inequality. The thesis of the critique of the division of labor is that historical reflection on rationality must consider issues of scarcity in order critically to reconstruct existing forms of intellectual activity and to consider possible and desirable forms of intellectual activity.

Postmodernism's perspective is, of course, quite different. Apart from its adoption of features of postindustrial conceptions, it rejects efforts to develop general perspectives of this sort altogether. Though presented as a way to combine critical impulses with resistance to utopianism, postmodernism's hostility to reflection risks falling into the kinds of practices it seeks to criticize. Rather than sustain its own criticism of knowledge-power, postmodern thought, I argue, contributes to the reproduction of scarcity of agency.

First we may consider how postmodern thought contributes to the social and self-understanding of intellectuals. We can approach this question by way of the modern tradition of an epistemological political culture. In certain respects, postmodern thought is at odds with such a tradition. Its rejection of systematic or epistemological reflection seems to clash with the reliance of modern politics on reflective claims about reason. In fact, the relation of postmodernism to this culture is more complex, as I noted in characterizing postmodernism as an antiphilosophical philosophy. It is a reflective activity, but it abjures the reflective strategies proper to the modern tradition. More precisely, in addition to foundational and transcendental strategies, it rejects all discursively organized reflections on claims to rational validity.

On the one hand, this means that in the context of modern knowledge-politics it in effect denies that power exercised through or in association with modern forms of knowledge can be defended rationally. But such a retreat from traditional philosophical strategies does not keep postmodernists from offering other kinds of commentary on modern knowledge. Various kinds of hermeneutic, deconstructive, and semiotic approaches allow for historicist conceptions of the constructive features of intellectual activity. These are conceptions that draw on various refutations of epistemological and methodological accounts to eliminate the claims to objectivity and universality that have traditionally been held to distinguish knowledge from literature.

If such commentary undercuts epistemological validation of intellectual practices, it by no means therefore repudiates these practices. Despite suspicions raised about knowledge-power and about intellectuals and politics, there is no corresponding retreat from claims to expert authority on the part of intellectuals. I have already made this point by noting the similarities of postmodernism to positivism. Postmodernist thinkers leave most intellectual practices unquestioned. But their reflective relation to such practices is quite different from that of the positivists. Rather than accept the positivist contrast between cognitive or scientific rationality on the one hand and literature or artistic use of concepts and language on the other, postmodernists tend to dispute any such categorical distinction. While this represents a break with the modern, Kantian differentiation of (what Habermas calls) value spheres, it retains an important assumption associated with this differentiation. Kant says that in matters of aesthetic judgment we assert claims we cannot help but take to be universally valid, yet we have no discursive means to justify these claims. We have to presuppose an agreement we cannot establish through rational argument (Kant 1987). Similarly, in rejecting reflective reasoning regarding specialized rationality and in linking knowledge with literature, the postmodernist does not reject specialist knowledge but says we have no means for argumentatively justifying it. Breaking the boundary between knowledge and literature has the effect here of generalizing the immunity to discursive reason said to characterize the aesthetic realm.

Consider the contrast between this line of thought and that of the critique of the division of labor, which also draws on language theory in seeking an alternative to traditional ways of reflecting on rationality. Postmodernism challenges traditional conceptions of theory by finding in knowledge linguistic similarities to fiction. The critique of the division of labor, in contrast, breaks with traditional theory by reconstructing knowledge in communications terms. Rather than diminish the claims of discursive reasoning, the communications approach reconstructs it as a social process. Rather than follow the postmodernist aestheticizing retreat from politics, the communications approach raises practical questions about theory understood as social practice.

As I have shown, despite its hostility to traditional philosophy postmodernism remains within the modern culture of reflexivity. While forgoing a rational reconstruction that would consider the validity claims of intellectual practices, however, it offers historicizing and aestheticizing interpretations precisely as an alternative reflection. Postmodern reflections on theoretical language offer a different kind of self-understanding of what intellectuals accomplish. And it does so in terms that leave the validity of these accomplishments beyond the reach of discursive argumentation. Neither for those intellectual practices it attacks nor for those it leaves unquestioned does postmodern thought engage in discursively resolvable argumentation.

This point is worth bearing in mind when we turn to what may seem a paradoxical combination of postmodernism's declared challenges to knowledge-power and the more general conservatism toward intellectual practices I am attributing to it. Its aestheticizing approach allows for arbitrariness in the exercise of its criticism. At the same time, it offers a way for intellectuals to understand their activity so that they can both address the challenges of movements and provide a reflective assertion of their expertise. This ambiguous relation to criticism allows for what I earlier described as the irony of postmodernism.

In general terms, then, postmodernism provides a self-understanding for intellectuals and contributes to the social understanding of expertise. Its aestheticizing reconstruction of intellectual activity allows for challenges to knowledge-power while excluding any stable or discursively accessible criteria for judging the social claims of experts. In this light speaking of postmodern thought as antiphilosophical philosophy is more than a matter of remarking on the logical paradox of its offering a kind of reflection when challenging philosophy as such. Rather it is also a matter of this kind of thinking continuing an important social function of modern philosophy, but doing so in a way that responds to contemporary conditions.

Now I have noted respects in which postmodern thought functions socially as philosophical mediation. The argument can be taken another step by considering how, in addition to constructing reflective accounts, postmodern thought contributes to that other feature of philosophical mediation I have identified. This has to do with working over elements of the resources other intellectuals have for their specific mediations.

In discussing mediations of modern epistemological philosophy, I spoke earlier of philosophers working on elements of genres, voices, and normalizing practices that contributed to the monological authoritative utterances of modern science and technology. While these remain important features of intellectual practice, the intellectual practices in relation to which postmodern thought has its mediating role bear somewhat differently on agency. The demise of epistemological concerns with objectivity and universality suggest that we are not concerned with traditional assertions of monological authority. What I have called the aestheticizing aspect of postmodern intellectual self-consciousness indicates a constructivist rather than a rule-following orientation. Historicist consciousness indicates context-specific criteria for successful practice, not the demands of universal standards.

Rather than provide elements of authoritative genres and voices, philosophers work on elements proper to mediating practices that are themselves mediating genres and voices. Rather than contribute to the construction of specific voices, they contribute to the shaping of voicings. The specific intellectual practices for which postmodern thought provides philosophical reflection are those which function in the management of communication. These are not the intellectuals working in "normal science" but those working on problematic forms of agency. Here I have in mind those kinds of expertise involved in the unacknowledged or quasi-politics I discussed earlier in the book. Philosophical emphasis on interpretation, the formation of subjects, the historicity of linguistic forms, and social construction reworks conceptual and pragmatic features of the intellectual mediations carried out by experts concerned with the interpretive, malleable, and unstable features of agency.

In addition to its role in general discussions of rationality, intellectuals, and modernity, then, postmodern thought plays a role in the discussion and refinement of features of specific kinds of intellectual mediation, ones that have a prominent place in the contemporary political impasse. In making this claim, I do not want to exaggerate the influence of philosophy. Undoubtedly, philosophy's role is reactive and secondary, though the reflexive qualities of modern culture foster discussions in which refinement and elaboration of interpretive ideas and devices take place. Practices that encourage and organize interpretative practices within contexts of instability and conflict require clarification and reflexive validation of their projects. Interpretation, self-interpretation, and negotiation are elicited and managed by intellectuals in a host of contexts, from hospitals to workplaces. Social pathologies associated with addiction, violence, and criminality increasingly become the target of therapeutic and psychologizing diagnoses that require specific kinds of reflection and communication aiming at stabilization and social adaptation. Other contexts for which postmodernist reflexivity has a special relevance include those concerned with the movement and effects of information and images; these include such diverse instances as management strategies, the news in its various forms, the promotion of political candidates and programs, and mass entertainment. Intellectuals engaged in various levels of these practices need reflective orientation, both to make public and institutional sense of what they are doing and to train others in their practices.

I explore some examples of this kind of politics in the next chapter. My claim about philosophical mediation is that it contributes to the terms of the more specific mediations that such politics involves. Discussion of narrative understanding, self-construction, contextually responsive problem-solving, along with the other themes I have mentioned, contributes to the vocabulary and strategies of intellectuals engaged in specific mediations. What I have called the aestheticizing direction of postmodernist reflection contributes to a sense of the constructivist relation of intellectuals to features of the agency of the citizens whose practices are their objects of concern.

I have already noted that this orientation to agency characterizes a host of quasi-political practices in the present period of structural change. From the standpoint of the critique of the division of labor, it is notable that the kinds of interventions mediated by postmodernist reflection are ones that reproduce features of the division of labor. Consider some examples. As the devices of mass culture are introduced into political campaigns, the political agency of citizens facing social crisis is targeted to manage perceptions, target information, and guide the formulation of alternatives. An acceleration of communications devices here involves a narrowing differentiation of perceptions and political capacities. Similarly, the introduction of therapeutic specialists in the context of social pathologies (addiction, violence, etc.), creates new dependencies as it seeks to stabilize social behavior. It does so in a setting in which received forms of collective identity and membership (notably the family) seem to be breaking down.

In the conception of the division of labor with which I have been working, differentiation and specialization mediate power relations. An important feature of this process is the way the various pressures on received patterns of agency include the initiatives of social movements that target the kinds of power relations reproduced in the division of labor. So far as expert action on agency reproduces the division of labor, it manages the scarcities associated with the various kinds of power being contested by movements. So far as philosophical mediation is involved in this reproduction, it contributes to the understanding and practices of experts in ways that construct new differentiations in which movements are both recognized and diffused.

In developing an account of postmodern thought as itself engaged in philosophical mediations, then, we can see ways in which the specifically intellectual practice of this kind of thinking plays a tacitly political role in relation to contemporary political evolution. So far as this kind of philosophy thus contributes to a larger political process, we may consider whether postmodernism may not be considered a feature of and an important contributor to political evolution.

Chapter 8

Philosophical Criticism of Postmodern Politics

Chapter 7 has treated postmodern philosophy partly for the purpose of confronting an important tendency in contemporary thought that would preclude the kind of democratic criticism I am attributing to the philosophical critique of the division of labor. I have questioned some of the claims of this way of thinking, but have also sought to rethink its arguments as figuring within a specific kind of philosophical mediation. In this way I have considered respects in which postmodernism continues features of liberalism and modern philosophy's knowledge-politics. Despite important ways in which postmodernism touches on the theme of knowledge-power, its hostility to theoretical reflection blocks it from developing the kind of argument that would allow it to achieve an adequate political understanding of intellectual practices or the division of labor in which they function. Postmodernism retains an ironic relation to politics and contributes a voice to contemporary culture that is continuous in important ways with the epistemological culture it claims to repudiate.

Viewed as a mediating practice, postmodern philosophy is a kind of politics. Among other things, it contributes to political understanding. It does so within a larger political context I sought to describe earlier in this book. We have now seen that in fact it can be regarded as a part of a larger postmodern politics. It provides mediating functions proper to a political culture that stands in an ironic relation to the practices and claims of liberal Enlightenment and to the epistemological culture it developed.

In discussing postmodern philosophical mediation I touched on ways the corresponding kinds of intellectual voices contribute to the kind of alienated politics I described in Part One. In this chapter I develop the notion of postmodern politics as a way of thinking about these trends. Such an account is a matter of philosophical criticism that seeks to advance reflection on rationality appropriate to a specific historical setting, a specific evolution within the context of modern epistemological culture and of the increasingly problematic reproduction of the division of labor.

Contemporary Politics and the Idea of Postmodernism

Characteristics of Recent Politics Reviewed

The themes of the critique of the division of labor have allowed me to treat postmodern philosophy as being directly political and as being part of a larger postmodern politics. With this latter term we can rethink some of the issues about politics I raised in Part One of this study. In speaking of postmodern politics, I do not claim that all contemporary politics exhibits the characteristics I stress, but that important problematic features of contemporary political evolution can be approached in this way. By way of a further initial qualification of my aims, let me emphasize that I do not mean to offer here a full account of postmodern politics, but rather to explore those features that have a philosophical dimension. In part, this is to follow out the relations in which philosophical mediation is set. In part, it is to locate ways issues about rationality figure within contemporary politics and so to locate possible areas of concern for democratic philosophical mediation.

First let me summarize some of the claims I made earlier about contemporary politics. I discussed an impasse of politics in the face of structural changes that fundamentally alter the terms of public life.

With the internationalization of production and distribution, the demise of the old power blocs, conflicts over nationality and nation states, the assertion of new identities and the challenge to modern values, the question of collective membership and social allegiance has assumed a variety of ever more pressing forms. Despite the triumph of free-market rhetoric, the interconnectedness, overlap, and yet tensions of the characteristic institutions of the modern world – the economy, the state, and the culture – have deepened so that none of these spheres is independent of the others, yet there is no good way to deal with the issues that arise from the blurring of their distinctiveness. Illustrative issues include immigration, the regulation of transnational corporations, the politics of education, and the role of the mass media in politics. Finally, I have touched on the increasingly problematic standing of labor and the principle of growth: both are the preoccupation of contemporary policy making and yet they embody profound dilemmas from an ecological as well as more conventional economic, political, and cultural standpoints. If we speak of these general features of social evolution as structural, this is to emphasize their objectivity, indeed their inescapability, but it is not to suggest that they proceed behind our backs. They both inform and are the objects of contemporary conflicts and provide the environment for social movements with diverse aims and effects.

To speak of an impasse of politics in this historical context means that our political language, procedures, and understanding have so far failed to enable us to address these structural changes and the problems and possibilities they contain in a way that is effective, much less in a way that extends democracy. It is in relation to possible democratic evolution that this impasse is most troubling. If we can accurately characterize our historical situation by reference to such structural issues as I have enumerated, then it seems obvious that prevailing forms of democratic politics need to be rethought and their scope and quality deepened.

But we confront an impasse precisely because the prevailing trend is a retreat from a reflective attempt to reconstruct and extend our political understanding and democratic capacity. This is not to say that we engage any less in political action, since the respects in which practices have become politicized or have taken on political characteristics point to an extension of politics in our period. The paradox with which I began my discussion, rather, is that we find simultaneous with this growth of various kinds of political power a diminution of the extent and quality of public discussion of political questions. Partly this has to do with a retreat from politics by a disillusioned citizenry; partly it has to do with the debasing of public debate; and partly it has to do with the fact that much of what is in substance political is organized in nonpolitical forms.

The presence of what I have called covert politics is especially important for my discussion because it so often involves the extension and application of specialized knowledge. Expertise plays an increasing role in a host of settings and does so in ways that bear on specifically political issues. Experts shape public policy, organize political perception and debate, design and promote the public understandings of our youth, and respond to pathological tendencies in the relation of individuals to society. To speak of covert politics is not to imply a conspiracy but to identify a tendency in the evolution of social powers exercised on public issues and frequently put into motion by explicitly political institutions. Part of the problem facing democratic movements is to find adequate political forms for the reorganization of covert politics.

I have identified two important features of the covert politics that characterizes the actual response to structural change. One is its reproductive function: while such practices contribute to the changes to which they respond, they do so in ways that resist systematic confrontation with issues about modern structure. Such practices are conservative in preserving the prevailing power relations, as rooted in economic and political institutions, though they inevitably contribute to the modification of these relations as they modify these institutions. The other feature of this covert politics is its relation to political understanding and the agency of which it is a part. If attempts to make this politics explicit are inherent in challenges to the power it organizes, then this power in turn relies on the promotion of appropriate social perceptions. To take note of the decline in explicit political discussion is not to assert the decline of activity concerned with the way politics is grasped. On the contrary, today the organization of power is thoroughly bound up with the mobilization of social appearances.

If much politics today is covert insofar as it falls below the threshold of explicit political understanding, this does not mean that there has been a simple diminution in the forms of political understanding. Later I develop the thesis that one feature of our political situation is the

proliferation of what are in effect displaced forms of political understanding. Power is exercised and at issue in politics, and our society
has become a veritable theater of power. I use the term "displaced
politics" to include ways mass culture has become a vehicle of the
interpretation of politically significant issues. I take this to be related to
ways mass cultural forms, including television news, have become
closely associated with more official forms of political discourse and
with the battle over public opinion.

Covert politics and displaced politics have to do with ways power is
exercised, experienced, and understood, and they have expanded in a
social environment in which explicit public discussion has become less
coherent and official political participation has declined. The impasse
of politics, or the paradox of simultaneously less and more politics, is
in part a matter of the evolution of citizenship. Below I develop the
claim made earlier that citizenship increasingly takes the form of
clientship and spectatorship.

Clientship and spectatorship represent erosions and evolutions of
traditional forms of liberal political participation. Clients relate to
politics as recipients of benefits in a quasi-contractual relation with
political operatives. Power relations are organized into strategic negotiations in which citizens face bureaucrats and expert mediators. Spectatorship follows partly from clientship, so far as the political process
appears as an object operating independently of the participation of
citizens. But there is a further feature: a political bond or charge is
established in the spectator relationship. Spectatorship introduces an
aestheticized agency that casts citizens as active interpreters for whom
power takes on an independent reality.

The emphasis on clientship and spectatorship isolates two features
of alienating politics: a welfarist redefinition of politics as serving
immediate interests and a politics as spectacle that helps compensate
for a decline of legitimation. Thus this pair of tendencies can be seen
against the contractualist and instrumentalist history of liberalism on
the one side and against its striving for legitimation on the other.

The distancing of citizens from consequential political discussion
provides one reason for speaking of alienation when characterizing
contemporary political trends. Since the idea of alienation may seem to
carry with it suspect philosophical presuppositions, let me emphasize
that with this idea I mean to imply a critical perspective that is historical rather than dependent on metaphysical or other notions of human

nature. Alienation implies a counterfactual relation to an objective historical possibility. In general, the idea of alienation provides a way of conceiving the paradoxical character of the forms of political activity that liberal political culture organizes in the present setting of structural change and political impasse. One of the difficulties with describing these practices as political is their lack of the appropriate kind of public quality as explicit questions facing the polity through its established way of confronting common concerns. The notion of alienation is useful in this context and not just because it evokes the idea of a loss or of being cut off (not just a matter of being cut off from politics). Alienation as a dialectical concept implies a relation to an unrealized possibility. As such, it is a normative idea, where existing practices are set in a critical light against possible alternatives. The particular focus of the alienation idea here is on the issue of agency: "unpolitical politics" is alienating by preventing the evolution of historically possible forms of democratic political understanding and agency. The idea of alienation is useful in describing contemporary practices because it includes this logic of suppression: these practices are not only "unpolitical" in appearance but have the effect of counteracting the development of a properly political understanding and the more democratic forms of agency that would go with it.

With the idea of political alienation, or alienated politics, I mean then to include more than constructed forms of social distancing that involve loss of access to historical possibilities. I have referred to historical forms of agency and experience that bear specifically on a relation to possible democratic politics. In my introductory discussion I associated the paradoxes of contemporary politics with paradoxes of modern rationality. Like political action, abstractly constructed and methodologically guided knowledge has grown in importance even as the value of rationality has become more questioned and questionable in mass and elite culture. While the connections between these phenomena are complex, my discussion of liberalism and knowledge-politics has attempted to show that these connections are close and profound. In contemporary politics, this is illustrated in the ambivalent relation to technological advance and to the expertise that goes with it. This ambivalence may be set against the fact that politics itself has assumed increasingly technological forms. Allegedly neutral technical knowledge and its specialist functionaries are a hallmark of contemporary society.

They figure within the way the impasse of contemporary politics appears and is organized, so far as this takes the form of crisis management. I am suggesting that political capacity is itself in a kind of crisis. This may seem an all too easy extension of the widespread readiness with which the specter of crisis is raised in the present. Indeed it is worth noticing that the language of crisis is a stock item of contemporary politics, not least because the viability, not just the stability, of many institutions repeatedly comes into question. If, nonetheless, the term is overworked, this is may be only a measure of the exhaustion of political discourse. Casting a problem in terms of crisis provides a language for setting one's aims: steering through, recovering equilibrium, and establishing normal functioning. It permits avoidance of normative questions and thus cuts short political reflection. The appeal to objective problems suggests the need for expertise that is above the fray of political debate.

The persistence of a politics organized around crises provides an appropriate style for a period of political impasse, even when the explicit crises are themselves evasions of more fundamental problems. The evocation of the imagery of crisis itself is noteworthy for the way it organizes social activity. It is as important as a means of organizing or shaping social agency as it is for identifying problems. As such it is a paradigm of the politics of appearances, that is, of the mobilization of apolitical understanding. The crisis context is precisely that in which the ordinary procedures of political discourse are to be suspended until the emergency passes. The rhetoric of crisis is designed to shape perceptions in a way that enables leaders to pursue their policies unhampered by popular participation. As such, it is a politics that focuses on appearances as a way of shaping forms of politically relevant agency on the part of the citizenry.

The point is not that crisis politics is simply a matter of cynical manipulation, though manipulation is often involved. Rather, crisis management is a way politics is organized in a period of more general uncertainty. It is a political style that contributes to a certain way of organizing political perception and establishing the relation between active and passive members of the polity. It is a politics of appearances and as such a politics that works on forms of agency while being itself a distinctive kind of political agency, one that is exemplary of a period of "unpolitical politics."

It is characteristic of the politics of crisis management that its construction of events pits reason against unreason. The tactical and strategic cunning of the crisis managers must confront forces that otherwise defy rational order. The construal of the given problem in these terms is part of the rationality of the managers. It justifies their active role as well as the passive relation to events allotted to ordinary citizens.

The kind of "apolitical" politics we are confronting can be described as political not only because it involves power, or because it has to do with common social questions, or because it shapes social relations, but also because it addresses the understanding of all these functions. Neutralizing questions of power by representing them as the exercise of reason is a way of providing social language about and perception of that power. This has been inherent in the knowledge-power of liberalism. While much of liberal thought has been the response to moments of conflict and crisis, the imagery of knowledge-power has been one of a smooth working mechanism. Such imagery finds its contemporary echo in systems theory, but the more common imagery of contemporary politics is that of crisis management.

Let me illustrate these claims by reference to the politics of the Gulf War. First, we can briefly note some of the ways it was an example of knowledge-politics: though appealing to moral ideals and political norms (self-determination, observation of national borders, a "new world order"), the administration emphasized the ways its policy embodied strategic rationality in the pursuit of economic and political-military aims (e.g., sustaining economic growth and assuring jobs, stabilizing oil prices, preventing the use of nuclear weapons, and maintaining regional stability). In these arguments, the administration tacitly asserted its possession of accurate information and expert analysis. Conjoined with this appeal to cognitive necessity and authority is the role of knowledge in the military side of the policy; here there was a massive appeal to secret information and to the promise of high technology, to strategic insight, and to the necessity of controlling the dissemination of information. As the last point reminds us, another dimension of the knowledge-politics of the war is the organization and conflict over the processes by which the conduct of the war is reported to the public. In the name of providing information that was accurate and as complete as possible, the media presented itself as the advocate of the public's right to know.

Reference to these aspects of the war illustrates not only the important place occupied by assertions and uses of knowledge but also the reliance on representational conceptions of knowledge. Of course, these cognitive claims were frequently disputed: questions were raised about the administration's understanding of regional politics, about the adequacy of its political and military intelligence, and about the reliability of the military's technology. The various experts brought in by the media to make sense of events for the public were themselves continually at odds. But here it is not the model of representation that is being questioned so much as its realization. If we look to the actual uses of these cognitive claims and counterclaims, we find the model itself being swept aside.

The manipulation of imagery and information by the contending forces has been a much-remarked-upon feature of the war. This manipulation overlapped with the complementary strategies of the media. It is important to emphasize that this was not solely a matter of concealment or misrepresentation of actual developments, because the play of social appearances was an exercise of power that affected the unfolding of the war itself. Using the distinction between events and their representations, we could say that events often became important as representations, just as representations were themselves important as events. An example of the latter is the use of the video replays of laser-guided bombings. These representations, evoking the rhetoric and culture of contemporary technology as well as making claims about developments in the air campaign, helped shape the nature of the war in domestic and international politics. Postwar disclosures that these tapes reflected a precision achieved in only a fraction of the bombings did not lessen their force as an event at the time they were shown, any more than they presently bring into question the authority of the officials who constructed and presented them at the time.

For an example of the way an event functions as a representation, I need only refer to the war itself, which frequently has been justified as "sending a message" to political outlaws everywhere. We need not restrict our sense of the rhetorical force of the war to such conventional claims. The frequent appeal to the experience of the Vietnam War and references to World War II suggest that the wars functioned symbolically in a number of respects. It is a message intended to shape the political understanding of a number of audiences, both domestic and international: beyond the issue of the "Vietnam syndrome" is the matter of the promise and threat of the United States as understood by its various allies, rivals, dependents, former opponents, and potential challengers in the Third World.

Of course it is artificial to speak of the event of war functioning as a representation when speaking of this kind of political communication.

So far as war assumes a linguistic character, it is through the interpretive and rhetorical functions of language rather than the representative functions, which have traditionally been emphasized by liberal knowledge-politics. Though contemporary strategy still appeals to representational mastery of the world, in fact the construction and uses of representations frequently are dictated by the aims of interpretation and rhetoric. It becomes more important to shape responses than to grasp objective conditions.

In this growing emphasis on the strategic manipulation of appearances, postmodernist politics contributes to a transformation within modern knowledge-politics. This transformation of liberal politics goes well beyond a de-emphasis on the representational functions of political language. The organizing rationality of modern knowledge-politics posits a coherence of strategy and agency that also declines in postmodernist practice. In this regard we can cite the difficulty the administration (or, for that matter, its critics) had in formulating a coherent and consistent account of the aims of the war. This is not to say that the war was arbitrary or inexplicable but that the received forms of political rationality do not provide terms in which to achieve conceptual or political clarity. Further, the emphasis on interpretation and rhetoric, along with this decline in the cogency of strategic political rationality, contributes to a decline in the coherence or consistency of agents themselves. A politics that has become increasingly a matter of response to unexpected circumstances, that is, a politics of crisis management, requires agents to adapt their identities and points of reference to new problematic situations. One may wonder if the president's inability to sustain a consistent articulation of policy before, during, and after the combat phase of the Gulf War does not reflect the larger conditions of contemporary power.

Why Call This Politics Postmodern?

In claiming that we confront an impasse in political life, I have referred to certain contemporary trends that I have also described as involving a certain kind of alienation from politics and from democratic possibilities. To justify talk of alienation and democratic possibility, one needs a conceptual framework in whose terms one can work out an appropriate historical perspective in which counterfactual references to unmet possibilities can be made intelligible and plausible. This is a task of the framework I am calling the critique of the division of labor.

With this framework, I argued earlier, we can also reflect on social issues about rationality in historical terms and can find an alternative to the epistemological tradition on the one side and its radical historicist critics on the other. Later in the discussion I show how the critique of the division of labor can connect its concern with rationality to democratic politics. Just now I hope to establish a relation between historicist trends in philosophy and some of the alienating qualities of contemporary politics. In terms of my discussion so far, establishing this relation involves showing how postmodernism in philosophy is related to postmodernism in politics. The immediate task is to show why, given my use of the term "postmodern," it is appropriate to apply it to the trends in contemporary politics I described in the preceding section. How is it informative to say that practices proper to the impasse of politics, or proper to alienated politics, are postmodern?

We can develop various parallels between the kind of politics I have just described and postmodern thought as reconstructed earlier. But I want to establish a closer relation, one that shows a politics that is postmodern because it embodies postmodern relations to rationality. To speak of postmodern politics is to speak of a politics with specifically philosophical properties. The aim, then, is to establish connections between these political practices and postmodern philosophy such that we can say that postmodern philosophy functions in a specific political way and that postmodern politics embodies an understanding and practice of rationality that involves the workings of postmodern intellectual mediation.

First, let us draw some parallels between what I have called postmodern thought and what I am now calling postmodern politics. Both involve the exercise of specialized activity, including sophisticated forms of knowledge, while dismissing received forms of reflection: among postmodern thinkers, we find the rejection of systematic philosophy; in postmodern politics, the diminishing of discursive political argument. At the same time, each kind of postmodernism emphasizes interpretive activity. Theorists reconstruct interpretive operations in what once were treated as impersonal forms of knowing, while the practitioners of postmodern quasi-politics engage in the extensive use of images, commentaries, persuasion. Both kinds of practice confront dimensions of agency as historically constructed and open to further intervention. Though historicizing the conditions of action in this way, neither confronts change itself as a practical problem worthy of sustained or systematic attention. This relation to the historical quality of the conditions of their own activity is associated with a kind of situational or pragmatic relation to the resolution of problems.

Now I want to establish how the presence of postmodern themes in contemporary politics is a philosophical quality of this politics. In other words, I want to show how the presence of these themes involves this politics in a reflection on rationality that contributes to the shift away from the epistemological reflexiveness I have associated with the political culture of modern knowledge-politics. My hope is to establish the plausibility of saying that postmodern politics includes the kind of reflexivity I have attributed to postmodern thought.

In philosophy, the shift from the epistemological tradition involves growing recognition of the dependence of thought on properties of language. Recognizing that meaning and validity orientations are dependent in some way on features of language that are themselves not always or as a whole subjectively available to agents leads to various constructivist reflections on linguistically organized experience. Theorists have developed a variety of approaches to the issues that follow from this line of reflection. I have characterized as postmodernist those approaches that treat thought in an aestheticizing constructivist manner. To this I have contrasted the communications approach, which contextualizes subjective experience within processes of interaction in principle subject to discursive rational considerations. My point here is that within postmodernist politics we find a reflexive relation to language that resembles that of postmodern thought.

As the example of the Gulf War indicates, contemporary politics too exhibits a reflective relation to language. It is a strategic relation as well, bound up with aims of constructing specific patterns of subjective response. Specific expert practices concern themselves with shaping political perceptions and responses by fashioning linguistic materials in strategically calculated ways. How is this philosophical? Certainly it is not primarily a matter of reflection on rational validity, though the extent to which contemporary political culture involves explicit reflection on normative issues is striking (even if it is not a particularly cogent reflection, e.g., on issues of the media and politics). It is philosophical insofar as reflective concern with language involves the preempting of traditional normative questions (political questions open for debate in a public sphere) through a specific constructive strategy that in a practical way historicizes the agency of citizens. In other words, it is philosophical in much the same way that postmodern thought is. It forgoes received forms of reflection with a conscious preempting of them by constructivist action that offers an alternative reflective relation to the world.

The key point here is that for postmodern politics, like much of the politics within modern epistemological culture, the concern is with making sense of alternatives in a context where justification is a live issue. This politics empties issues of justification without forgoing reflective relations to choice. To be sure, this politics is philosophical in a peculiar way, but this is precisely the way of postmodern thought. As a result, we find within this politics the same quality of irony regarding issues of rationality that we find in postmodern thought itself.

In saying that postmodern politics is philosophical, I am not saying that this politics is shaped or controlled by philosophers. Perhaps philosophers play less of a role here than they did in the more consistently epistemological culture of earlier modern knowledge-politics. In any case, the role of philosophers could only be recovered through a reconstruction of the various intellectual mediations that are involved in the formation and reproduction of this kind of reflective culture. And to lay the emphasis on mediation here is, as in the case of other phases of modern politics, to treat intellectuals generally as communicatively interacting in complex ways with the rest of society.

Indeed, the point of saying we can speak of features of contemporary politics as postmodern because they embody features of postmodern thought is to contribute to my more general discussion of the social understanding of rationality from a democratic perspective. To see features of the political culture as postmodern is to see ways intellectual practices, even when concerned with the abstractions of philosophy, are embedded in social process. Bringing out philosophical features of political culture is a way to see how philosophy is embedded in politics. And the equivocal relation to philosophy of postmodern thought corresponds to the equivocal relation to politics I have described as a feature of the contemporary political impasse. Further, the irony postmodernism exhibits toward reason coincides with a postmodern irony regarding politics.

I have associated postmodern irony with an arbitrariness in its relation to the criticism of knowledge-power. More generally, I can posit a postmodern arbitrariness in relation to the various kinds of power that are mediated within the division of labor. Because of this, postmodern political understanding can contribute to the reproduction of the scarcity of agency, even as its constructivist dimensions de-naturalize existing configurations of shortage.

In sum, postmodern politics is philosophical because it is reflective regarding rational capacities, and the most significant respects in which it exhibits this reflectiveness have to do with political relations to the formation of agency. In the historical setting as described above, we can see these political relations in terms of the reproduction of the division of labor, and in particular in the reproduction of aspects of agency articulated to scarcity. This is the effect of the covertness of this politics, its frequent displacement, and its subordination to the imperatives of crisis management.

Features of Postmodern Politics

Language and the Manipulation of Social Appearances

Having given some reasons for speaking of features of contemporary politics as postmodern, I now turn more closely to specific features of this politics in order to bring out some of the corresponding issues about the intellectual mediations it involves. In postmodern politics we find the equivalent of postmodern philosophy's appropriation of the "linguistic turn" of earlier twentieth-century philosophy. Positively, this has to do with practices that rely on the interplay of elements of language with one another, or, in different words, the self-referentiality of linguistic activity. It provides a practical expansion on themes theorists have explored in terms of intertextuality and the interplay of signifiers. Negatively, this politics corresponds to theoretical challenges to representational and instrumental conceptions of language and to the subordination of the signifier to the signified. We find a practical emphasis on language as a medium of interpretation and imaginative construction rather than as a medium primarily concerned with the representation of an independent reality.

We need to consider how this relation to language becomes incorporated in politics. We can do this by referring in nonlinguistic terms to an important feature of contemporary politics that we can describe as the strategic manipulation of social appearances. Speaking here of appearances allows us to emphasize the perspectival and interpretive dimension of this politics. In various contexts, including foreign policy, political campaigns, and consumerist culture, we can see ways in which power is exercised and pursued through the manipulation of appearances. In these contexts language functions to elicit linguistic responses appropriate to strategic requirements. Representational language assumes an ironic relation to extralinguistic states of affairs. The manipulation of appearances figures in strategic practices within linguistic frameworks in which intralinguistic relations are ordered in strategic and conflictual ways.

In speaking of appearances, I am emphasizing respects in which the ostensibly representational features of language become the focus of action. In speaking of strategic manipulation, I am contrasting this action not only to representational speech that makes claims about objective states of affairs, but also to communicative action that seeks to achieve common understanding among interlocutors. To use Habermas's terminology, language is here not primarily functioning to depict states of affairs or to foster reasoned agreements through communicative action. Statements ostensibly depicting objective states of affairs, as well as those ostensibly seeking rational consensus, are strategically used in such communications to achieve desired practical responses from the audiences to whom they are directed. From the validity judgments of those they address, strategic speakers do not seek rationally motivated agreement either about states of affairs or about practical understandings. Rather, they seek judgments that lead to desired patterns of action.

Perhaps one can say that in postmodern politics a strategic relation to language is set up within language itself. Language is manipulated in the pursuit of linguistic outcomes. Crudely, we could say messages are crafted to elicit linguistic responses. For example, on the basis of an opinion poll taken before the Gulf War, the Bush administration determined that the most popular reason for attacking Iraq was to block the development there of nuclear weapons. Though this had not previously figured as a major administration argument, it became for a while a key rationale for the policy against Iraq. These arguments, then, figure in a complex play of strategic communications: the opinion polls themselves, the use of their results in public argument, the related elicitation of communication in talk shows, letter writing to senators, the subsequent communications of senators, and even the initiation of military activity as "sending a message."

What is characteristically postmodern about this kind of politics is not the strategic use of ostensibly representational language but the functioning of such strategies within a wider politics oriented to effective communicative strategies. From the standpoint of the division of labor and the scarcity of agency, what is characteristic of postmodern politics is the way such a politics functions not only with regard to specific outcomes but within the ongoing practice of politics. In this regard, we need to see that specific strategic initiatives contribute to a political culture. In the context of the reflexiveness of modern politics, a pertinent feature of this culture is the explicitness of linguistic strategies themselves. The strategic use of the nuclear weapons argument became almost immediately itself an item of commentary within news broadcasting. Typically, government officials discuss (without attribution) their media strategies with news reporters and commentators, and this all becomes part of the publicly available language of politics. The truth value of ostensibly representational speech becomes all the less relevant as public discourse rates it for its effectiveness.

To illustrate this kind of politics, and particularly how it includes a reflexive relation to the knowledge that is deployed in strategic action, we can turn to certain features of a key domain of displaced politics. I shall trace some of the functions of knowledge in popular culture. My main reference point in the following is television, but the claims I make are meant to have a wider application. I consider four ways knowledge functions in popular culture, and in the course of sketching these I discuss some of the theoretical issues that arise for their conceptualization. Knowledge figures in popular culture first, as a means for its production; second, as content that it conveys; third, as a dramatic force represented in popular culture; and fourth, as being itself reproduced in the audience reception of popular culture.

Knowledge figures in the production of popular culture in a number of ways, some closely tied to the physical apparatuses of the technological means of this production—the cameras, studios, satellites, and so forth. But even the most purely technical forms of knowledge function within a division of labor organized by fairly well defined social goals. The social content is explicit in some of the organizing forms of knowledge, for example, strategies for writing scripts, research on potential audiences, psychological theories, marketing strategies, economic calculations. Social relations beyond the sphere of cultural production are themselves pursued strategically. Perhaps one should speak of a complex of strategies, for example, producers against corporate networks, both against advertisers, and all of them against their "targeted" audiences. Thus, strategic rationality coordinates the production of popular culture and designs the social relation between producers and consumers of culture. This involves a specialized intelligentsia that is responsive to corporate demands and political constraints and that targets an audience it both fears and tries to manipulate. The role of knowledge here is no doubt shaped by a variety of factors, including the massiveness of the audience, the complex technology employed, constraints of time and of material resources generally, but these are in turn inseparable from the kind of social context culture develops within, its prevailing social relations and dominant interests. In any case, knowledge's role cannot be separated from the quality of the relation established between producers and consumers of culture.

Within the strategies of popular culture, culture is a product designed for an audience schematized and treated as a mass of consumers. If this conception of the audience is to some degree a fiction, it is one that is constitutive of real cultural strategies; and further, to the extent these succeed, it is a fiction that contributes to a very real reduction of cultural experience to consumption, rendering it episodic, distracted, mechanical, and repetitive. By treating the audience as passive, such production contributes to making it so. Of course, this passivity is a matter of degree, and the strategic calculations of the producers of mass culture are notoriously prone to error. Audiences themselves are constructs, and if the conditions for achieving them can be abstractly formulated, this is the case only in so general a way that any specific project carries with it considerable risk.

Knowledge is here associated with a power strategy whose aims are political in seeking to establish patterns of response in its audiences. But how we are to understand the mechanisms of this process is a question that in turn raises a host of basic questions of social theory. I approach some of these in a general way once I have discussed ways abstract knowledge figures not only in the production of popular culture but also in its content.

Here I turn to the second way abstract knowledge figures in popular culture, namely, as knowledge conveyed to an audience. A great deal of television time is given over to the presentation of real or alleged factual information, research findings, theoretical claims, reports, studies, commentaries, consultations, and so on. Advertising looms large in this context, and seems in fact to have assumed a virtually paradigmatic status, though much time is also given to news, special reports, documentaries, interview programs, commentaries, press conferences, and news analysis. There are all sorts of knowledge specialists—on-the-spot reporters, interviewers, poll takers, weather experts, veteran commentators, scientific specialists. Even sports is subjected to abstract analysis, statistical comparisons, strategic profiles, and the games themselves come to be seen as the projection of complex plans, precisely monitored and subject to close and appreciative reconstruction by expert commentators.

If this seems to indicate an enormous popular appetite for information and scientific insight, the presentation such knowledge receives of course provides grounds for a more ambivalent assessment. Advertising assumes paradigmatic status in the conveyance of knowledge not only because it is ever present, occupying vast quantities of time distributed in a regular and inescapable rhythm of brief though highly compressed messages. Advertising also most clearly embodies the strategic relation between the producers and consumers of culture; but what is of most immediate concern to us is the consequence of this relation in the way knowledge actually appears in these cultural productions.

One way of putting this is to say that the knowledge content conveyed tends to be overwhelmed by the form of its presentation. Soap may be recommended on the basis of alleged scientific findings, but one can hardly register the character or even the coherence of these findings amid the orchestrated chumminess between washer repairman and housewife or among neighbors, or the against the backdrop of the husband's renewed confidence in his wife's laundry know-how.

If the scientific findings explain her happy outcome or justify her restored self-confidence, these results in turn reduce the appeal to science to a kind of ritual that a certain percentage of commercials seem obliged to repeat. That something similar happens with the news has been the focus of much criticism. As newscasters become media stars (though reassuringly capable of informality with one another and with us), and as the technical presentation (color, computer graphics, sophisticated editing, immediate worldwide coverage, etc.) becomes more impressive, the content of news seems more and more meager, events seem staged, analysis artificial, and the whole enterprise given over to an unseemly self-congratulation. This elevation of style over substance poisons not only the media coverage of politics but the conduct of politics itself. Showing open concern for credibility rather than truth, government leaders improvise the truth as they go along, calculating shifts of media attention before their fabrications have been methodically refuted, perhaps assuming that their public has been made cynical about truth in any case. Aspiring politicians recognize that vague slogans implying competence are more effective than boring attempts to justify these claims with analysis and programs. Their opponents rise to the challenge by sneering back in the slogans of fast food commercials ("Where's the beef?").[1]

If news tends in the direction of entertainment, it remains a striking fact that it is precisely news that has become entertaining, that specifically knowledge has here become a fetish. This bears on the third way I have said abstract knowledge figures in popular culture, namely, as a dramatic force within popular entertainment. Various genres make use of abstract knowledge in this way: the resolution of problems with abstract knowledge is a regular feature of programs about police, private detectives, doctors, lawyers, even coroners and teachers, not to mention astronauts, social workers, and reporters. No doubt the prominence of knowledge in such entertainment is tied to the fact—which itself deserves careful reflection—that much popular culture draws from the grim realities of everyday life, from which one might have thought it would provide a diversion. Armed with knowledge, skill, and insight, leading characters negotiate their way through the often bewildering and menacing forces operating in our fragmented social world. If rationality is required to keep external forces at bay, forms of therapeutic insight are equally necessary to tame the inner demons that threaten to poison personal relationships and to destroy individual psyches. Series like *Hill Street Blues* combine these themes in a striking way.

Here, as in the case of the presentation of knowledge in popular culture, it is the imagery, effects, and prestige of knowledge that are stressed over its actual content. Here too the fetishism of knowledge permits it to supplant or obscure value questions. Knowledge becomes virtually a moral force in a world depicted in a way that lacks any genuinely coherent moral framework. This may not be surprising, given the same absence in the social world on which popular culture is parasite for its content. But what is noteworthy for my purposes is the function abstract knowledge plays in providing a surface coherence for stories in which orientations to ideas of good and evil retain some force. In the absence of genuinely moral or political values, competence itself takes on moral authority, especially when combined with integrity or authenticity of feeling. If all this is to be expected in a technocratically inclined society, it nonetheless invites criticism from the standpoint of democratic values, not to mention experiential plausibility. But if the content analyses of the presentation and dramatic roles of knowledge in popular culture that I have sketched here raise issues for both the understanding and criticism of popular culture, one must still question the relevance of this kind of analysis to an understanding of the actual cultural process in which this content functions. One cannot presuppose a passive audience any more than one can presuppose an audience that is homogeneous or static in its makeup. An account of popular culture, like that of any kind of culture, must assess the process of its reception, which involves an audience response that may be relatively passive and accepting, or distracted and bored, or angry, frustrated, cynical, ironic, and so on. Since audience reception involves an interpretive interaction, one must be able to treat the way cultural processes intersect with preexisting capacities, knowledge, expectations, and so on.

Such considerations bear on my fourth way knowledge figures in popular culture, which is really a subheading under the theme of the social effects of popular culture. This is the way popular culture contributes to the reproduction of social knowledge itself. By now it should be clear that the kind of knowledge at issue here goes well beyond theoretical knowledge or even the knowledge that is explicitly presented or dramatized in popular culture. Knowledge includes the abstract strategies and beliefs proper to coping with a fragmented social world and the problems of constructing a self adequate to the demands of the practices characteristic of this world. The reproduction of such knowledge involves not only the propagation of appropriate beliefs about the world and about knowledge itself but also the integration of the individual into prevailing schemes of rationality, that is, the integration of individuals into the existing division of intellectual from manual labor.

The reception of popular culture closes a circuit of practices that begins with its strategically organized production. If the producers of culture schematize their task and audience in terms of the seduction and manipulation of consumers, their strategies are frequently thwarted by a fickle public. As I have just noted, we need a way of grasping the audience relation to popular culture as an active interaction that admits of resistance as well as acceptance. This is not a purely theoretical requirement, since popular culture in fact does continuously incite resistance despite its hegemony in the cultural sphere. This is resistance that has gone well beyond the rejection of given programs to systematic critique and programmatic initiatives in the construction of countercultures. Whatever the prospects of such oppositions, they remain a key feature of the social process and relations within which popular culture operates. The communications approach is useful here, since it treats the various kinds of validity claims as points at issue in the reciprocal relations of speakers and hearers. The suspension and confusion of claims provides a way of thinking about the process by which knowledge is fetishized, since these claims are in principle open to challenges that demand justification, as well as a framework for conceiving how opposition and resistance may be mounted within a cultural sphere.

Viewed in this light, strategic manipulation of political language can be seen as contributing to the shaping of specific historical forms of political agency. These forms of agency involve specific kinds of interpretation and participation, understanding and relation to power. Parallels can be drawn between the formation of specific kinds of political agency and the formation of other contemporary forms of agency, for example, consumerism. At issue here are complexes of perception, dispositions to act, forms of satisfaction, expectations regarding outcomes, and so on.

This comparison between strategies in explicit political contexts and those in apparently nonpolitical settings may be justified partly because the latter settings are not so nonpolitical as they first seem. Earlier I argued that the manipulation of agency in advertising and other features of consumerism should be counted as a covert kind of politics. It illustrates the breakdown between the economic and cultural spheres so far as reflective concerns with forms of experience inform practices that supplant appeal to the economic subject of traditional political economy. This is a breakdown that has a political aspect because it mobilizes power relevant to matters of general social concern. Another reason the comparison of explicit politics and consumerist economics is relevant is that the citizen within the field of strategic manipulation of language (of social appearances) becomes a citizen of a kind that echoes forms of social being outside the explicitly political realm.

The communications approach to action on agency is nonreductive in the sense that it treats agents as agents even as they undergo action upon their agency. This action "upon them" is an interaction in which they make validity judgments within processes of reception. So far as this is an interaction in which features of modern knowledge-power are at work, we can explore how this action upon agency figures within the evolution of this characteristic of the modern division of labor. A relation to knowledge-power may involve the exercise by a citizen of some genre or voice proper to this knowledge-power (e.g., filling out a tax form, taking an exam, doing office work). At the same time, it may involve the use of a reflectively deployed genre of knowledge-power by an expert (e.g., not just the making up and evaluating of the test, but application of a theory of education or a strategy for evaluation). The citizen may be placed in a quasi-reflective relation to issues of knowledge-power as such (e.g., attending a debate over the health-care system, watching a movie with an antibureaucratic theme).

As these references suggest, there are various relations to knowledge-power that can come up in interactive relations in which action on agency takes place. These can involve immediate outcomes, the quality of relations between citizens and experts, reflective under-standing of regimes of power, and so on. They can strengthen the hold of normalizing and disciplinary practices or elicit a conflict that loosens it (e.g., testing that integrates a "subject" or that antagonizes one against the testing process). In any case, it should be clear that the nonreductive quality of this analysis projects an applicability of com-munications concepts across social contexts, though it allows for varia-tions on their use. As bound to conceptions of learning, judgment, and reflective abstraction that allow for a wide range of applications, the communications approach accommodates a range of conditions—economic, political, cultural, psychological—that affect how communi-cation proceeds. Thus, although this approach resists reducing away the linguistic dimension, it treats that dimension as subject to condi-tions and constraints of various kinds.

In the case of the postmodern relation to language, we want to combine this analytical resistance to reductionism with some historical sense of the overloading of the linguistic dimension that results from the increasing reliance on strategic manipulation of language. The thesis of the political impasse in effect asserts that contemporary politics resorts to manipulations of language as a way of deflecting attention from structural questions. A critical aim of a communications approach that refuses to absolutize language is to identify salient features of a politics that veers precisely toward such an absolutization. In considering one feature of the practical logic of this politics, I shall show how this absolutization contrasts with the subjectivism of politics one might infer from talk of the manipulation of social appearances.

With the strategic manipulation of language, we see, I have argued, a practical version of the collapse of the signifier/signified distinction. Rather than unambiguously orient itself to a world apart from language, postmodern politics seems to concentrate on the play of language itself. It would be misleading to imply that this increasingly self-referential, even self-enclosed play of signifiers cuts itself off from a world that goes on in its own disturbing ways. Rather, the world itself is increasingly reworked and interpreted in linguistic terms. The collapse of the signifier/signified distinction amounts to an attempt to bring what previously counted as the signified (concepts) or that to which reference was made (particulars) all into the play of signification. In other words, the strategic manipulation of language, though associated in my argument with the impasse of contemporary politics, is not purely an evasion of social problems but a certain way of trying to encode and manage them.

This analysis allows us to locate some of the kinds of intellectual mediation for which postmodern thought provides a historical self-understanding. The organization and pursuit of manipulative strategies is the work of various specialists. Not only do they employ language in ways that admit of postmodern interpretation, but this interpretation allows them to avoid or respond to traditional forms of criticism. Besides drawing on various kinds of specialized knowledge for these practices, such intellectual specialists frequently use knowledge as a source of the appearances they manipulate. This is one way they contribute to the more general interpretation of knowledge that characterizes postmodern politics.

With the communications approach we can see how these features of postmodern politics involve a specifically contemporary division of labor. Moreover, we can see how this division of labor thus includes practices that promote an understanding of the necessity of the scarcity of agency and thus the necessity of the continuation of the division of labor itself. The various mediations of specialists contribute to political outcomes that not only reproduce specific power relations but reproduce the more general framework in which their powers as specialists are established as fixed and necessary features of the social landscape.

Though I have spoken of an instrumental relation to language, this is a matter of the practical standpoint of these strategic undertakings more than an adequate characterization of the relation between speakers and language. The speakers are themselves historically constructed, in part by language, so they cannot stand in a strictly instrumental relation to language. In this respect, a communications approach agrees with postmodern reflection. But it does not reduce agents to figments of linguistically conceived processes. Rather, by emphasizing social practices within which individuals function historically with more or less coherence, the communications approach absolutizes neither strictly linguistic relations nor purely instrumental or strategic forms of action. We can reconstruct the play of signifiers in terms of historically shaped strategies, and we can reconstruct these strategies as figuring within social practices.

Reconstructing this politics in communications terms allows us to see how it is context responsive, how the necessities to which strategy appeals are themselves historical and shifting. Strategy extended to the materials of language undercuts assumptions about fixed practical points of reference and destabilizes intralinguistic grounds for common understandings. Crisis management provides a model for the kind of self-stabilizing logic appropriate to this politics, but it is also a creature of power relations and reproduces such relations by achieving specific crisis resolutions.

There is an apparent paradox in the emergence of strategic communication, since the understanding of language that accompanies this kind of practice in effect dismisses the distinction between agents and thought on the one side and language on the other. We cannot stand in an instrumental relation to language if language does not stand in a representational relation to the world but is instead a constitutive feature of it. An increasingly strategic relation to specific utterances thus involves a decreasing sense of any independence of language or of any instrumental relation to it as a whole. Instrumentality becomes a style that is context dependent.

This point bears on the themes of political metaphysics that follow. They in turn bear on the quality of reflection and the coherence of the relation to politics. Absolutizing the strategic not only erodes clarity about the world apart from language, it also erodes clarity about the terms of action, the aims and the presuppositions. Moving toward an exclusively strategic orientation is also becoming increasingly context dependent and unreflective, despite the considerable reflection expended upon relevant features of communicative strategy.

Though there are moments of idealism, even solipsism, in this kind of politics, it does not exactly amount to a linguistic turn away from the world. While my general historical theses imply that this kind of politics of language is inadequate for dealing with the issues posed by structural change and thus is a politics of impasse, I do not mean to imply that such politics tries to imagine away conditions I am discussing in structural terms. The idealist tendency here lies not in substituting language for the world but in recasting the world in linguistic terms and as being open to linguistically conceived intervention. Postmodern politics has to respond to events; in fact it is characterized by its qualities of episodic and contextual responsiveness. But it responds by casting events into language, by trying to reconstruct issues as linguistically organized and susceptible to strategies of various sorts.

The paradox of strategic perspective being adopted within an inherently noninstrumental, perhaps interpretive situation, then, is not so much a matter of a contradiction as of limits to coherence. It is episodic and context specific, and in this respect quite consistent with postmodern intellectual arguments against totalizing perspectives. Intellectual arguments provide terms for thinking the virtues of a political reflectiveness that is inevitable. In practical terms, postmodern politics exhibits an orientation that defies normative determinateness as much as it abjures normative justification. Its context responsiveness assumes the forms of what I have spoken of as crisis management. Rather than have stable aims or objective claims, it responds to problems in ways that reproduce dominant power relations.

Constructing Citizens: Beyond the Modern Subject

By way of the idea of strategic relations to language, I have tried to establish some connections between postmodern intellectual mediation and postmodern politics more generally. This politics involves action upon agency, which I have been arguing is a crucial dimension of the quasi-political action upon agency that characterizes contemporary mediation. Thus its action contributes to reproduction of the division of labor. Reflexiveness in relation to language characterizes both the theoretical and the political repudiation of the metaphysical tradition. In the latter case, the practical assumptions of liberal metaphysics are at stake. The theoretical repudiation of the modern subject has been a central theme of postmodern discussion. It has its correlate in the destabilization of the liberal political subject.

I have already referred to ways postmodern mediation acts upon agency. I discussed examples of the working of mediation on forms of reception, perception, and judgment. Now I want to expand on this point as a way of contrasting other features of the philosophical functions within postmodern politics. To the extent that it makes the issue of agency political, postmodern politics breaks with the metaphysical relation to politics I have attributed to classical liberal knowledge-politics. Of course, even classical liberalism did not simply take forms of agency as given. Like ancient politics before it, liberalism had an important place for the cultivation of political capacity, an important concern with political education (Esquith 1994). In some respects, the covert politics of agency proper to postmodern politics continues traditional liberal practice. But traditional liberalism's readiness to modify aspects of agency presupposed an epistemological and metaphysical point of reference that postmodern thought—and politics—abandons.

This break with metaphysics occurs in postmodern thought via the various influential challenges made to the idea of the subject. My claim now is that the historicizing of the subject in postmodern thought corresponds to a relentless politics of refashioning subjects in postmodern politics. What were once fixed points of reference are now explicitly or tacitly made problematic. I have already touched upon features of action upon agency and on general ways this can be approached in communications terms. And I have touched upon two kinds of political agency characteristic of postmodern politics, the agency proper to citizens cast as clients and that proper to citizens cast as spectators.

The Citizen as Client

The idea of the citizen as client figures in liberalism. Already with conceptions of the calculating self-interested individual as citizen, a conception tied to market relations, we see features of what I am calling the client-citizen. But now I are referring to something more historically specific, an evolution of this kind of practical orientation in specifically postmodern conditions. Here I am interested in ways clientship evolves as a political agency that is appropriate to postmodern conditions and that is sustained through specifically postmodern mediations.

Clients stand in relation to an increasingly corporatist state. These are not isolated individuals within the competitive relations of the market but atomized individuals confronting a state whose services and reliability are both in question even as citizen dependence on the state grows. As recurring themes of the tax revolt indicate, the relation to the state is frequently cast in exchange terms. The relations themselves are organized bureaucratically. One reason the exchange relation retains its hold on political perception is the frequent organization and articulation of state services along consumerist lines. Citizen clients stand in political relations to the state and experience these relations as a matter of services or of isolated problem solutions in exchange for taxes and loyalty. Political relations here tend toward exchange relations conceived in specifically postmodern ways.

The client is a political consumer open to all the manipulations and influences visited upon consumers in general. The introduction into political campaigns of the advertising and public relations strategies proper to consumerism is not adequately grasped by complaints about the dilution or trivialization of politics. This evolution involves an intensification and extension of politics of a peculiar sort. Within the explicitly political realm, it involves an increase of public political talk, but of a sort that remains distant from involvement in or challenges to power. I can cite here not only the considerable amount of mass media time given over to explicit and tacit political questions (a theme I consider further in a moment), but also various kinds of quasi-involvement orchestrated by television and radio, for example, through talk and call-in shows, and "town halls." Such an evolution of public discourse can be examined for the content of what is discussed and can often be criticized for substituting secondary or false issues for substantial questions (e.g., focusing on personal lives of candidates, on hearings over nominees) or for failing to pursue substantial themes in adequate depth. But of more immediate concern here is the relation to politics that these forms of discussion fashion for citizens. In particular, we need to notice the role of intellectual mediation in organizing this relation of clients to power.

I have been relying on terms from economic life to characterize this relation: exchange, consumption, and client. To appreciate what is historically distinctive about this quality of contemporary politics, we need to recall the theses of covert politics and the blurring of the distinction between the economic and the political. The economic itself has become deeply politicized and has become so in a distinctively postmodern way. So if we speak of consumerist citizens, we refer to a tacitly politicized realm so far as consumers are themselves the object of various expert interventions addressed to facets of agency, to perception, need, and identity. In what conventionally passes for politics, but also in material production and consumption and in the various spheres whose status is unclear within public understanding (e.g., schools, health care, mass culture, perhaps even the family), specialists intervene in ways that deepen the political stakes while avoiding political identification. As I have noted, it is the language of modern knowledge-power that allows for this paradoxical accomplishment.

Clientship as discussed so far indicates citizen relations to structural changes: the welfare state is charged with maintaining labor and economic growth but is unable to elude long-term stagnation in the standard of living and the decline of work and investment in important sectors of the economy. Clients make greater demands on the state (in the form of social services, schools, and heath care) as family relations fragment and reorganize. Despite the economistic understanding of the state, client-citizens stand in relation to an economy on which they make political demands and whose political dimensions are accompanied by cultural initiatives. Clients confront state institutions that are increasingly charged with preserving conditions for social identity and moral stability. The respects in which clientship illustrates structural change are complex.

To speak here of mediation is to allude to the constructed character of this kind of citizenship. This is more than a matter of agency being historical. Here we find strategic intervention into aspects of agency, for example, by social service agencies concerned with drug abuse, teen pregnancy, and violence. It is not just that agents are targets of strategic intervention, but they are presupposed to be permanently open to such intervention. And if agency is not just historical but the target of complexes of conscious strategies, it is also marked by fragmentation and instability as citizens are solicited and pressured from a variety of directions in keeping with the varied imperatives proper to the different institutions in which individuals live and work.

In speaking of mediation that is reconstructed communicatively as utterances that involve validity claims whose recognition is a condition of their effectiveness, we avoid any suggestion that this kind of politics is simply manipulative. Citizens are not passive stuff in the hands of state and corporate power. If they were, there would be no point to mediating action on their agency. Nonetheless an account of the quality of their compromised agency is required. In fact, this is the analysis clientship is intended to initiate, since it points to specific ways of receiving messages and relating to power generally. Moreover, in speaking of the agency of citizens as clients, I refer to actual and potential participation and conflict with prevailing forms of power. In referring to the tax revolt, I have already mentioned one respect in which clientship can be a way of organizing a resistance, however problematic, to the state. As such it is a variable interpretative standpoint that allows for identification of different issues and the formulation of specific aspirations and goals. In the context of social movements concerned more explicitly with political programs, the formation of political clients has a depoliticizing effect, though it does not free the state of serious political costs and pressures.

Citizens as Spectators

To speak of spectatorship as a mode of citizenship is plainly paradoxical. But as in the case of political clients, this kind of citizenship involves a kind of activity even if it is largely interpretive. It is an activity whose distance from decision making is not a separate matter from its relation to social conflicts. Spectatorship as I mean it is not only an involvement in displaced and covert politics but an involvement that reflects the contestation of movements.

I have already spoken of ways postmodern politics extends the liberal appeal to objective necessities. When power is experienced as the expert application of insights into objective necessities, citizens become spectators of power and clients of specialists. If politics becomes the application of abstract objective knowledge rather than a matter of debate, interpretation, and initiatives, then it tends toward adaptation to objective necessity. But this application takes place in the context of dissatisfaction and social contestation.

The democratic aspect of the new social movements thus partly consists of their making political interpretations and operations explicit and contestable. Challenges to technocratic politics have exposed various kinds of reification and made the quality of agency a matter of social debate. But it is in keeping with the quality of technologically minded politics that these challenges have in turn elicited significant responses that seek not so much to repress the aims of such movements as to absorb them into technological politics. Let me illustrate by referring to a way in which such politics is pursued in the sphere of popular culture. There is a kind of television programming that, either in the form of specials or themes within series, functions as a kind of cultural management of political perception. I call this kind of programming "disaster entertainment." Here one finds portrayals of ongoing social problems as encountered by stylized versions of newsworthy social figures. Often these include experts and sometimes proponents of social movements. Shortly after the release of toxic chemicals in Bhopal, India, ABC broadcast a program that constructed an analogous chain of events in a small midwestern town in the United States ("Acceptable Risks," Sunday, 2 March 1986, 9:00 P.M.).

Featured here were various stock figures (a beleaguered plant manager, shortsighted city officials, indifferent or complacent plant personnel, unscrupulous real estate developers, innocent families in affected areas) as well as figures drawn from recent social history (a single mother entering a workplace dominated by men, a black woman who has become city manager on the basis of new opportunities for minorities, a community activist who on health grounds opposes permits for homes near the plant, a workaholic plant manager).

The unfolding of the disaster provides for the dramatization of various social perspectives. The chemical leak is attributed to negligence and the indifference of distant corporate officials, but we also learn of international economic competition and the possibility of the plant being moved to Mexico. Larger social forces dwarf the responsibility of individuals, and we are shown the mistakes and moral compromises of individuals representing diverse and perhaps irreconcilable points of view and interests. Finally, in the wake of the disaster itself—reconstructed according to the imagery of the news coverage of such events—the program concludes with a screen showing the addresses of representatives of government, industry, and environmental groups. The disaster receives dramatic resolution by appeal to various experts to whom we may turn if the reduction of politics to entertainment does not provide an adequate substitute for more active involvement.

Drawing from media reconstructions of events that embody fundamental social dilemmas, this cultural construction provides a kind of political sense making, though one proper to what I have called displaced politics. The program provides a substitute politics rather than promote a real debate. Diverse perspectives are not given a voice but are represented in terms proper to the aims of the program itself. One need not suggest a conspiracy to observe that corporate programmers are faced with the need both to respond to the concerns of their audience with social issues and to avoid adopting a standpoint that will alienate a significant part of their audience or sponsors. The result is a caricature of various political standpoints, combined with an appeal to the experts. Despite the portrayal of politically charged perspectives, in the end the appeal to expertise contributes to the sense that we confront processes guided by necessities that overwhelm the understanding and the practical powers of ordinary individuals. The program reasserts the necessity of the division of labor even while it is itself the product of a division of cultural labor in which specialists reconstruct social issues for a passive audience of spectators. Here we have a process of political sense making that acknowledges the breakdown of credible authority, the existence of real crisis, and even portrays experts in a critical light. But while this sense making incorporates the fact of the social conflict over political interpretation, its own interpretation helps blunt impulses for wider participation. If it tacitly acknowledges a breakdown in received appeals to objective necessity and expertise, it nonetheless manages the challenges to past technological politics in a way that asserts their unavoidability.

By making citizens political spectators, disaster entertainment helps manage social crisis through an interpretation of crucial problems and conflicts. As an instance of strategic politics in culture, it treats citizens as the clients of cultural and political experts. By portraying disasters, this kind of popular culture responds to what it takes to be real concerns of its audience; but by making political issues into matters of entertainment, it helps construct a passive relation between citizens and public issues. Though there are tacit and debatable political claims built into the portrayal of the disaster, the most significant political act lies in the relation that is being constructed between citizens and the exercise of power. At issue here is less a particular controversy than the construction of a relation to politics through the tacit politics of the programming itself.

Disaster entertainment, then, illustrates what earlier I called the politics of agency. It contributes to political understanding and the relation of individuals to political action. Moreover, in doing so it explicitly refers to ways political understanding has recently itself been the object of conflict. Thus it makes sense of a politicized realm by interpreting the sense making of the representatives of social movements. It illustrates a politics of agency by illustrating ways contemporary political practices manage social problems by acting upon the perceptions, capacities, and identities of individuals. In probing human sensibility such practices bridge the realms of politics and aesthetics.

By cultivating the role of political spectator, disaster entertainment provides an example of postmodern politics. Other examples, both within and without the sphere of explicitly cultural activity, can be cited to illustrate action on the agency of citizens, placing them in a spectator relation to social power through the employment and depiction of expert knowledge. In the explicitly political domain, such practices are found, for example, in the use of presidential commissions, television interview programs drawing on academics and insiders, expert testimony at hearings, and reliance on regulatory agencies for defining public interests in various controversial settings. In such contexts, we can see the way power is exercised beyond the reach of ordinary citizens and the way it is exercised on citizens by cultivating their understanding and capacities in relation to power. All these practices both draw upon experts and display the need for expertise by portraying the world in terms of necessities and abstractions that place political competence beyond the reach of the nonspecialist.

Having located the political operation of casting citizens as political spectators, we can also see that the devices of popular culture have been adopted in other political and economic spheres as well. In the political realm we can cite again the examples given above as well as televised debates, the news, and so on; in the economic realm, advertising, public relations, personnel administration, and scientific management. The construction and imposition of interpretive frameworks, the manipulation of images and associations, and the substitution of calculated rhetoric for the respective rationalities (bureaucratic, economic) all point to ways such practices shape the relation of citizens to political agency. In shaping capacities and social identities these practices are cultural forces, and in carrying out such functions they are playing a significantly political role.

These political mediations not only provide social interpretations but shape the interpretive capacities of social individuals. They promote capacities that accept passive political roles, and the need for social experts. I have argued that the new social movements have in effect challenged postmodern politics through their challenges to aspects of the division of labor. Demanding transformed capacities, recognition of new social identities, and redefinition of social goals, these movements in effect promote a different kind of politics, a different kind of participation for the majority of citizens. As the example of disaster entertainment indicates, the management of this political challenge has itself become a problem for postmodern politics, requiring new interpretations to recuperate the more passive orientations of political spectatorship.

The features of spectatorship I have been discussing bear on the respects in which this kind of citizenship embodies a postmodern reflection on contemporary uses of rationality. Thus spectatorship exhibits the contemporary evolution of the epistemological dimension of modern politics. As a kind of reflective relation to power, it is at once also a kind of reflective relation to rationality and politics.

Beyond Liberal Metaphysics

So far my aim in this section has been to discuss ways postmodern politics supplants the political metaphysics of modern politics with its own more historically self-conscious shaping of agency. I am showing ways the demise of the subject announced in postmodern thought plays itself out in politics. Postmodernism's philosophical dimension provides terms for making sense of intellectual activity in a world characterized by mediations that combine extraordinary degrees of reflexiveness about the formative features of agency with little normative orientation. The extent and variety of powers seem to expand without limit, but so do uncertainties and instabilities. The ironic sensibility associated with postmodernism is surely inseparable from these paradoxes of the contemporary period.

If citizens formed (through the complexities of communicative practices) as clients and spectators possess little in the way of what is usually thought of as political power, neither are they particularly fixed or stable. That does not mean that they are capable of transforming rapidly into democratic citizens, but it does illustrate the provisional qualities of a world oriented toward crisis management. The self-consciousness of this instability manifests itself in the various ironies I have remarked upon. It also can be seen in features of the agency proper to experts and leaders. Here too, features of the modern political subject coincide with the postmetaphysical interpretations of post-modern thought.

By "modern political metaphysics" I mean the basic terms in which the conditions, actors, issues, relationships, and possibilities of political life have been understood in the modern period. I have in mind the idea of the independent individual capable of acting from considerations of self-interest as well as of morality, the ideals of well-being and freedom achieved by private gain, the idea that though the world is competitively structured, it nonetheless can be organized into political wholes capable of a rationality analogous to that of the individual, and so on. Linked with these ontological and practical perspectives are epistemological ideas about the structure and power of reason, including the capacity of thought and language to represent an objective world. Though this framework is the result of a complex historical process, it is fair to call it a metaphysics, if only because it has typically been regarded as such from within, namely, as providing timeless and universally applicable ways of understanding society. Though it has undergone evolution, this framework has proven a rather stable conceptual structure, open to use in a variety of practices and by a variety of different political and ideological perspectives. Thus it has provided the terms of reference for Marxists and conservatives alike. Its appropriateness comes into question practically when the conditions of politics can no longer be approached metaphysically, that is, when political action becomes explicitly preoccupied with the nature of the political sphere itself.

Contrary to the received metaphysics, in which language and thought is assumed to represent the world, postmodernist politics treats language quite explicitly as an object of manipulation and as itself a medium in which political effects are to be achieved. Politics becomes the target of politics in the specific sense that appearances become the focus of strategic thought and action. The Reagan administration's preoccupation with imagery was not so much a simple debasement of democratic discourse as the fashioning of a new mode of political agency, a new kind of power. For example, with the idea of the "Vietnam Syndrome," the administration and its allies conceived popular reluctance at the prospect of U.S. interventionism as a psychological sickness. To combat this reluctance, the administration worked on the terms of public debate and response, from patronizing right-wing think tanks to staging successful token invasions, from countless photo opportunities to inflated Fourths of July, embracing Olympics-style chauvinism and draping itself in Ramboist imagery. With its manipulation of imagery, postmodern politics indulges in the play of signifiers celebrated by postmodern culture. Though this politics is effective in shaping specific political responses and in affecting political agency as such, its relation to political culture is mainly negative and tacitly ironic. It alters and manipulates received terms rather than provide a new vision or language.

Conventional political forms take on the function of symbols. This can be seen in the case of electoral politics. Once defended as an efficient means for securing interests and blocking arbitrary rule, electoral politics has become a kind of political theater in which participation is managed so as to absorb opposition and mediate elite conflict. The political organization of power is inseparably bound up with the deployment of symbols. This is evident in what Herman and Broadhead (1984) call "demonstration elections." In El Salvador, for example, the electoral process was designed and managed by the United States for a world audience. In the language of our politicians, such elections are designed to "send a message" and to do so to a variety of targeted audiences—Congress, domestic critics, allies, and so on. This is not to deny the local significance of such elections, though the workings of symbols and power there too has little in common with traditional liberal conceptions of democratic process. Elections are externally imposed, and in their outcomes often are manipulated, as when the United States blocked the rise of Roberto D'Aubisson.

In this case, liberal democratic procedures are subordinated to the imperatives of a complex international politics. It is not just that Salvadoran elections were incomprehensible independent of the war effort in which the United States played so central a role. The war itself cannot be taken as a starting point for explanations of the symbolic dimension of this politics, since it too was an exercise in the symbolics of contemporary power. Whatever else is the case, this intervention was designed to send a complex of messages to other potential insurgencies in the Third World, to the Soviet Union, and, not least, to the population of the United States.

Warfare, once the paradigm of strategic action, becomes a tactic within the symbolically organized strategies of contemporary politics. For this dimension of politics, quite a different paradigm is in order, that of advertising. One reason to invoke advertising as a paradigm is the loose relation to truth values that characterizes contemporary political discourse. Like advertising, with its use of repetition and its appeals to the unconscious, contemporary politics makes truth claims and argues in fragmented and arbitrary ways that reveal a lack of discursive seriousness if not an entirely open irony. It leans heavily on the self-referential features of language: with vivid images, crude assertions, and truncated arguments, it downplays the need for analysis or discussion of the historical events themselves. An illustration was the Reagan administration's repeated characterization of the Nicaraguan counterrevolutionaries as freedom fighters and the president's comparison of them with the Founding Fathers. These were contrasted with images of Sandinista state-sponsored terrorism—though the charges against the Nicaraguan government were never documented—at the same time the CIA's guidance of contra terror had become a matter of public record (condemned by the World Court).

Postmodernist politics, then, is characterized by an ironic relation to modern political metaphysics in its politicization of appearances. This is not a subjectivization of politics, since it shifts the nature of agency itself. By making the framework in which politics is understood itself an object of manipulation, it acts against received forms in which power has been articulated. By loosening the referential force of the received political vocabulary, it loosens the framework in which it must itself chart policy and take decisions. With the opportunistic manipulation of discourse, the terms in which agency is conceived themselves fragment. This is reflected in the lack of strategic coherence that characterized administration policies. Though fixated on strategic rationality, its policies lacked clarity of focus or consistency of execution. We see a familiar paradox of heightened technical efficiency with declining practical orientation, increased competence to manipulate appearances and decreased ability to control events.

Modern political metaphysics posed the conditions of social action from the standpoint of an individual subject able to formulate and act upon conceptions of self-interest. The state's agency in turn was organized with reference to this model, however ideological it may have been. The construction of such a subject is possible only by positing coherent and stable notions of goals and the means by which they are to be secured. That the practice of postmodern politics forgoes a commitment to the ideal of a coherent political subject is illustrated by an unwillingness to articulate fixed practical perspectives through the consistent use of strategic reason. The resulting fragmentation of agency does not, however, exclude fixation on specific goals. Indeed, such fixation is virtually required by the absence of a general practical perspective that would permit flexibility in specific matters as relevant conditions change.

U.S. foreign policy is formulated in language that treats its practical orientations ironically. For example, in the case of its characterizations of Nicaragua, the Reagan administration shifted between such depictions as served its immediate concerns. When challenged for its grounds for opposing the present government, it shifted between explanations. In one context Nicaragua was a Soviet forward base and so an emerging military threat to the United States itself. In another context, it was an aggressor state, a menace to its neighbors. In a third setting it was totalitarian, an unacceptable affront to the supposed democratic commitments of the Western Hemisphere. Each of these depictions was given as the reason for seeking the overthrow of the Sandinistas; yet they are not intrinsically related, nor do they obviously demand the same response. They were treated as equally compelling grounds for a U.S. policy that was represented as having commitments to regional order, defense against a Soviet threat, and to democracy. The issue here is not whether any of these claims was true, much less whether they were sincerely held. Rather, the point at issue is the kind of social practice that results from an ironic manipulation of discourse.

Noteworthy here is the way the administration used these claims over time, responding to developments (whether in the region, among allies or enemies, or in Washington), making demands, shifting in ways that made its intentions and requirements ambiguous and virtually impossible for Nicaragua to meet without giving up its revolution. Early in the Reagan administration, for example, claims of massive Nicaraguan support to Salvadoran rebels were made, but these were never substantiated. Subsequently, the Nicaraguan government offered to end all aid to the Salvadoran guerrillas, even to the extent of expelling their representatives from Managua, and to guarantee its borders bilaterally with its various neighbors. In the meantime, the administration shifted the focus of its criticism, stressing the allegedly tyrannical hold of the Sandinistas over their population. In the wake of elections in which the Sandinistas received a majority support somewhat larger than the Reagan ticket itself achieved, the administration changed its focus to Soviet designs and created a crisis over MiG's that had, in fact, never been sent to Nicaragua.

Later the focus shifted back to the internal structure of Nicaragua, with the administration demanding reforms that it admitted required the overthrow of the Sandinistas. Even if this was in fact the fixed aim of administration policy, my point is that its statements lacked the internal stability and consistent focus necessary for them to function within a coherent foreign policy strategy. Rather, claims about the Sandinistas had the character of pragmatic adjustments to events, used or dropped opportunistically, designed to sustain a political fixation that remained largely unstated. This is of course to repeat the claim that politics today is characterized by a strategic manipulation of appearances. Rather than serious (much less credible) representations of either Nicaraguan reality or administration aims, policy statements cohere strategically only with regard to the manipulation of appearances.

As the representational force of language declines in favor of its strategic use, the kind of agency that results strays from the ideal unity of purpose and understanding to which modern politics is in principle committed. In the practice of postmodernist foreign policy, the integrity of the subject, even the primacy of a single, centered subject gives way to a fragmented agency that is unproblematic from the standpoint of the dominant politics. This can be seen in the way foreign policy is enunciated. I am referring here to the common practice of undercutting or qualifying public statements by "background" remarks that are attributed only to "unnamed officials." When, for example, the Reagan administration reversed its support of the Contadora treaty in the face of Nicaraguan acceptance, its explicit statements about newly discovered problems over verification were elucidated off the record by officials who spoke of Sandinista duplicity regarding agreements of any sort. Frequently the president would say one thing, the State Department another, with qualifying commentary being supplied in background statements made to the press only. This is a familiar pattern: statements are made and then explained away in tactical language by anonymous officials. This may be in the form of explanations of intended effects, of underlying motives, or assurances to certain audiences that might otherwise get the wrong impression, and so on.

Following the discourse itself offers no reason to take any administration statement at face value, whether it is issued officially or presented as background information. When, after public disavowals of administration intentions to invade Nicaragua, writers reported un-named officials as speaking of a growing willingness to use the military option, we might just as easily have seen this as a tactic to raise the paranoia level in Managua as a reliable account of true intentions. That is, the repeated strategic use of language renders all statements open to multiple interpretations; all statements become objects of suspicion, since any may be deployed tactically.

This is less an epistemological point about the difficulties of knowing what administration intentions really were than an ontological point about the practice of foreign policy. With the ironic play with political appearances, the nature of agency itself changes. If this dissemblance gives rise to pride regarding technical skill at manipulating language, the nature of the resulting agency exposes this as an anachronistic appeal to an ideal of a coherent and centered subject conceived in terms of the metaphysics that is being violated. Rather than self-conscious masters of language, the agents here may be as much the fragmented creatures as they are the manipulators of their discourse. Yet to speak of them as alienated would be to miss the point and the effect of the strategies they do exercise.

Representational claims are used not only to establish the authority of the dominant subjects in this discourse but also to establish their identity as the subjects this discourse depicts them as being. Thus the social identity as well as the claims to authority made by numerous participants in this discourse rests on the claim that their statements represent social reality. This is true of journalists, academic consul-tants, and scholars, in addition to state officials themselves. Very much in keeping with the discourse of modern philosophy, these knowledge claims are associated with privileged episodes of experience, involving immediate access to the facts themselves; and these validate the broader analytical claims made in the discourse of foreign policy. Access to and possession of facts is treated in much the same way as modern epistemology treats the basis of warranted cognitive claims, making use of what Derrida (1976) calls the "metaphysics of presence." In methodological discussions, the most influential version of this today is still positivism. But one finds this schema as well in such contexts as the reporter's use of privileged and unidentified sources to write an inside account of debates among presidential advisors, or the administration's appeal to the results of intelligence operations (the specifics of which, to protect sources, cannot be revealed) in accusing the Sandinistas of regional subversion. Similarly, scholars and consultants appeal to research and data that are effectively inaccessible to most of those whom they address, and base their claims on this material, to which they have a unique access, given their place in the division of labor.

Within the metaphysics of the discourse of foreign policy, language provides a host of representations—descriptive, theoretical, technical, and political—as it expresses a privileged access to a grounding reality, whether this validates the statement of facts, the proof of laws, the conferral of certificates, or the tallying of votes. This metaphysics depicts a relation of language to the natural and social worlds and sets the terms in which power is described and justified. The relation of representation amounts to a claim of equivalency between language and the reality—the facts, empirical evidence, competence, consent— that is represented. By virtue of this relation, descriptions, scientific laws, claims to expertise, and assertions of political power receive their authorization. Within the sphere of foreign policy, this may be illustrated by the key role played by policy experts whose credentials are based on empirical social science, access to intelligence reports, and experience in the field, and by the political leaders they serve, whose own claims are couched in terms of a mastery of national interests and the backing of majority consent.

Social authority is the emphatic or practical form of a kind of social being, that of a representation; that is, power is depicted and justified as flowing from the authoritative subject's having attained the standing of a representative, whether this be the representative of social facts, laws, technique, or of the people itself. But today the practice of this discourse refutes the metaphysical relations depicted in its language. Far from treating its descriptions as factual representations, the administration seeks to shape the facts to fit its policy, as "insider" critiques of State Department white papers have shown. Similarly, the careers of Kissinger and Kirkpatrick illustrate the way expert influence is as much a matter of self-promotion and political alliances as it is of intellectual achievement. Given the control, shaping, and restriction of information (the use of secrets, the engineering of media events, the staging of phony crises, and so on), the government can hardly claim to represent interests and consent that it is so actively trying to manufacture. Its penchant for appointing presidential commissions to give the appearance of technical impartiality to strategies for neutralizing the opposition only provides another example. The representational claims of the press are undercut as well by its habit of building up the events it can then report as news, or the more dangerous practices of self-censorship and of reporters working for intelligence services. Confronted by the practices of which they are a part, representational depictions of foreign policy discourse turn out to be tactics in the power operations they simultaneously facilitate and distort. As the repeated violation of the standards to which they appeal, manipulation of representation undermines the kind of stable discourse in which it might be brought to account.

The claim I have been developing is that as ironic practice manipulates key elements of the received framework of political understanding, it becomes itself less comprehensible in terms of the modern ideological framework. Its practice less and less approximates either the normative or analytical assumptions of modern political metaphysics. From an democratic point of view, this restates the problem facing the critics of U.S. policy: how to avoid being trapped by the rules that the administration both manipulates and flouts.

With reference to the goals of action, to the unity of the political agency, and to legitimating claims, I have shown that representations repeatedly undercut themselves as actions refute claims formulated in terms of the modern political framework. Analysis and criticism are less and less able to make use of the categories of the modern political metaphysics. The demise of this metaphysics undercuts not only the appeal by conservative critics to genuine national interests but also the analyses by radical critics who presuppose coherent class or imperial interests. While this suggests that agency today is not well conceptualized in terms borrowed from modern metaphysics—and so criticism and explanation must adjust themselves accordingly—it does not imply that action is arbitrary or incomprehensible.

I have stressed aspects of the Reagan administration's foreign policy that suggest incoherence and fragmentation. Yet the fact remains that there was a good deal of constancy in its resolve to overthrow the Sandinistas and to avoid a revolutionary regime in El Salvador. In denying that this constancy can be grasped in terms of the modern ideals of state rationality, I have characterized it as a fixation on specific goals. Despite its psychological connotations, this term is meant to suggest a structural feature of postmodernist foreign policy: its finding points of stability in particular preoccupations around which policy makers fight their battles and enunciate their ironic general formulations.

For another example of the evolution of political agency in post-modern politics, consider uses of the idea of terrorism. Within domestic political discourse, the idea of terrorism contributes to the kind of postmodernist practice I have already described, and to the same statist and massifying alienation. We can see this first in the way the use of the theme of terrorism contributes to the manipulation of political appearances: terrorism figured as a key part of the Reagan administration's attempt to reframe the terms of debate (Secretary of State Haig said at the beginning of the administration that "[i]nternational terrorism will take the place of human rights in our concern because it is the ultimate abuse of human rights" [Armstrong and Shenk 1982, 189]). For challenges to prudential and moral resistance to interventionism, the theme of terrorism was used to marginalize conventional levels of debate. As a term of abuse, terrorism has enormous flexibility, supplanting to some extent the ideologically more precise anti-Communism. It permitted attacks on the Soviet Union as a supporter of terrorism, while also allowing friendly relations with China despite that country's support for forces otherwise identified by the United States as terrorist (e.g., the PLO, Libya).

Talk of terrorism thus has contributed to the shifting, inconsistent, fragmenting political agency I have associated with postmodern practice. For example, it figures in the changing explanations for U.S. opposition to the Sandinistas (as well as figures in the different ways they are demonized, as supporters of terrorism, as terrorizing their own population, and so on) (Kornbluth 1987, 157–98). Further, it figures in the way statements are undercut or supplemented by background information (e.g., reference to secret intelligence that is leaked but not substantiated). As such it figures in the ironic use of legitimation through appeal to representational relations—intelligence information, authority of military and police competence, and so on.

These operations are alienating in that they integrate individuals into power relations while undermining democratic political capacity. The threat of terrorism makes citizens more dependent on the state, which possesses the needed information, expertise, and firepower to combat it. It erodes political judgment by reducing the social issues linked to violence into issues of criminality. While terrorism today is generally a symptom of the inadequacy of existing political frameworks, it is characterized by the state simply as illegality rooted in depravity. Being outside the terms of political understanding, terrorism becomes a technical problem for the police and military. The result of this reductive politics is a degradation of political culture that permits social decisions affecting a host of political, economic, scientific, and technical issues to be crystallized in strategies against terrorism.

That the rhetoric of U.S. policy toward terrorism exhibits the same ironic relation to modern political metaphysics as the postmodernist practices I discussed above is not surprising, since terrorism reflects a basic failure in existing organizations of power. Whether the tactic of the disenfranchised or the policy of a state, the resort to actual or symbolic terrorism typically follows from the unresponsiveness, uncertainty, or fragility of political institutions. The prominence of the theme of terrorism within U.S. domestic politics reflects legitimation problems of the state. And this seems to be one facet of the profound uncertainties attached to the internationalization of power relations.

To explore the international politics of terrorism, we may first look to some further aspects of the rhetoric I have already discussed. In addition to the alienating functions regarding the relation between citizens and state, this rhetoric contributes to the political culture of a significantly internationalized world by influencing the domestic population's understanding of its relations to the people of Central America. This holds for general themes regarding economic and political-military relations to the Third World, as well as for specific issues regarding borders, immigration, domestic unemployment, bilingual education, international economic competition, and so on. The theme of terrorism contributes to a depersonalization of peoples with whom there are complex daily relations, and helps organize a complex social space across and within national borders.

And in the context of the present technology of communications, this domestic rhetoric assumes political functions within the political life of U.S. allies, rivals, clients, and countries who risk U.S. hostility. Given the United States' predominant role, its political claims shape the international political culture in ways similar to those in which it affects the domestic understanding of internationalization, encouraging Europeans to understand Central America and the Middle East in similar terms, for example. Moreover, terrorism provides an interpretive framework in whose terms the United States defines its global role, organizes the collaboration of its friends, and establishes the terms in which it condemns and warns its enemies. This is not to say that terrorism is the only framework in which this is done or that it is used consistently. That would contradict the postmodern character of U.S. policy: the language of terrorism permits a fragmenting, opportunistic, and to some extent unpredictable exercise of international power. Rather than provide a global conception or a unified strategic vision, it figures within the kind of political world in which no such vision is possible. Just as acts of terrorist violence are themselves fragmenting, the organization of state political power in terms of this theme is also episodic, fragmentary, and set within other kinds of initiatives.

Yet this does not mean that the U.S. approach to terrorism is not strategically organized, any more than it implies that this policy is purely rhetorical. The use of the theme within political language often exhibits the kind of strategic manipulation discussed earlier, just as it exhibits the same combination of strategic mastery and political incapacity. While the theme is used to great effect, the direction and aims of policy remain ill defined. But the role of strategy goes beyond the organization of language to other dimensions of terrorism.

The interpretation of unrest, insurrectionary movements, and revolutionary states in terms of terrorism feeds a logic in which attempts at social change are equated with kinds of instability that can only be confronted with police and military techniques. The rhetoric of terrorism has accompanied extensive aid programs for regional police forces in addition to massive injections of aid to local militaries. The lines between military and civilian, war-related and humanitarian aid blur in a perspective that sees the erosion of existing power as the proliferating threat of terrorist violence.

U.S. aid to regimes in Central America has sometimes gone beyond supplying the means and tactics with which to confront proponents of change understood as terrorists. It has contributed to the strategies and material used in state-sponsored terrorism in El Salvador and built an army that routinely employed terror in its attempt to overthrow the Nicaraguan revolution. The use of terror has long been associated with counterinsurgency doctrines and remains a part of them in their most recent formulation as strategies for "low-intensity conflict."

Thus the reductiveness of counterterrorism strategies leads to the use of violent tactics that aim to remove the causes of instability. But even here the role of terrorism is not purely negative. Once again we see what is by itself a largely negative device being put to political use in attempts to reconstruct Central American societies along nonrevolutionary lines. In Guatemala, for example, the working of politics on the political framework is evident in the combination of state terrorist methods with limited social reforms, imported food and medicine, forced labor, cultural homogenization of indigenous populations, use of psychological techniques of indoctrination and confusion, uprooting, and so on (for an overview of U.S. policies in Guatemala, see NACLA 1984). This has involved U.S. aid despite ruptures in formal relations between the countries. Support from South Africa and Israel has made this truly an international project in social reconstruction. Present attempts to resettle rural areas in El Salvador are following the same approach.

Here selective uses of terror fit into a complex of activities that together constitute a remarkable experiment in social engineering. Consistent with the general pattern of postmodernist politics, we see a response to inevitable political change that both resists innovations that would alter the structure of power and treats the political world as a framework to be manipulated strategically. The fact that the conservative aims of these strategies lead to tactics that are often as negative as they are opportunistic and episodic should not blind one to their constructive dimension and so to the way they abandon the modern metaphysical treatment of social relations and roles as fixed in the nature of things.

A final set of examples of the evolution of postmodern political agency comes from the politics of the Iran-contra affair. Surrounding the Iran-contra affair was a typical practice of what we may call the multiplication of spokespersons. Numerous voices, most of them unidentified, presented claims, attitudes, reactions from the government, whether the White House, top advisors, the Departments of State or of Defense. To some extent this represented the manipulation of publicity in internal power struggles. Sometimes it reflected confusions among policy makers or within the presidential mind. On other occasions, it represented strategic attempts to fool opponents, test responses, stall for time, or cover actual intentions. All of these seem to have figured in statements regarding Central America policy, for example.

As I have noted, this kind of practice corrupts political discourse as understood in liberal terms: like plausible deniability, it undercuts responsibility on the part of leaders while disrupting the conditions for judgment on the part of citizens. In these ways, the manipulation of appearances undercuts the exercise of agency as provided for in liberal discourse. A further aspect of the shift away from the world in which liberal discourse makes political sense can be seen in the changing

content of statements even when made by a single recognizable political agent. Thus, as I noted above, the official position of the administration on Nicaragua changed repeatedly. At some points, the issue was
aid to the Salvadoran rebels; at others, Soviet presence; and at still
other times, the reason for opposing the Sandinistas was their allegedly totalitarian proclivities. Given the very different practical implications of these different lines of criticism, the relation between
administration rationales and their other actions was loose.

While it is possible, as I have already claimed, to see this kind of
politics as symptomatic of an evasion of fundamental structural dilemmas, its being such does not prevent it from also being quite
effective in dominating the existing field of political debate. At least one
can say that this sort of postliberal politics of appearances has proven
itself effective in the face of the challenges of liberal critics. From a
democratic perspective, it is important to consider the implications for
an effective criticism.

Let me illustrate the kind of issue I have in mind by referring again to
the debate over U.S. policy regarding Nicaragua. Critics argued that
the persistent efforts to overthrow the Sandinistas conflicted with,
rather than served, U.S. interests. For example, the economic reforms
instituted by the Sandinistas not only did not exclude economic relations (including foreign investment from the United States) but could
well have made Nicaragua a more attractive source of markets. Similarly, U.S. military interests would not have been jeopardized by a
socialist Nicaragua, especially one that had agreed to forgo Soviet
bases. At the same time, intransigence over Nicaragua threatened
further to isolate the United States within the hemisphere and fueled
the forces it claimed to oppose.

During a period in which the administration had controlled the
terms of political debate, these arguments proved ineffective. I do not
deny that, under other circumstances, politicians mounting such criticisms may successfully change policy. But if they do, it will be within a
political discourse that resembles current practice more than it differs
from it. That is, the liberal argument projects a kind of political rationality that can only itself become part of the play of ironically deployed
appearances under present circumstances. It could be otherwise only if
the terms of liberal criticism could acquire a representative force in
relation to current structural realities. But the ideal of collective national rationality (even if analyzed in class terms) and the notion of a
collective entity to which definite interests can be attributed have (like

those of purely economic processes or strictly national military objectives) declining relevance in a world of transnational economic power and multinational political organization.

Rationality and Postmodern Politics

Aestheticized Politics

So far I have shown how philosophical issues, that is, reflective relations to rationality, figure in postmodern politics. For example, issues about the relation between language and the world, the makeup of subjects, and the relation of politics to historical time have figured in my account of tendencies in contemporary politics. I have argued that the strategic manipulation of social appearances within contemporary political language, the various workings on the agency of citizens (as clients/consumers and as spectators), and the organization of practical problems as matters of crisis management all contribute to a distinctively postmodern understanding of rationality and, in doing so, contribute to a dynamic but conservative relation to the issues of the division of labor and scarcity.

As a prelude to the practical criticism of this kind of politics, I offer one further characterization of it. In so doing I develop further the claim that grasping the specifically philosophical dimension of this politics is of political as well as philosophical interest. For this purpose I turn to a theme Walter Benjamin introduced into the discussion of politics in the twenties and thirties, namely, that of the aestheticization of politics. I consider ways the political trends I have described above contribute to a distinctively postmodern aestheticization of politics. This term seems apt for a number of reasons: the role in contemporary politics of the techniques of mass culture, the corresponding setting-into-motion of processes of sensibility formation, and a resulting applicability of themes from Kant's aesthetic theory to such politics. More generally, the term alludes to features of this politics that bear on its uses and reflective relation to rationality and does so in ways that place this politics in a distinctive relation to conventional forms of political criticism. The aestheticizing features of postmodern politics contribute to its successes in resisting conventional liberal and radical criticism and do so above all by virtue of the ways this politics reorganizes and disarms conflict and protest.

We can approach the idea of aestheticized politics by way of the themes of spectatorship and displaced politics, but I do not mean to restrict the application of this idea of politics to these phenomena. In the account of displaced politics and the construction of citizens as spectators, I showed that citizens are engaged in utterances over politics that affect features of their political agency, including modes of interpretation, conceptions of identity, and forms of activity. These all involve specific kinds of reasoning and reflect the operations of specialized forms of cognitive mediation that in turn often mobilize representations of knowledge or rationality. The reflective relation to rationality proper to such communicative patterns bears on the understanding and practical relation to social movements and to conflict and challenges to social stability generally. In various ways, aestheticizing politics casts citizens in passive relations to power.

Political passivity as I mean it is connected to the idea of alienated politics, to the combination of more political intervention and less explicit political involvement. Passivity does not here imply the absence of activity, since communicative engagement in these political practices implies specific kinds of agency. Rather, passivity characterizes the relation to the exercise of power that these kinds of activity yield. To speak of this passivity as having an aesthetic or aestheticizing quality is a way to characterize the way it combines a distance from the exercise of power with a reflective relation to that power. The passivity of aestheticized politics involves a sensuous apprehension, and often enjoyment, of the exercise of power. To say this apprehension is sensual is not to say that it is nonconceptual or noncognitive. But it is to characterize this apprehension in terms of Kant's separation of aesthetic judgment from theoretical and practical reasoning. Without taking over Kant's account, we can find in it suggestive themes for thinking about how a certain historical kind of political experience casts the relation to power in a form that minimizes or virtually excludes practical reasoning. To approach the point in slightly different terms: emphasizing here a sensual relation to politics or power is to speak of an apprehension that responds to matters of interpretation and choice in ways that fall below the threshold of adequate practical reasoning and adequate communicative action. Political issues are not typically matters of taste, where this means they cannot be discursively resolved, but in aestheticized politics issues are often experienced as if they were.

We can compare Kant's (1987) conception of a free play of the understanding and imagination to a contemporary play of information and fantasy. This is perhaps at best a suggestive allusion, but it points to an experience that involves modern forms of rationality without being cast in a coherent form of reasoning (that is, it does not reach the threshold of practical reason or communicative action). The equivalent of Kant's aesthetic pleasure on this comparison may or may not involve pleasure, but it contrasts with both a conventional theoretical or practical understanding and involves a symbolic construction that plays on feelings and motives tied to social issues, without yielding a practical resolve. It appeals to the interests of the citizen, an interest in power, but this is not converted into a political orientation.

Kant treats aesthetic experience as contemplative so far as it is disinterested. Aestheticized political experience is disinterested so far as coherent interests are not articulated within it, but it is not truly disinterested in the sense of being aloof from practical concerns. The equivalent here of disinterestedness is distancing from power, from actual decision making. Aestheticized experience itself creates a social space between agents and politics.

In addition to the theme of a passivity in relation to the exercise of power where this passivity is organized as sensuous apprehension, the idea of aestheticized politics also includes the theme that this passivity is a feature of agency that results from a complex of interventions on the part of expert mediations. These are mediations that concern the sensibility of citizens and so have an aesthetic function in this respect. Although this function tends to aestheticize political understanding, it does so precisely in the modern context where this involves an understanding of rationality, hence the philosophical aspect of this understanding.

Having drawn together various features of the idea of aestheticized politics, I turn to this as a relation to the division of labor, in particular to the scarcity of agency. Aestheticized politics is differentiated process, a heteroglossia of speech and of interpretation. This specific heteroglot combination is a key part of the division of labor; but so far as it is a matter of the apprehension of power, it is also a kind of practical reflection on this division of labor. Passive apprehension of the division of labor involves the apprehension of the necessity of parceling out agency and of agency exercising power, and the acceptance of some variant of this parceling. It thus involves the citizen's apprehension of the necessity that power be exercised elsewhere, by others, in relation to reified necessities, and without clear grounds of rational determination. Thus this apprehension of power also cedes a kind of absoluteness to power itself. Here we see respects in which postmodern reflection on knowledge-power is echoed in the aestheticized relation to reason in postmodern politics.

Understood in communications terms, aestheticized politics involves interactions that interpret contemporary heteroglossia by a process of massification and differential revoicing. Postmodern political language is differential in addressing a variety of audiences, but it massifies citizens by reducing significant difference and in offering rearticulations of differential experience. This reconstructed or solicited heteroglossia avoids the conflict and identification of power issues that a radical response to the division of labor on the part of social movements brings out. So the reconstituted differentiation represents a solicited experience of the division of labor. It is part of the aestheticized relation to the power relations and political operations proper to the division of labor.

The aestheticized citizen experiences a relation to power as reified in the necessities enshrined in the cognition of experts and in the differentiation of agency to which this contributes. The distance from politics/power is experienced in part by way of the acceptance of these reifications. They set the terms in which specific interpretations possess their aestheticized political meaning.

If we can speak of an aestheticized relation to politics by way of postmodern politics of communication, perhaps we can treat this relation to power as being at the same time a relation to politically charged language. I have noted that the organization of linguistic powers and positions is an important aspect of power. This includes power over language itself so far as experts who mediate aspects of communication, including semantic potentials, operate on linguistic possibilities and options. Aestheticized politics involves specific disposition to linguistic process and possibility. It involves a specific management of linguistic possibility and a corresponding relation to historicity.

With the theme of aestheticized politics, we identify a way the paradox of modern politics is experienced politically. This is a kind of alienating relation to alienated politics, a kind of adjustment to a postmodern relation to power. Grasping the philosophical aspect of this politics is important politically because the understanding and organization of judgment is itself a political issue. In certain respects, the reorganization of knowledge-politics in recent years has brought with it a characteristic form of social understanding.

To speak of a function of the aestheticizing qualities of postmodern politics is not to imply a functionalist approach to politics. Nor does identifying here a function of absorbing conflict and stabilizing protest imply the achievement of a kind of manipulative stabilization on the part of this politics. But this idea does provide a way to think of the problem of closing off criticism and undermining protest. To see how this approach avoids a reduction of political agency to a point that would exclude democratic criticism or the prospects of a democratic politics, let me briefly draw a contrast with an idea of Herbert Marcuse's.

Aside from proposing a way of thinking about what is often posed as the question of the role of the media in politics, the conception of aestheticized politics offers an approach to the phenomena Marcuse (1964) conceived with his account of one-dimensionality. Following Horkheimer and Adorno (1972), Marcuse was interested in the diffusion of conflict potential in the face of manifest relations of domination and material inequality. The one-dimensionality thesis employed the reliance of first-generation Critical Theorists on claims about the political and cultural force of instrumental reason. The present claims about aestheticized politics are indebted to these arguments, so it is not a matter here of pretending to have devised an alternative to them. What the account of aestheticized politics may provide, however, is a conception that is more consistently social in thinking about the processes by which conflict is defused, retains a relation to conceptions of rationality as functioning in this process without collapsing the form of a kind of reason to the social content of a process, and maintains a more open-ended relation to possibilities of politics. Power is here conceived more consistently in terms of social relations. The theme of conflict and criticism continues to pose difficult questions, however.

Problems for Critics

The need for a politically minded alternative to the one-dimensionality thesis is not just an internally generated problem following from the claims I have been making about postmodern politics. It is a reflective problem attached to the difficulty encountered by contemporary social criticism and perhaps most pointedly summarized in the "end of history" thesis that has been argued following the demise of Communism (a debate responding in part to writings of Fukuyama [1992]). The issue concerns the range of meaningful historical alternatives to be considered by contemporary political debate. For the "end of history" position, like that of the "end of ideology" before it, debate should now confine itself to rather local and specific issues, since more general questions about social organization are moot.

Obviously, the historical assumptions of my argument are very much at odds with this view. The thesis of aestheticized politics is one approach to some of the reasons for the surface plausibility of arguments for a narrowed range of alternatives. It offers an account of the political environment within which democratic critics must proceed and to which they must find effective ways to respond. As a kind of transitional discussion that takes us to themes of democratic criticism, I want here to take up the issue of criticism and to discuss why, in the contemporary setting, criticism is so often unsuccessful, so often short-circuited by the culture within which it operates.

First let us consider what is at issue in the question of criticism. In part this has to do with the fate of challenges to specific policies, and in part it has to do with the fate of political trends at odds with the status quo. It also has to do with the quality of debate within a public and the extent to which the aims of communicative action are accommodated and cultivated. Criticism, then, is not only a matter of the success of the opposition but has to do with the articulation and interaction of a variety of voices within highly differentiated societies.

In this light, we can understand the thesis of the aestheticization of politics, and my claims about postmodern politics more generally, as ways of thinking about a politics that undermines criticism. We should be able to see how critics are undermined through the operations of this kind of politics. If trends in contemporary politics possess the postmodern characteristics I have been describing, then one would expect difficulties for critics. We can refer to ways aestheticizing politics undercuts criticism both as a way of emphasizing aspects of this kind of politics and as anticipating issues for democratic reflection and politics.

To say aestheticizing politics works on agency is not to say that it manipulates or controls agency even if it typically employs strategic forms of action. While the organizing aim of such interventions may be manipulative control, they respond to crisis situations marked by conflict and are themselves partners in conflict. Therefore the issue is not whether criticism disappears but how successful it is or can be under circumstances altered by postmodernist interventions. Since these interventions, by working on features of agency, affect the terms in which political situations are organized, we can expect that the issue for critics will not just be a matter of specific disputes or issues. That is, critics come up against the qualities of postmodern politics as well as specific policies pursued in a postmodern way.

To see the nature of the difficulty, we can refer to various features of political situations as transformed by postmodern practice. I have touched in particular on general properties of postmodern political language and the fate of modern political metaphysics, especially the subject and the framework for coherent and stable strategic action. By referring to examples I have used above, we can discuss some of the problems critics face when confronting postmodern politics. These problems arise when it comes to challenges to specific policies. During the eighties, U.S. administrations pursued policies in Central America that were widely criticized on moral and strategic grounds and that, by many standards, have been discredited in retrospect. There was considerable congressional opposition and a notable lack of public enthusiasm for these policies. They occurred in the wake of the U.S. defeat in Vietnam, in the context of the intensified rivalry with the Soviet Union and the political success of conservatism on the domestic scene. Despite considerable criticism and public opposition, three administrations pursued policies of intervention that were minimally affected by these challenges.

Consider typical patterns of criticism from within the liberal camp. Critics would question the morality of policies, their effectiveness regarding anti-Communist goals, the relevance of anti-Communist rhetoric, the relation of these conflicts to Cold War rivalry, the impact on domestic political life (e.g., uses of secrecy, public misrepresentation, lying to Congress). Critics would also note the contradictions in administration statements regarding various of these factors, for example, changing justifications for intervention, representations of actions by client armies, and projections of successful outcomes.

As a narrow matter of logic, many of these criticisms were unanswerable (and, to a large degree, they were unanswered). As I have noted, there were indeed inconsistencies within policy, between policy and stated moral and political principles, between statements of policy, and so on. The relevance to the Cold War was seriously in doubt, the contribution to the well-being of these countries dubious, and so on. But, as I have also noted, these patterns fit into a specific postmodern quality of politics that for the most part went unaddressed by critics. My first aim is to see why these critics would likely fail.

Following my analysis of postmodern politics, we can suggest that one source of the ineffectiveness of critics was their inability adequately to confront the self-referential qualities of postmodern political language. Since language was being strategically deployed to elicit specific effects, challenging it on the grounds of misrepresentation or inconsistency would be to the point only if this affected the outcome of that use of language. The frequently made point that refutations of misrepresentations always come too late reflects one feature of the workings of postmodern political language. Refutation of administration claims about a specific event are politically irrelevant when public/media attention has shifted its inconstant focus.

Critics would question the consistency of administration statements about its policy aims. As I have noted, these shifted between a variety of quite different and sometimes contradictory goals (U.S. strategic interests, economic interests of the region, Cold War influence, Communism, etc.). Apart from the fact that critics here maintain the representational assumption about language and assume that utterances about aims are to be measured by their plausibility as the presentation of actual or acceptable aims, critics are in such cases assuming that action has or could have in this setting a stable and coherent strategic organization. Similarly, they are assuming that action does or could have a stable agent-centered standpoint (e.g., that of the nation, the government, or the administration).

Both assumptions, of course, have been questioned in the account given above. If postmodern politics is a contextually responsive matter of crisis management, then the idea of abiding aims as regulating policy must be replaced by a conception of a more unstable and variable set of goal orientations and strategic standpoints. Similarly, if we see politics as a heteroglot field in which structural conditions militate against stable subjects, we need to treat such representations as idealizations that, depending on circumstances, may be quite imaginary and counter to the facts.

It is important to see that these points do not only hold for conventional liberal or conservative critics. Similar arguments can be made about radical critics who are unwilling to accept many liberal premises.

For such critics, standards of morality might be relevant in making public appeals, but are not assumed as affecting policy makers. Similarly, administration claims about the economic or political development of Central America were not taken at face value. But, like liberal critics, many radicals retained the framework of modern political metaphysics when developing their analyses at the structural level. Thus, explanatory appeal might be made to economic interests or U.S. imperial interests. And foreign policy language was challenged for its misrepresentations, for the manipulations and secrecy it involved. Thus, a representational notion of language prevailed along with a conception of stable political subjects and coherent, if veiled, strategic frameworks.

How can we summarize what is wrong with the approaches of these critics? On the one hand, they are not responding to the way language functions in postmodern politics. In saying that they retain a representational conception of language along with other features of liberal political metaphysics, I am indicating how they fail to recognize the rules by which the new political game is being played. This is not to imply that they should adopt the ironies and cynicism of postmodern politics. In any case, it is a game they cannot win, since the rules favor a conservative outcome, that is, reproduce forms of political action and response that make genuine challenges to policies unworkable.

To imply that critics must challenge the postmodern game is in part to avoid the impression that critics fail because they do not act as though the language of politics is self-enclosed. If their acceptance of liberal metaphysics reveals a mistaken sense of historical conditions, their attempt to measure claims by appeal to objective conditions fails not only because it mistakes the way postmodern language works but also because it works with anachronistic terms for grasping objective structural conditions.

I have earlier treated the postmodern one-sided concentration on the self-referential properties of language as a kind of linguistic idealism. Rejection of the terms of modern political metaphysics has limited my own resources for explaining the course of postmodern politics to admittedly general reference to structural change, conflicts in which movements play an important role, and the increasingly problematic standing of the division of labor. With these references I am at least making clear that my account of postmodern politics, and so of the problems facing critics, does not follow that idealism and does not exclude structural analysis that refers to production, political organization, the preconditions of culture, and so on. These are themes to which I return in the discussion of democratic criticism.

My discussion points to two general considerations. First, it is not only specific outcomes that are at issue, but qualities of politics as such. Both from the standpoint of the aim of advancing the fortunes of specific critical voices and from the more general standpoint of advancing a democratic heteroglossia, the concern of critics must be to counteract features of postmodern politics as such. Second, this cannot be a matter of trying to revive the kind of political discourse with which postmodern practice breaks. Postmodern approaches represent, by hypothesis, an avoidance of adequate response to structural changes that make the classic politics of liberal knowledge-politics no longer viable. Thus the weakness of a politics working from liberal metaphysical assumptions is not only a matter of the tactics of the present disposition of power. It is also a matter of changing conditions to which these tactics are one kind of response.

The problem of criticism is thus inseparable from the problem of democratic politics. In terms of the argument so far developed, one can attach more specific content to this idea: democracy implies the democratic articulation of voices, a democratic heteroglossia, including in the short run the articulation of movements and interests that have suffered the reworkings of aestheticized communication. This implies a politics of language, agency, and political process that would counteract the force of postmodern practices.

At the risk of making this schematic pronouncement even more abstract, let me pose the issue in terms of the philosophical aspect of postmodern politics. My claim has been that, as a kind of continuation of modern knowledge-politics, postmodern politics involves a reflective relation to power and reason. If the nature of the response postmodernism provides to structural change is to be made explicit, and to be made a practical issue, this must be by way of a challenge to the reflective relation this politics establishes to historically acquired powers. Thus, bringing out the philosophical aspect of postmodernism and contesting it democratically is part of the task of democratic criticism, one of the conditions of its potential effectiveness.

In view of my argument for philosophical reflection understood as the critique of the division of labor, this appeal to a political criticism of postmodernism that incorporates a philosophical dimension amounts to linking this issue of criticism to the themes of the division of labor and the challenge to scarcity.

Part Four

Democratic Philosophy

In these final chapters I turn directly to the idea of democratic philosophy. In doing so, I summarize and argue for the conception of philosophy that I have been developing throughout this study. In Part Two, I presented a conception of philosophical practice in historical and social terms appropriate to the critique of the division of labor. In Part Three, I used this conception to discuss postmodern trends in philosophy and politics. My first aim in that chapter was to challenge an important contemporary opposition to philosophical reflection, one that builds on a sense of the need to consider the problem of thinking about reason in the light of the intellectual problems with modern philosophy and the social legacy of intellectual specialists. My other aim in Part Three was to illustrate philosophical criticism proper to the critique of the division of labor by discussing features of postmodern politics. When we see the links between postmodern philosophy and the political world to which it contributes, we see how reflection on rationality in social terms can contribute to political understanding.

This argument about postmodern politics, which includes argument about intellectual mediation within this politics, is one aspect of democratic philosophical criticism. Viewed as a social initiative, it aspires to contribute to a democratic intellectual mediation. In Part Four, I discuss more directly the idea of democratic philosophical mediation. One issue concerns what such mediation consists of. Another concerns its specifically philosophical character, including the kind of reflection on rationality it provides. Here we must confront normative issues that I have for the most part sidestepped in the discussion to this point.

The intellectual framework I have offered for thinking about and engaging in philosophical criticism is that of the critique of the division of labor. Historical, narrative, and reconstructive, this critique is more of an "approach" than a theory. While it involves systematically conceived claims and proposes a sweeping view of history and contemporary society, it does not follow traditional aims or standards of philosophical theory. Partly this reflects the historical and empirical nature of much of its argumentation. Partly it follows from treating this framework as a basis for ongoing questioning and research rather than for offering ambitious systematic claims. Another way this "approach" differs from traditional theory follows from its being conceived as mediation, as practical as well as conceptual.

Understood as mediation, democratic philosophy's conceptual content must be placed in practical or communicative relations. This requirement holds for thinking about how democratic philosophy can contribute to democratic politics as well as for how it must reflect on its own rationality. This reflection on democratic philosophical rationality is inseparable from the practical engagements such philosophy might undertake.

So, having explored some of the issues proper to the conceptual concerns of democratic philosophy, I now turn to the problem of relating these concerns to this philosophy's own social orientation. As critique of the division of labor, it is concerned with understanding power relations whose democratic overcoming remains its normative point of reference. I discuss some of the intellectual and practical issues proper to sustaining this perspective. By making plausible the historical relevance of the critique of the division of labor, I hope to develop a sense of the social mediations in which democratic philosophy is involved. These discussions contribute to such justification as this philosophical perspective can receive. Following these considerations I discuss the prospects of democratic philosophy today.

Chapter **9**

Historical Conditions for the Critique of the Division of Labor

I first return to the theme of the historical conditions for this kind of democratic philosophy and for democratic politics more generally. This includes concern about the objective possibilities I am citing when arguing from a counterfactual critical standpoint. In particular this has to do with the possibility of overcoming scarcity. So the first objective is to explain why a politics of agency articulated to relations of scarcity can be challenged from the standpoint of a politics of agency that rejects appeals to scarcity and seeks a democratic politics of agency. In clarifying the respects in which this seems a plausible historical project, I clarify some of its features.

My strategy is to explore the relation between the themes of scarcity and growth so as to argue that overcoming scarcity becomes plausible in important respects if putting an end to imperatives to growth is possible. Scarcity, I have shown, sets boundaries to politics. The democratic critique of the division of labor seeks to extend and transform the way we think about politics. Overcoming scarcity involves replacing imperatives of growth with politics regarding production and consumption. This extension of politics directly challenges the scarcity of agency reproduced by postmodern politics.

Scarcity, Growth, Necessity

To counter the charge of being unrealistically utopian, the project of overcoming the division of labor has to confront reasons for thinking that the division of labor is unavoidable. I have already tried to make clear that overcoming the division of labor as I mean it does not mean the elimination of the differentiation and specialization of tasks, nor does it imply the feasibility or even desirability of direct or participatory democracy, at least as a sweeping principle of political life. Rather, overcoming the division of labor means overcoming scarcity of agency, which is to say, overcoming the respects in which specialization serves the reproduction of relations of domination and inequality. The positive program related to this negative formulation is developed to some extent later in this chapter. The aim now is to explore the idea of overcoming scarcity as this bears on general considerations regarding the necessity of the division of labor.

In addressing scarcity, I mean to consider the strongest argument against the feasibility of overcoming the division of labor. Although I am speaking of scarcity in a way that departs from common usage, the distinction I draw between scarcity and shortage should allow us to confront the strengths of this objection to the democratic program I have in mind. Scarcity figures as a justification for the division of labor, but I have claimed that it is in fact its operative principle. That is, the division of labor is a differentiation, specialization, and coordination whose organization of power and inequality makes elements of agency scarce and makes the reflective orientation to the historical formation of agency itself scarce. This reflective orientation is inherently political, though in contemporary conditions the intellectual mediations in which it takes place often lack an explicit character.

As I am using it, the term "scarcity" does not refer simply to there being fewer goods than people want. For this apparently permanent human condition of wants outstripping supplies, I am using the term "shortage." Scarcity is more specific, and refers to shortages when these figure in the understanding and organization of inequality and power relations. Scarcity may not be inevitable, though shortage is. That is, although both are historically shaped and experienced, it may be that, under certain conditions, regimes of scarcity can be overcome and shortage be confronted in an egalitarian and democratic basis.

As I have repeatedly noted, scarcity is not just a matter of things, but bears on the social formation of agency and so on the division of labor.

It is in this regard that we can speak of scarcity as the operative principle of the division of labor. And when we think of the division of labor as having to do with social activity as a whole, we have a basis for speaking, as I have, of the scarcity of politics. Further, the argument about scarcity is not just that it is constitutive of the division of labor but also that it is historical. Its forms evolve, with the specific evolution of modern and postmodern intellectual practices being important features of this evolution for contemporary democratic reflection and politics. It is also historical in the sense that its necessity can be brought into question. The distinction between scarcity and shortage is a practical concern for democracy. Making the politics of agency explicit, that is, making these issues of power an explicit theme of contemporary social discussion, includes considering whether scarcity can be replaced by shortage. This amounts to the question whether the specializations and lacks proper to the differentiation of activity can be regulated democratically.

For considering how we can argue against the necessity of scarcity, I turn to a closely related idea that figures in discussions of scarcity and what it requires of society. This is the idea of growth. Though extremely abstract, it is precisely as a rather indeterminate abstraction that it figures in political debate. Of course it has a very specific social embodiment so far as it refers to the expansion of market activity. But the importance of growth as a political idea lies partly in the fact that it is not only a matter of economics.

First let us consider growth as a way of justifying, even interpreting, scarcity. Growth is typically presented as the remedy to scarcity: through growth we will overcome poverty, improve opportunities, and diminish inequality. The idea of overcoming scarcity through growth often figures in claims about the relation between market economies and prospects of democracy, both in the formerly Communist countries and the so-called Third World. In the setting of the economic stagnation of recent years, growth has been the buzzword of recovery and well-being. Despite rhetoric about an "age of limits," the need for growth as the solution to existing ills seems almost universally accepted within public discourse. Yet in other respects not only the means for achieving growth but the desirability, even acceptability, of growth has arisen as a repeated theme in political discussion. For good reason, the specter of destructive growth haunts these political discussions.

The uneasiness about growth that may be detected in contemporary politics may follow from the closeness of the relation between it and scarcity. As the proposed remedy to scarcity, growth figures indirectly in making existing scarcity acceptable. Appeals to growth acknowledge that something is wrong about existing scarcities. If growth were impossible or undesirable, then some other response to the inequities of the regime of scarcity could justifiably be demanded. Further, if growth tends to justify scarcity, it also provides an interpretation for it, namely, as a matter of there not being enough. The appeal to growth is the interpretation of scarcity as being in essence a matter of shortage. So we can speak of the idea of growth as providing a representation of scarcity as remediable shortage.

Or we might say that orientations to growth provide us with ways of living out the fact of the scarcity that characterizes our world. I want to press for so close a relation between growth and scarcity in part because I argue against the necessity of scarcity by citing arguments against the necessity and desirability of growth. Another reason is that with the idea of growth, particularly in its abstract and often equivocal usages and in its multiple applications, we find a distinctively modern orientation whose evolution is directly bound up with the postmodern features of contemporary politics I have already discussed. Growth is a way of thinking about historicity. The aims of growth, the relation of growth to the actual course of experience, and the ability to orient ourselves to issues of growth in a conscious and effective manner all bear directly on the Enlightenment legacy and the role of intellectual practices.

Let me then say a bit more about how I understand growth for purposes of this discussion. First, in the modern setting growth does not figure so much as a value as it does as a structural imperative. It is for this reason that we can speak of the respects in which growth has become problematic as being ones that raise issues of structural change. To speak of growth as a structural or objective imperative is in part to acknowledge respects in which the need for growth is bound to modern institutions, especially the market. It is also to note that an orientation to growth is one factor in our experience of modern social objectivity. Speaking of growth as a way scarcity is lived out, a way scarcity appears, can be defended by reference to the way requirements of growth organize the evolution of activity, indeed of the scarcities proper to the division of labor. Growth mandates innovations, transformations of work, changes in wage structure, individual and social opportunities, and so on.

In discussing growth as institutionally rooted, we can refer to the quantitative side of this orientation. It is worth emphasizing the obvious here, since it is necessary to make clear that an orientation to growth is not to be equated with an orientation to change. And growth is by no means the only way to think of progressive change. An orientation to growth involves ongoing expansion, an idea that receives some coherent application in the case of economic value. Whatever else it can mean, in this setting growth means more exchanges, more realized value.

The second point I want to emphasize about growth is that its economic dimension is only one facet of its role in modern and postmodern experience. I have already remarked on the abstractness of the idea and on its multiple uses. Growth figures awkwardly in the context of art, yet the modern period has witnessed a kind of artistic mimicry of economic expansion with its cult of novelty. In science and technology, the quantitative model is more apt: more knowledge, more applications, more powers. Growth as I understand it is not to be equated with development, but in the modern setting, the issues of social and individual development, so crucial to questions of identity and fulfillment, are haunted by quantitative ideals. Further, an orientation to growth affects political culture by reducing the scope for conscious decision making. The imperative of growth establishes the framework within which reactive initiatives are to be taken.

Regarded as a form of appearance of the various scarcities organized by the division of labor, the growth imperative functions as a depoliticizing feature of social understanding. Despite the historical connection between modern commitments to growth and arguments for historical progress, the growth imperative survives postmodern criticism and figures as a given within postmodern politics.

A critique of growth, then, is inherent in the project of overcoming the division of labor. Before I turn to arguments against growth, let me emphasize that what is at issue is a relation to politics, not the existence of shortage. The critique of growth contributes to the critique of scarcity. Rejecting the necessity of growth and so of scarcity is not a matter of declaring we live in an age of universal abundance. There can be little doubt that an increase of goods is desirable for much of the world's population. It would be obscene to think otherwise given the hunger, disease, and inadequate housing experienced by many of the world's people today. Nor would rejecting growth simply be a matter of asserting that meeting these needs requires redistribution of exist-ing goods rather than more production. That would be at best an oversimplification of the issue, since it neglects issues of forms of production, participation, forms of investment, and so on. Another reason why speaking of redistribution is misleading is that it suggests that this is a technical or strictly economic issue to be managed by the appropriate politics. But from the standpoint of my argument, the core issue is politics itself.

Arguments Against Growth

I take up two kinds of arguments against growth. The first has to do with a theme I have just anticipated. It concerns the respects in which growth is ideological, even illusory. That is, if we take growth to be the promise of overcoming scarcity yet interpret growth as the way scarcity appears politically, then we see it as containing a contradiction. The second argument takes what may seem the opposite tack, by address-ing the all too real and destructive qualities of growth. If it fails as the resolution of scarcity, it nonetheless unleashes processes of material transformation that have become threatening to civilized existence. I turn to this ecological argument after saying a bit more about the paradoxes of efforts to "grow out of scarcity."

The first argument against growth points to the respects in which actual growth reproduces old scarcities and creates new ones. Marx's critique of capitalist growth, itself indebted to classical political economy as well as to Hegel's own arguments about the "system of needs," remains paradigmatic in this regard. With his account of the relations of production, Marx (1976, chap. 15) shows how capitalist expansion repro-duces class relations. In contemporary terms the argument can be made by referring to the comparative inequities that characterize even the expansion of the industrially advanced societies and the absolute impov-erishment that has resulted on a world scale (for an overview, see Frank 1980). A detailed discussion could explore the new kinds of inequities that characterize the most recent phase of economic development, in which various forms of internationalization coincide with growing un-employment and impoverishment in even the most wealthy societies (Frank 1980, chap. 2).

Marx's argument does not consider forms of state intervention and redistribution devised in the twentieth century, but though these may have contributed to the frustration of his political expectations, they do not seem to have refuted his structural economic projections so far as inequality is concerned. In any case, from the standpoint of the present argument about scarcity, economic inequality is only one factor to be considered. Modern growth has reproduced scarcity in the other senses I have discussed as well. It continues to transform the nature of work and participation in it and so continues to create new forms of specialization and fragmentation. Beyond the sphere of production, growth has created new differentiations of political and cultural activity, some of which have been mentioned in the discussion of postmodern politics. Of particular relevance to my considerations are the ways recent forms of growth have resulted in covert and displaced politics. Expansion of the culture industry, social services, and the professions have brought reflective action upon agency into the division of labor itself.

From the standpoint of my argument, this illustrates how contemporary growth figures within the evolution of scarce agency as it bears directly on politics. In particular, it contributes to a scarcity of political agency even as it increases the extent of political interventions.

The second argument against growth is that growth is intolerable because of its ecological consequences. The problems are by now familiar: the increasing expense and ultimate exhaustion of resources (especially fuels), the damage to health and the ecosystem caused by pollution, the destruction of biosystems, and the weakening of the gene pools relevant to agriculture all point to the impossibility of maintaining growth along lines followed during the industrial era. Such growth cannot continue in the wealthy industrialized countries, and it cannot be emulated in the poorer countries, in which the world's majority lives (Brown et al. 1992, 57–64).

To be sure, this argument uses an imprecise sense of growth. It is conceptually possible that capitalist economic growth could coincide with an end to ecological devastation, but there is little evidence that this is a possibility that in fact can or will be pursued. And if existing economic institutions cannot be reformed to break with destructive growth, this does not show that alternatives are available. Nor does it show that such possibilities as might be possible would or could abolish scarcity.

Yet if my claim about the closeness of the relation between the growth imperative and scarcity is sound, a struggle against growth would have to be also a struggle against scarcity, since it would have to address the power relations and challenge the interests that are advanced through a system oriented to growth, and this would involve questioning the inequities and dominations reproduced through relations of scarcity. I am in no position here to consider the possibility of such a challenge. More to the point in my present concern to support the possibility of doing away with growth and so the possibility of doing away with scarcity is to cite arguments that suggest that growth in certain relevant respects is dispensable.

In moving, then, from arguments against accepting the growth imperative, I turn to arguments for the possibility of living without growth. I frame this question narrowly, treating growth here as an institutional commitment to the ongoing expansion of the production of goods. What can be said for denying that such an expansion is necessary? Let me put the issue in terms of the distinction between scarcity and shortage. Why think that we are in a position to confront shortage without resorting to systematic domination and inequality? To confront the issue narrowly is to consider why we might think that material conditions exist (or are in sight) such that growth, considered as the form of appearance of the power relations of scarcity, can be dispensed with. Since this is a question of doing away with the power relations of scarcity and the division of labor, it is also the question of the existence of the material conditions for democracy in the sense in which I have been speaking of it in this study. To focus on the material side of the argument is to set aside for a moment political and cultural issues that cannot in fact be set aside for long.

Now I am returning to a point mentioned earlier in discussing structural change as it bears on labor, which has been up to the present the most important social activity for most individuals in the modern period. By referring to the diminished role of material production in the modern economy (some figures show it occupies only a fifth of those employed),[1] to the increasing level of unemployment and underemployment, to the extensive presence of waste production (including most notably objects that one hopes are never used—military armaments), and to the promotion of buying and using up things in the consumerist economy, we indicate reasons for believing that advanced industrial societies have reached the threshold of quite new material possibilities. While this raises all sorts of possibilities for the cultivation and use of what we now call "free time," including the possibility of new kinds of politics, the immediate point is that these developments suggest that there may be little need for expansion when it comes to the quantitative production of things. To suggest that more goods are not required does not imply that the quality and distribution of those that are presently produced would not require massive transformation for democratic purposes (Gorz 1980).

On this argument, growth viewed as the requirement for a certain necessary minimum well-being for all members of society is no longer defensible on grounds of material shortage. To summarize the argument differently, we can say that it points to an enormous surplus productive capacity whose disuse and misuse suggest a superabundance of material goods. This claim assumes that is it is possible to establish an account of real social needs such that much of what passes for productive labor is in fact unnecessary and would be dispensed with under democratic conditions. It assumes that there is some rational limit to consumption demands such that if our productive capacity were turned to full use, and if all individuals were provided the full extent of their consumption needs, there would still be excess productive capacity. As this formulation suggests, the point of the argument goes beyond asserting that further productive growth is unnecessary to saying that existing productivity is sufficient not just to eliminate the need for more labor but to reduce the amount of labor time currently expended. In fact, such a reduction is needed to pursue the kind of democratic practices I discuss below.

Let me point to two kinds of issues this argument for the possibility of eliminating growth must face. First, even if this general line of argument is sound, it does not show that such an end to growth would be adequate to put an end to scarcity in the sense required for a democratic overcoming of the division of labor. The second has to do with how this argument is made, and specifically with the claims it makes about real needs.

Regarding the first issue, recall that eliminating scarcity means establishing democratically manageable shortage. The claim that establishing an adequate level of material well-being requires less labor than is currently expended does not deny that shortages would persist under these hypothetical conditions. We must assume that there would be shortages in opportunities (within work or within leisure, not everyone could do what they wanted when they wanted) and in goods (whether matters of social or private consumption). And, obviously, the fact that labor would still be needed implies that besides not always being able to do what they want, there would be circumstances in which individuals would have to do what they did not particularly want to do (Green 1985). There is no a priori guarantee that these shortages are not such as to elicit conflicts that can only be resolved by the imposition of scarcity, that is, the management of shortage through relations of domination and inequality. In these truly postmodern conditions, scarcity would no longer be organized by growth.

Rather than attempt the complex and somewhat speculative task of exploring the plausibility of a democratic response to this question, we should consider the importance within it of the second issue about ending growth cited above. The extent and implications of the shortages that would be experienced under these hypothetical conditions would turn on the quality and force of the needs by which they would be defined. Already in postulating a notion of minimal well-being for which sufficient productivity presently exists, we have tacitly distinguished between qualities of needs. To speak of wasteful or unnecessary production is to posit an idea of appropriate consumption.

While there are complex psychological, sociological, and cultural issues raised in distinguishing between needs, let us consider only the political side of the question of needs that are socially legitimate. The question is not so much whether it is possible in principle to distinguish "true" from "false" needs.[2] Such distinctions are common in all effective cultures of morality and, more generally, are found where virtues and dispositions are a matter of social concern. Rather, the question is how to think about these distinctions in a way appropriate to contemporary democratic politics. Some issues of legitimate needs are already a matter of social debate, for example, regarding weapons production and environmental regulation. Others presently occupy an uneasy place in public discourse: the effect of television on children, the connections between pornography and violence against women, and so on. Some are issues about the desirable workings of institutions, others about the felt needs of individuals.

Although I touch further on these themes in the next chapter and in discussing democratic mediation, I do not go very far with them. The general point that I want to urge as part of the claim that these are political issues is that specific questions of needs can become matters of public debate. To put the point differently, the only way a relation to needs can be consistent with democracy is if conflicts over needs are themselves resolved by democratic process. This injects into the discussion the specter of two kinds of circularity: one regarding the conception of a need consistent with democracy (i.e., it is consistent if confirmed by democratic process) and one regarding the historical process of achieving a culture of needs that has overcome scarcity (i.e., a democratic process is required to establish the standards democratic evolution must attain). Neither of these circles is vicious in the sense that it undermines the claims of democratic reflection as I am pursuing it here, but both represent serious conceptual and political problems.

Politics "After Growth"?

So far I have discussed reasons for thinking that overcoming the division of labor is a thinkable historical project. Such an overcoming is not presented simply as a conceptual possibility but as a way of reading actual historical trends, and thus is introduced as a plausible critical perspective on such trends. The issue of true and false needs raises basic questions for the resulting kind of democratic perspective. It also brings us back to themes taken up in the discussion of postmodern politics. By returning to the issue of aestheticized politics, I bring the kinds of issues I have just been discussing into connection with the more historical orientation of the earlier account of contemporary politics. In this way we can perhaps see some connections between these issues and actual political tendencies, in particular those represented by contemporary social movements.

I characterized postmodern politics as aestheticized politics, as a kind of relation to power on the part of citizens in which the scarcity of agency is reasserted. In this argument I noted how aestheticized politics makes citizens into spectators and clients and undercuts an active political relation to questions of power while intensifying covertly political activity on agency. The term "aestheticized politics" has a twofold force, concerning the aesthetic relation to politics (spectatorship, but also the entry of aesthetic appeals into political life, e.g., political spectacles like Desert Storm and mass culture techniques in advancing political programs and politicians) and the active targeting of the sensibility, the interpretive and practical makeup, of citizens.

With earlier claims about recent social movements, I have been arguing that not only are the division of labor and scarce agency in principle contestable, but that, in important respects, they have become contested. Scarcity and the division of labor have been made problematic in the absence of a sustained and explicit politics addressing the division of labor. Now I want to argue that, although tentative and ambiguous, these contributions to a democratic politics can be seen as asserting an alternative to aestheticized politics.

First, the division of labor has become an issue for feminist, ecological, and minority movements. They see the distribution of social skills and decision making as matters that should become the focus of political debate. Second, each movement raises qualitative issues about agency: assumptions about capacities and their distribution, about perceived needs and ideal goals, and about the formation of individual and collective identities. Third, these movements frequently challenge the exercise of power through conventional forms of expertise, whether in the use of scientific evidence or even the presuppositions of specific theories or in the development and application of technologies. They have, for example, identified ways in which scientism and objectivism obscure debatable questions of social power.

In transforming aspects of the modern division of labor into matters of political discourse, social movements may be seen as contributing to the elements of a political culture quite different from that of liberalism, at least as it has been depicted here. The various political challenges I have reviewed represent a challenge to knowledge-politics and suggest the possibility of a different construction of modern rationality. In so doing, they show how challenges to the division of labor can promote a political culture that does not make the structural presuppositions earlier attributed to liberalism. For example, in disputing gender-coded forms of agency, feminists have made the social reproduction of power relations in the differentiation of tasks explicit and have questioned the various mystifications of technocratic and economistic analysis and policy. In these ways they have indicated how economic, political, and cultural issues are now inseparable. Simultaneously, they have questioned economic growth as an unquestioned social aim and have made the definition of labor itself an issue. With the rethinking of historical experience, they have contributed to various notions of collective identity that deprive nationality of its central importance. Similar claims can be made for the politics of minorities, ecology, gay rights, and so on.

One cannot confidently make sweeping historical or political claims about the significance of these developments. But they do indicate ways in which contemporary politics addresses issues about the division of labor and does so in ways that posit quite different structural possibilities than those taken for granted by liberalism. To say that they do this while making the division of labor a political question is also to say that in making the division of labor a political question they are challenging the dominance of knowledge-politics characteristic of liberalism and extended by postmodern practice.

In various respects, then, the critique of the division of labor can claim to respond to historical conditions and possibilities. There are reasons to think material conditions exist for challenging modern forms of scarcity organized as growth, and in various ways these challenges are being made. The politicization of agency raised by the challenges of movements exists in a reciprocal relation to conservative, postmodern action on agency, and both represent ways the liberal metaphysics of agency have been superseded by politics. Despite the democratic impulses of some social movements, this is a politics that is not sufficiently explicit nor sufficiently understood from the standpoint of democratic needs and possibilities.

These are the historical terms in which we can return now to the theme of democratic intellectual mediation, particularly as this involves philosophical activity.

Chapter **10**

Democratic
Philosophical
Mediation

Chapter 9 provided an argument for thinking we stand at a historical moment in which challenging the division of labor is a viable project. In this chapter, I discuss ways a democratically conceived philosophy can contribute to this challenge. In part this is a matter of clarifying the kind of mediations within which the arguments made to this point might be thought to take place. More generally, it is a matter of specifying types of activity through which philosophers can contribute to greater democracy.

Though I refer to other kinds of intellectual mediation, the main concern here is to concentrate on specifically philosophical practice. Given philosophy's role in developing the understanding of rational capacities in general and expertise in particular, the problem of such mediation is precisely that of contributing to a democratic culture and polity in which reflection on rationality does not function, as in the epistemological culture of modern knowledge-politics, by licensing authoritative voices and genres but instead contributes to processes of political understanding and decision that are democratic in the positive sense of being consistent with egalitarian and popular power as well as in the negative sense of blocking the historical forms of domination identified by movements.

Democratic philosophical mediation must thus contribute to a democratic political culture. I say more about the idea of such a culture after developing the theme of democratic criticism, since such a culture seems to be the likely outcome of a twofold process, one negative and the other constructive. Though internally related, it is possible to draw some distinctions to bring out what is at issue in both. So first I consider the theme of democratic philosophy as criticism and then turn to its role in the formation of a postliberal democratic political culture.

Democratic Philosophical Criticism

Challenging Knowledge-Power

What I mean by democratic philosophical criticism is illustrated by many of the arguments developed in my earlier discussions. In particular, this is philosophical reflection that draws on the narrative perspective of the critique of the division of labor to reconstruct intellectual practices in their contribution to relations of knowledge and power. I claimed Marx provides such criticism in his treatment of political economy, and I suggested ways that modern epistemological philosophy could be subjected to similar criticism. The discussions of postmodern thought and politics have had the same general objective. Such criticism is specifically philosophical by providing reflection on reason as embodied in social activity. I need to say more about how it this is a philosophical *practice* and how it has a specifically philosophical function.

Let me start with respects in which this criticism is philosophical. It maintains continuity with the philosophical tradition by offering reflection on rational validity claims. But it departs from the tradition by couching these reflections in social terms. In considering aspects of what I have called embodied reason, that is, by thinking of reason in terms of social practices and in particular as intellectual mediation, this kind of criticism advances another traditional philosophical concern. This is the effort to confront skepticism. As I have noted, the significant skepticism today is aimed not at the reality of knowledge but rather at its universality, viewed from the standpoint of claims about knowledge-power. A philosophical aim of the critique of the division of labor is to advance a criticism of the interrelations of knowledge and power that avoids the historicist renunciation of universalistic claims for reason. Such a renunciation has been associated here with postmodernism, and I have therefore treated democratic philosophy as confronted with the twofold task of rethinking modern rationality and of providing an alternative to postmodern criticism. These tasks have a particularly close interrelation if postmodern thought turns out, as argued above, to figure within postmodern knowledge-politics.

In a moment I discuss the conception of rationality that figures in this criticism. First, let me make more explicit the kind of criticism proper to democratic philosophy. It is a challenge to the workings of knowledge-power from a democratic standpoint. Democratic criticism examines intellectual practices for respects in which power functions in them. I have reviewed several examples of this criticism: political economy as reconstructed by Marx, in which the intellectual interpretation of such theory functions in the reproduction of voices and genres proper to the practices of market capitalism; the epistemological tradition, in which we find the construction of voices and genres that assert the autonomy of experts and that are taken over in various aspects of the liberal social practice; and various dimensions of postmodernist practices, in which ironic relations to rational claims figure in the reproduction of scarce agency. Generally I have shown that democratic philosophical criticisms can provide instructive reconstructions of the intellectual practices associated with liberal political culture and its postmodernist aftermath. We can critically reconstruct the practices associated with the liberal commitment to the knowability of the world and the possibility of its being made rational through the appropriate cultivation of the modern institutions of market, constitutional state, and secular culture. And we can reconstruct the practices associated with the postmodernist relation to this confidence, a relation that includes a retreat from explicit philosophy and politics while advancing covert philosophical and political operations articulated to the same modern institutional framework.

These discussions have developed an explicit philosophical criticism aimed at social practices, but they have also treated philosophical reflection as part of the larger political culture. Criticism that is implicitly philosophical thus takes place in a context of other kinds of political argumentation. This contextual relation is understood by the fact that in the critique of the division of labor, challenges to knowledge-power do not treat power as an abstract and generalized phenomenon, but rather interpret it in terms of the various social conflicts that mark modern society. Thus, although it presupposes power relations specific to the division of labor, democratic criticism in my sense of the term concerns itself as well with a variety of power relations and operations. Accordingly, we can find implicitly philosophical criticism within the political challenges raised by social movements so far as they touch upon the validity claims of intellectual practices. Thus I have claimed that much feminist criticism contributes to what I am calling the critique of the division of labor, even if it does not target the powers specific to intellectual practices. When, for example, such criticism locates ways assumptions in science reproduce gender relations, it contributes to an account of the workings of scarcity in this context. Similarly, challenges to ways racism is reproduced in the schools provide material for thinking about this aspect of the power mediations proper to intellectual practices within the division of labor.

Criticism of this sort contributes to a philosophical reflection by challenging validity claims about rational accomplishments. It locates such claims within the genres and voices proper to various intellectual practices. In doing so, it seeks not so much to locate errors by appeal to an unproblematic rational principle. Rather, it makes an explicit issue of what counts as valid. That is, it raises a question for what is in effect philosophical debate. If it does so typically in the course of political arguments (e.g., over sexism and racism), this retains a philosophical dimension so far as it bears on the philosophical features of political culture. Of course, these validity issues can be abstracted from the political context. This I have claimed is one of the functions of philosophical mediation: to interpret and rework the understandings of rationality functioning in the social world. In political debates, the issue of social understanding is broached directly. In technical philosophical debates, the issues of social understanding are broached indirectly, though here the technical details of rationality become the explicit theme. To speak of philosophical criticism, then, is ambiguous to the extent that it can be carried out in different contexts with different degrees of explicitly philosophical elaboration. Nonetheless, the key point is that challenging knowledge power is a matter of entering a social debate over validity claims. With this point in mind we can turn to the second issue I raised about philosophical criticism, namely, how it is a practice.

I have already touched on what I take to be the central issue in thinking about democratic philosophical criticism as a practice, namely, that it functions explicitly within various contexts of social debate. But to make the point more clearly, let me recall the contrast drawn earlier with traditional theory. In rejecting the idea of purely contemplative reflection organized by the imperatives of a rationality detached from social and historical reality, I propose a contrast between the practice of democratic philosophy and that of the tradition, with its monological, authoritative voices. To say that rationality is practical and social is, from the standpoint of a communications approach, to say that it is intersubjective and dialogical. In this regard I have followed Habermas and Bakhtin in speaking of the validity claims inherent in the interactive processes proper to all utterances, including those with a philosophical dimension. For thinking of philosophy as a practice, the consequence of such a communications approach is to see reflection on validity claims as itself taking place in the making and assessing of validity claims. On this basis we can think of philosophy as a mediating practice. What distinguishes democratic philosophy is that it makes this interactive feature of its reflection on rationality explicit. Consequently it departs from traditional notions of theoretical demonstrations that proceed monologically, according to necessities available to the solitary thinker.

In this light we can distinguish between more or less purely philosophical practices, that is, practices that to a greater or lesser degree focus exclusively on reflective issues about rational validity claims. There may be a philosophical dimension to practices that have no explicit philosophical intent or self-understanding, as may be the case in various kinds of criticism advanced by social movements. It is the presence of philosophical features in various kinds of practices that makes philosophical mediation socially important, particularly in contexts in which intellectual validity claims play a large role in the exercise and representation of power. And if strictly philosophical practices construct abstractions that allow for a more sustained and explicit reflection on such validity claims, they still do so communicatively. In emphasizing the dialogical side of philosophical mediation, I am of course setting aside other respects in which philosophy is a practice. But this emphasis is justifiable because of the relation between the explicitness that democratic philosophy gives to this dialogical aspect and the nature of the democratic conception of rationality itself.

Democratic Reason

I have reiterated the break with epistemological argumentation in democratic philosophical reflection. As I show in Chapter 11, the critique of the division of labor can provide certain kinds of arguments for its conception of reason, but these do not attempt to achieve the necessity and certainty that characterize foundationalist and transcendental arguments. In contrast to postmodernism and positivism, democratic reflection does not conclude from the rejection of these traditional epistemological projects that no illuminating reflection on rational claims is possible. It asserts rather that reflection can establish distinctions between different kinds of thinking and intellectual practices and that it can establish lines of justification that are powerful enough to confront the kinds of concerns about rationality that need to be addressed. These are concerns about the degree and extent of the universality achieved in modern uses of reason. More specifically, they are concerns about the respects in which the Enlightenment promise is betrayed by modern intellectual practice.

Arguments that reconstruct rationality for philosophical purposes draw from a variety of sources and need not achieve the kind of necessity sought in traditional epistemology if they can respond to the question of the relation between knowledge and universality in an adequate way. I need not go into the kinds of intellectual construction that underlie the conception of democratic reason I propose to work with here. The issues are too complex for a discussion here and are discussed better than I could by the relevant authors. The most significant author in this regard is Habermas, whose communications conception of rationality has played a basic role in my discussions. Though I must acknowledge disputes over the historical character of his conception of a discourse ethic and over the extent and way this conception relies on transcendental argumentation, neither of these sets of issues hampers the use I propose of the discourse ethic as a conception of democratic reason. Later I show how this can be conceived of historically, and the argument I give for my use of it as a political ethic does not rely on transcendental arguments.

For now, let me discuss how this provides what I am calling a democratic conception of reason. As I have just noted, democratic philosophical criticism is to be construed as an activity, as initiating a debate in which a more rigorous understanding of validity claims becomes part of political discourse. The mediations of which democratic criticism is a part aim to contest forms of political understanding that go with modern and postmodern knowledge-politics. Criticism involves demystification that is effective only if it goes beyond scoring intellectual points to informing the understanding of expertise by citizens. It is with this concern in mind that the value of Habermas's discourse ethic as a conception of democratic reason becomes evident. To move toward seeing how it offers an understanding of democratic rational reflection, let me first review the general features of Habermas's conception of discursive reason (Habermas 1990, 43–115).

According to Habermas, the rationality of practical (i.e., not technical) arguments consists in conformity to the ideal of a provisional consensus achieved by all participants in a discourse guided only by the best arguments and characterized by the free participation of all concerned, by their access to all relevant resources for debate, and by their mutual recognition as interlocutors. The communications ethic evokes such an ideal speech situation as both the presupposition of rational discussion and as a normative standpoint. This is an ideal of genuine reciprocity, unhindered participation, and equality of information on the part of all speakers.

Habermas is interested in exploring how this ideal provides a way of reconstructing the rationality of theoretical and practical arguments. He is concerned to reconstruct the claims inherent in universalistic norms that govern such discussions. My interest here is somewhat different, since it bears more directly on articulating a political ethic appropriate to contemporary democracy. While this concern does not exclude the need for some reflection on the status of this norm, my immediate aim is to make clear how we can see this ideal as a principle of democratic reason proper to democratic philosophical criticism of the sort I have been discussing.

Viewed as a critical instrument, the ideal locates the points at which the power of experts overreaches an authority that can be justified by appeal to rational powers. Thus experts deny recognition to nonexpert interlocutors, just as they manage participation and maintain a monopoly on relevant cognitive resources. Thinking in terms of the division of labor allows us to concretize such critical assertions, and it provides historical terms for conceiving the practical implications of the ideal speech situation as a political standpoint.

The abstractness of the values of the communication ethic allows them to be employed by specialists within practices that are alienating in ways I have associated with alienation politics. For example, the ideal of participation, when lacking clear conditions and aims, can be employed as a way of absorbing discontent among industrial workers in manipulated forms of involvement managed by paternalistic experts. Similarly, the ideal of reciprocity can be manipulated in negotiations between debtor nations and multinational financial institutions whose policies follow economic necessities calculated by expert advisors. The ideal of sexual equality can be instrumentalized by advertisers in practices that preserve class privileges and sexist stereotypes.

Such considerations suggest that the communication ethic can best assume democratic content in contexts where the problem of knowledge-power is already an explicit theme. And within such contexts this ethic is particularly suitable for the criticism of power exercised through expertise. By evoking the ideal of genuinely discursive participation, one can specify ways in which linguistically mediated interaction structures power relations. For example, it can be used to show where appeals to expertise cut short possible discussion and withdraw recognition of others as full participants. The devices that achieve power can be reconstructed as linguistic performances, and the specific distortions of potential forms of reasoning and collaboration can be specified. The communication ethic need not be seen as a categorical imperative from which any departure stands condemned as undemocratic. Rather, it provides an ideal from which any departure should be explicit and must be justified. For democracy what is crucial is not universal participation or unquestionable equality of all citizens in every context in which knowledge and power are at issue, but rather a political culture in which needed specialized abilities are not mystified and made the medium of undemocratic power.

In a context in which knowledge-power is already an issue, the values I have equated with the ideal speech situation can be used to reflect upon the mediations carried out by experts. For example, the discursive ideal helps us conceive a relevant notion of *inequality* in which experts monopolize relevant information and use mystifying language. The value of *participation* can be applied to investigate the various types of speech and response that different participants in cognitively loaded situations are assigned. Relative degrees of activity and forms of spectatorship and clientship can be examined. Similarly, the norm of *reciprocity* helps us sort out tacit practices of assigning discursive roles that have been contested, for example, by feminist and minority critics.

At issue here are the practices of experts within the division of labor. The communication ethic provides a standard by which critics of expertise can challenge mystification and covert domination, just as it provides terms in which specialists can work out the practical implications of such democratic commitments as they may possess. Here I am not thinking of the ideal speech situation as a kind of professional ethics but rather as a practical standpoint from which contemporary professionalism can be put into question. Questions about professionalism or expertise, about the division of labor, and about forms of social agency are inseparable. If contemporary alienated politics is marked by the reduction of citizens to the status of spectators and clients, this is in large part because power is so frequently exercised as the application of a person-neutral expertise rather than as a matter of debatable politics. If more democratic forms of politics are to be achieved, they must be achieved with the aid of a critique of expertise.

In this regard one can make two claims about the communication ethic. *First*, it offers a standard by which criticism of expertise can proceed. While the norms of the ideal speech situation can be used within practices of knowledge-power, they in turn provide terms with which such practices can be critically challenged. Contrary to those who find the forms of modern rationality to be intrinsically complicit in domination, I have followed the more cautious view that the interconnections between rationality and domination are historical. My *second* claim has been that these interconnections can best be understood in terms of the evolution of modern social structure and the division of labor. The communication ethic develops modern ethical abstraction in a genuinely critical way insofar as it allows us to address power exercised through the kinds of expertise that characterize contemporary alienated politics. But I have noted that the critical promise of this ethic depends on the context in which it figures. It provides a standard for those already engaged in challenging the division of labor and alienated politics. Moreover, although it evokes an ideal of democratic agency, the concrete forms such agency might assume also depend on the forces and aspirations proper to specific historical conditions.

Having shown how the discourse ethic provides a standard appropriate to democratic criticism, let me return to the theme of the dialogical character of the philosophical practice in which this standard can become an explicit point of reference. The standard, after all, is presented as a norm inherent to dialogical activity, as a model of discussion to which philosophical practice might itself aspire. As a conception of process the ideal speech situation articulates a norm that may seem incompatible with expertise of any kind. It certainly promotes the goal of conversation between experts and citizens that aspires to genuine equality and reciprocity. Working out how this idea is compatible with democratic differentiation is a topic to which I shortly turn. My point now is that so far as this norm articulates the highest ideal of democratic reason, it sets for philosophers the problem of democratizing the conversations in which conclusions proper to reflection on validity claims are to be reached.

Contributing to a Democratic Political Culture

So far I have shown how democratic philosophical mediation involves criticism and presupposes commitment to a conception of democratic reason I have identified with a historical version of the discourse ethic. Criticism is utopian in the sense of anticipating universalistic possibilities to which its criticism is to contribute. The communicative ideal projects historical forms of participation and collaboration that avoid the forms of domination and inequality democratic criticism of knowledge-power is able to identify. We face the theoretical problem of how we are to think about the abstract ideal speech situation in sufficiently historical terms to establish an appropriate relation to feasible social practices. We face the more directly political problem of how intellectual mediations can contribute to such practices. This political problem, which, following the guiding theses of this study, I take to be a philosophical question closely related to the theoretical question, can be approached in terms of elements of a democratic political culture. I turn to this theme before taking up the theoretical question, which I treat in terms of the kind of justification this democratic ethic can receive.

With the discourse ethic we have seen the outlines of a communications conception of democratic process. The issue of democratic culture is how to conceive the embodiment of this ethic in a social differentiation that provides a democratic alternative to the division of labor. This requires thinking about constructive democratic mediations carried out by intellectuals in general and philosophers in particular. Our problem, then, is to specify some of the qualities of a democratic culture that would allow it to sustain an alternative to knowledge-politics, and we need to do this explicitly in contrast to abstractly utopian schemes that wish away the complexity of the modern world. On the one hand, it is impossible for everyone to be knowledgeable about everything that bears on important social choices, and on the other, it is undesirable for everyone to be directly involved in as many contexts of choice as are theoretically available. Although democracy requires a broadening of our understanding and practice of politics, it will not succeed if it demands of individuals that they become exclusively political animals.

So we are concerned with a culture that balances a differentiation of tasks with popular regulation of experts. Democratic responsibility of experts requires breaking the link between expertise and systematic power and instituting the regulation of experts by a democratic public. Such a public needs to understand the boundaries of competence as well as what is debatable within those boundaries. An abiding role for philosophical mediation is the discussion of the corresponding issues in a way that bridges the languages and self-understandings of experts with the discussions in the public sphere. For this to be possible, nonexperts, a category that includes all of us most of the time, must have the capacity and time to engage in such discussions. By helping identify and cultivate such capacities, democratic mediation would contribute to a democratic culture that has surmounted scarcity in the relevant sense. Though philosophers are not in a position to create the conditions in which such capacities actually emerge, trying to define them seems in part a genuinely philosophical task.

Culture of Democratic Competence

In speaking of democratic political culture I refer to the conditions for establishing and reproducing democratic agency. With the evolution of modern politics in mind, I am specifically concerned with the philosophical features of democratic culture, that is, with the reflective relation to rationality proper to it. And in the context of the present discussion, I am concerned with features of a culture that would be regulated by the ideals of the discourse ethic, which is to say, a culture that aspires to an appropriate historical embodiment of its ideal. Only such an embodiment would establish the democratic validity of the practices of a differentiated and highly productive society. And to speak of validity in this way is not to mean an abstract standard by which a detached observer might judge the workings of such a society, but rather the basis for the acceptance of social decisions and processes by democratic citizens themselves.

The question for concrete embodiment of the values of participation, equality, and reciprocity concerns the way these values can be respected sufficiently to avoid relations characteristic of the division of labor. I am putting the point negatively to emphasize that the critical use of these ideals in identifying knowledge-power must acknowledge that only a qualified realization of them is possible, and so must explore what kind of qualified realization would be sufficient to avoid the reproduction of the division of labor.

This negative concern points to one feature of a democratic culture, the enabling of citizens to carry out critical challenges to possible forms that the reassertion of scarcity might take. Thus, while a democratic culture could not aspire to making everyone competent in every field, it would have to provide every citizen with the capacity to spot expert mystifications and to challenge expert claims. Citizens would have to be able to engage experts in discussions in which the specific weight of their expert claims could be isolated and recognized for its relative merits and for what might be controversial about it. It is to some degree a matter of political experiment to find out how such democratic engagement of citizens with experts might proceed, and it might proceed differently for different kinds of expertise. Let us imagine briefly the role of experts in contributing to this democratic engagement.

To speak of the formation of democratic capacities here suggests a background of democratic educational processes, with corresponding innovations in the contents and forms of learning. Similarly the sustaining of a democratic culture suggests the existence of a popular scientific culture with appropriate forms of journalism, museums, television documentaries, and so on. In settings of controversy over specific questions, democratic intellectual mediation might also involve the juxtaposing of alternative expert viewpoints in the setting of the public discussion by citizens.

In contrast to the apparently unrealizable conception of overcoming the division of labor by eliminating or generalizing expertise, that is, by eliminating dependence of citizens on experts, this conception assumes that citizens need not be experts to assess expert claims. No doubt the plausibility of this assumption varies from field to field. The assumption is that in a socially problematic use of expertise, citizens can, with feasible preparation and reliance on other intellectual mediation, confront experts in a way that allows them to assess the claims made by experts so far as they bear on politically relevant concerns.

Throughout, the aim of democratic intellectual mediation would be the avoidance of the emergence of scarcity in the setting of the inevitable shortages of knowledge and experience on the part of citizens. The philosophical dimension of this mediation would focus specifically on the respects in which political discussion involves the discussion of expert validity claims and the understanding of specifically democratic process. Thus abstractly developed philosophical claims about the uncertainties of a specific kind of knowledge or about its cognitive scope would inform the mediations of other mediators as well as the discussion of citizens. The consequence would be the development of genres and voices proper to a democratic public.

Obviously the existence of this kind of culture of democratic competence requires a high level of education for all citizens. An argument for the feasibility of this culture draws from the experienced ability of educated citizens to challenge experts in contemporary political debates. Those who take the time can inform themselves about the specifics of ecological, medical, or geopolitical issues so as to arrive at a sense of what the experts know and do not know and of what is a matter of conflicting interests and power claims. But education and time is necessary for this capacity; hence it would be available generally only on the basis of the significant reduction of labor time I have already argued present levels of productivity make possible.

Yet other objections have to be acknowledged, especially concerning the capacity and will of all citizens to acquire this kind of education and actively to use it in subsequent political debates. Here I believe conservatives are on as weak empirical ground as are democrats.

Recognizing that a qualified realization of these values would suffice for a democratic alternative to the division of labor allows us to avoid the impression that the discourse ethic makes impossibly utopian demands. In particular, it allows us to see that it may be possible to accommodate the unavoidability of the differentiation of tasks and the corresponding pursuit of expertise without preserving the division of labor. To say that differentiation and expertise are unavoidable is to recognize the implications of the complexity of modern society, the unavoidable abstractness of many of its relations, and the reliance of society on a variety of highly specialized powers. But this recognition is not a covert reintroduction of scarcity, so long as participation, equality, and reciprocity are sufficiently achieved to keep differentiation and expertise from becoming the media of power relations.

With this proviso, we see the general problem of a democratic culture. It must be a culture in which experts are effectively responsible to the judgment of nonexperts so far as this is required to avoid a covert transformation of expertise into social power. That a differential distribution of expertise is compatible with a critical perspective on knowledge-power follows from the way contemporary criticisms of expertise illustrate that one need not be an expert to see that power is being exercised, as well as to see how it is being exercised, through expertise. Movements, to be sure, draw upon expertise, but frequently in ways that have less to do with the self-criticism within specific fields than with intellectual criticism developed from a variety of perspectives. Indeed, the possibility of self-criticism without the informing insights of perspectives beyond professionally constrained fields may be doubted. In any case, the claim I mean to support is that a critical relation to expertise requires less a generalization of expertise than the existence of a certain minimum level of knowledge and reasoning combined with an appropriate framework of communication and debate.

On such a basis, specialization could give way to flexible and variable development of various kinds of expertise, and the identification of expertise with specific privileged strata could end. It would in effect draw the appropriate conclusion from the fact that within the division of labor experts are always nonexperts in most social contexts. Eliminating specialization and generalizing access to differential expertise imply a society in which everyone is both an expert and a nonexpert and is neither intimidating nor intimidated by this fact. Such a culture would imply a different kind of agency both with regard to specific exercises of expertise and with regard to the evolution of individual powers.

Overcoming the division of labor implies less the end of complexity or differentiation than the end of a specialization of individuals in a world in which social decisions respond to social requirements apprehended as objective necessities grasped by expert knowledge. Overcoming the division of labor in this sense does not imply a world without specialists or one that does without highly developed, abstract, and often esoteric knowledge. Rather, a democratic alternative to the division of labor is one in which such knowledge does not have the last word in social choices and the bearers of such knowledge do not derive political authority directly from their cognitive capacities. Experts instead must always be responsible to democratically capable citizens whose political discussions generate social decisions.

Responsible Intellectuals

Democratic responsibility of experts requires breaking the link between expertise and systematic power and instituting the regulation of experts by a democratic public. Such a public needs to understand the boundaries of competence as well as what is debatable within those boundaries. An abiding role for philosophical mediation is the discussion of the corresponding issues in a way that bridges the languages and self-understandings of experts with the discussions in the public sphere. In speaking of a democratic political culture, I referred to ways philosophical mediation might inform the political understanding of citizens. My general thesis about modern philosophical mediation has been that it has functioned to provide a self-understanding of intellectuals. In the democratic setting, the corresponding task for democratic philosophy would be to contribute to a democratic self-understanding on the part of experts. Democratic orientations have to be developed within the practices of experts to complement the cultivation of democratic competencies by citizens.

In considering what this might involve we should remember that the democratic formation of citizens and that of experts cannot be separate processes if citizens are all to be experts in some contexts and experts are to be nonexpert citizens in most contexts. This point is worth bearing in mind also to forestall concerns that experts might have interests that would inhibit their development of the genres and voices of democratic responsibility. Undoubtedly such interests presently exist, but they come into question when the democratic aims of movements are pursued, and these movements embrace experts and nonexperts alike. In other words, while there are important issues specific to the cultivation of the democratic practice of expertise, what stands in the way of this cultivation is not so much expert resistance per se as it is the various resistances to the various kinds of power that are reproduced in the division of labor.

Perhaps the single greatest reflective task for philosophical mediation concerned with the democratic self-understanding of experts is to explore the implications of the communicative reconstruction of rationality. Such an exploration would be necessary to consider the genres appropriate to democratic mediation and thus the embodiment of a social understanding of rationality in various contexts of democratic communication, for example, journalism, teaching, television, and public debate. But a more theoretical problem would be reflection on the communicative dependencies of experts for the possibility of their specialized work. In many contexts, these two issues would be closely connected. For example, a communicative reconstruction of social science research could inform attempts to recast the relation between social scientists and citizens. Similarly, a reconstruction of the historical conditions for technological innovation might contribute to rethinking how technologies could be reworked in the present.

In this respect, the issue of intellectual responsibility is not so much a matter of moral demands on experts in view of the powers they possess. It is more a matter of rethinking those powers, both as they have been historically acquired and as they might be cultivated in the future.

Democratic Philosophy and Aestheticized Politics

I have discussed democratic philosophical mediation from the standpoint of criticism of knowledge-power and from the standpoint of the counterfactual historical ideal of a democratic culture. I have presented the latter as a way of thinking about the historical embodiment of the democratic values of the discourse ethic. Now I complete this discussion of democratic philosophical mediation by turning briefly to how it bears on the alternative, promised by a democratic politics, to the aestheticizing politics I have presented as an important feature of postmodern practice.

Such mediation would be democratic partly in the specific way it continues the modern philosophical tradition's reflective concern with the role of abstract, methodologically self-conscious knowledge in society. It would be democratic by continuing this reflection as social argumentation that connects the nature and function of such knowledge with the politicization of agency that has deepened during the modern period. As itself a kind of social mediation, such argumentation figures in this politics of agency. But its concern is to do so in a way that makes the politics of agency a democratic concern of all citizens.

Earlier I touched upon various aspects of philosophy's mediating activity: it contributes to social and self-understanding of intellectuals, to genres and voices proper to intellectual mediators, and thus to the epistemological features of modern political culture. Democratic philosophical mediation aims at reflection and argumentation that contribute to a different political culture, one in which citizens can draw upon expertise freed of the power relations and inequalities reproduced within the division of labor. The relation of democratic philosophy to postmodern aestheticizing trends, then, is one of reflection and debate that aims at citizen capacities that are very different from those of clients and spectators.

I have shown that philosophical action on agency concerns itself not just with specific argumentative claims but with the genres, voices, and relations to semantic potential characteristic of particular political culture. A specifically democratic philosophical mediation is concerned with the genres, voices, and relations to semantic potential characteristic of a political culture that confronts scarcity of agency as a political evil and that equips citizens to approach issues of the social formation of agency in a democratic way. Now let us see how we might develop these claims in thinking about the alternative democratic mediation can advance against aestheticized politics.

We can focus on some features of the politics of spectatorship discussed earlier. First, let us refer to some pertinent features of aestheticized politics. I have noted that the idea of aestheticizing applies to the formation of citizens as spectators in a double way. It refers to the observer relation to politics made into spectacle and displaced into entertainment where political judgment involves corresponding aesthetic norms. And it refers to the activity of aestheticizing politics on political sensibility such that this aesthetic relation to politics becomes a regular relation to politics. The contrasts with democratic competence are clear. Spectatorship involves a fetishism of expertise in various respects, generally reducing the capacity for democratic judgment.

The question is how we are to think about the democratic alternative to such an aestheticizing politics of agency and in particular how we are to think about the role of democratic philosophical mediation in this alternative politics of agency. One approach to these questions is by way of the social movements that have contributed to making the division of labor a contested issue. By referring to these movements we can cast the issue of democratic mediation in more historical terms, and we can draw from mediations that are part of the intellectual trend I am identifying with the critique of the division of labor.

At issue is bridging between the general requirement for democracy of what I have called a democratic culture of competence and existing conflicts. The social movements address relevant features of agency that bear directly on the workings and results of aestheticized politics. Their political challenges include concern with voices, genres, and semantic potential in ways that bear on aestheticized politics.

Movements of minorities and feminists frequently address the relation to politics as itself a contested terrain. This may include direct attacks on media images and devices, but in any case it makes a theme of the constructed relation to politics as proceeding beyond the control of those it affects. Critics associated with these movements have identified ways depoliticized social roles are constructed for members of these groups and ways that seemingly unpolitical preoccupations (e.g., organization of the household) involve politically loaded assumptions and practices. Devices of mass culture that reinterpret the aspirations and strategies of movements have become in turn the object of criticism as a necessary part of a critical reflexiveness about politics that seeks to manage away social contestation. So these movements make themes of the targeting of sensibility by contemporary covert and displaced politics and so set into motion the kind of criticism that a democratic culture builds upon.

Movements also offer ways of counteracting features of political spectatorship. Minority movements and feminism assert politically charged identities that promote active political agency. These sometimes demand new practical opportunities, denied by the existing division of labor, and they challenge traditional understandings that justify scarcity along gender, racial, or ethnic lines. In contrast with the aestheticized relation to politics, here we find assertions of a creative relation to one's sense of values, needs, and self. Another example bearing on political sensibility that counteracts an aestheticized relation to politics is the assertion by ecology movements of the need for a different relation to nature. This involves an explicit politicization of sensibility and includes attacks on various devices of contemporary covert and displaced politics, for example, those proper to a consumerist culture that reproduces a productivist relation to nature.

I have already referred tacitly to some of the roles played by intellectual mediations in this kind of democratic politics. Scientists, journalists, teachers, political organizers, and so on, contribute to the articulation of criticisms and counterassertions that make features in the formation of agency a political question. What specifically is the role here of philosophy?

Concerning specific issues about scientific claims (e.g., regarding gender, race, or environmental impacts), philosophical arguments about method, interpretive presuppositions, and so on, have played a role. Similarly, so far as movements have been matters of identity, philosophical criticism of metaphysical assumptions, of the guiding themes of traditions, and so on, have contributed to work that has recovered past traditions and alternative possibilities. Here we can refer specifically to ways new genres, voices, and relations to semantic potential have been cultivated through philosophically informed intellectual mediations. Movements have been engaged in a politics of language that not only affects specific usages but has encouraged new literatures, new ways of arguing, and new ways of teaching. They have cultivated new senses of communicative potential for individuals and groups, and through scholarly and imaginative works have developed new relations to possible meanings and interpretive standpoints.

These observations provide some basis for thinking that social movements and the intellectual mediations that have figured within them have contributed to a democratic political culture whose outlines I sketched in the previous section. They contribute both to the explicitness of the politics of agency and to efforts to cultivate kinds of agency that contrast with those of aestheticized politics. Philosophers I am including within the tendency of thought I am calling the critique of the division of labor have contributed to the assertion of this democratic relation to agency by contributing to a more democratic understanding of rationality. At the same time, the democratic promise of movements has sometimes been challenged, and certainly intellectuals and the standpoints to which they have contributed have not typically stated overcoming the division of labor as their aim.

In acknowledging the undemocratic features of some movements or the fragmenting potential of the identity politics some movements pursue, I mean to combine recognition of ambiguous features of some of these historical experiences with a claim for the value of making the democratic potential of such movements as explicit as possible. From the standpoint of my systematic argument, this means urging on specific movements and those engaged in democratic politics generally the value of making the issue of the division of labor an explicit analytic and political concern. Because the problem of the division of labor connects issues of agency and the specific forms of power addressed by specific movements with corresponding concerns of other movements, it provides the kind of democratic perspective that allows such movements to retain a universalistic perspective. In this respect, the argument for the critique of the division of labor as a philosophical standpoint is also an argument within the sphere of contemporary democratic politics.

Chapter **11**

Normative Justification in Historical Reflection

After presenting aspects of a critical use of the idea of the division of labor, I have characterized some of its reflective and practical uses for philosophy. Now I summarize some of the kinds of arguments that can be used to justify this philosophical use of the division of labor. The shift to themes of justification from the political themes of the preceding chapter is not so abrupt as it may first appear. Understood as a feature of democratic philosophical mediation, this justification figures within debates about the self-understanding of democratic practice.

It is not obvious what is an appropriate justification. It is necessary to defend the historical claims regarding the past and present significance of the division of labor in relation to scarcity and the possibility of overcoming it. But this is a long way from providing a foundationalist or transcendental refutation of skepticism regarding the transhistorical perspective or normative force I have attributed to the critique of the division of labor. Even if we agree that abstract skepticism is an arid impulse, we should take aspects of skepticism seriously. In particular, we need to take seriously skepticism about the independence and political innocence of intellectuals, a skepticism I earlier associated with some postmodernist rejections of philosophy. In this light, the critique of the division of labor is faced with the challenge to show that it does not simply provide another ideological framework for intellectuals seeking and exercising power.

It is toward the satisfaction of such doubts that the work of justification must be directed. In particular, we can pursue this kind of justification by considering three issues about the universality of this perspective. First, why think that a transhistorical perspective like that asserted for the critique of the division of labor can arise within history? How is it possible that the division of labor can be challenged from within the division of labor? If we agree that the paradox of such criticism can be explained, we are still left with issues about the feasibility of abolishing scarcity and constructing a democratic alternative to the division of labor. Why think it is now possible to establish a political regulation of shortage that avoids the relations of inequality, domination, and conflict that, by my hypothesis, characterize the division of labor? Finally, establishing that it is possible to abolish scarcity is not the same as showing that it is or should be a compelling goal. How do we justify the critique of the division of labor, which I have argued provides a historical reading of the discourse ethic, as a political ethic? The way we answer this question bears most directly on the concern about intellectuals and power.

Transhistorical Reflection

First, let us consider what can be said in support of thinking that the kind of transhistorical perspective claimed by the critique of the division of labor is possible today. At the outset we need to recognize that such a transhistorical perspective is not itself ahistorical. The critique of the division of labor is a project of reflection proper to a specific conjuncture and proceeds with conceptual resources proper to that conjuncture. This reflection does not require ahistorical conceptions of society or human nature, but the means for positing certain constants and contrasts over the sweep of historical societies.

To make the possibility of transhistorical reflection plausible is to claim that this kind of intellectual reflection finds in contemporary experience the materials that can be conceptually reworked so as to provide the posited degree of universality. Thus the critique of the division of labor can be shown to be possible by reference to specific features of contemporary society. I have already made reference to some of the relevant features. For example, in referring to ways social movements have made political issues of various aspects of agency, I touched on ways they make agency a matter of social reflection. The politics of these movements has been in part a response to the covert forms of political intervention into dimensions of agency, which, in turn, can be related to structural changes: for example, the transformation of the relation of production and consumption within the economy; the blurring of institutional boundaries between economy, state, and culture; and changes in large-scale organization and identity associated with the internationalization of economics, politics, and culture. I am not implying any particular relation between these aspects of our historical situation. Rather, they illustrate the kinds of factors that can be cited to make intelligible our ability to think in terms of the critique of the division of labor. They contribute to a reflexivity about agency, and the powers constructing and conflicting over agency, in terms that allow us to think generally about the prospects for eliminating scarcity.

So the claim is that reflection on the division of labor as such and on the workings of scarcity has become possible because structural evolution, quasi-political initiatives, and social conflict have jointly made the constructed nature of agency an evident fact of our world. This fact has emerged often in the form of political issues and has tacitly brought into question the adequacy of existing forms of political understanding and action. To speak of the constructed nature of agency as a fact should not divert us from how this fact emerges only in the articulations of intellectuals, particularly those engaged in what I have collectively labeled democratic reconstruction. In probing the workings of scarcity, democratic reconstruction thinks transhistorically by evoking the counterfactual possibility of overcoming scarcity of agency or economies of powers and thus of instituting a politics that directly confronts the issue of shortage. At issue are a host of specific questions about the relations of society to humanity's outer as well as inner nature. Unavoidable in these is the question of the promise of the productivity of contemporary labor. But whatever the course of debates over these questions, I believe it is plausible to claim that contemporary conditions enable the formation of the kind of reflective criticism of the division of labor that makes these genuine matters for further debate.

The Contingency of Scarcity

Perhaps, then, such a transhistorical perspective from within history as proposed by the critique of the division of labor is possible. It does not automatically follow that we can abolish scarcity and the regime of the division of labor that goes with it. Let me indicate the kinds of issues facing the question whether such an abolition is plausible. To establish that scarcity can be abolished requires first showing that productive powers are such as to reduce shortages to a level that permits the formation of a democratic culture in which this shortage could be faced by means other than the division of labor. Earlier I argued that existing productive powers permit a drastic expansion of free time and the redirection of social energies toward the formation of such a democratic culture. Whether such considerations establish the material basis for a democratic culture can be argued only with a fuller account of such a political culture than can be attempted here. At issue is providing all members of society with the capacity to judge the claims of experts so far as these bear on the exercise of social powers. The formation of this capacity is the precondition for eliminating the division of labor and counts as the elimination of the corresponding scarcity of agency and of politics. There is another reason these considerations are inclusive. Establishing an account of the limits to which productive powers must be mobilized for material needs presupposes a definition of real needs versus the false needs that sustain demands for continued economic growth. Such a distinction between needs could itself arise only as a result of the politics of the hypothetical democratic culture, which would address the more general political questions of shortage.

I have claimed that this kind of circularity is not fatal to arguments for the critique of the division of labor. Besides illustrating a way theoretical reflection depends on the evolution of politics, however, it points to historical features of the political rationality of the discourse ethic. I touch upon these in discussing the kind of argument this ethic can receive from the kind of philosophical reflection provided by the critique of the division of labor.

The Discourse Ethic

I have shown that historical arguments can be made to account for the critique of the division of labor as a historically located reflection that makes transhistorical claims and to establish the material conditions for the elimination of scarcity this critique counterfactually presupposes. The final task of the kind of justification of this philosophical perspective that both is necessary and possible concerns the respects in which the abolition of the division of labor represents a rational advance. In discussing the normative commitments of this critique I claimed that a historical version of Habermas's discourse ethic can provide an appropriate normative conception. The third task of philosophical justification consists in showing how the discourse ethic can be suitably historicized.

The Ideal Speech Situation

As the demand that all norms be validated by a discussion in which all those affected by its adoption can participate with equality of discursive resources and in genuine reciprocity, the discourse ethic evokes a utopian speech situation that effectively cancels any division of labor. The values of participation, equality of resources, and universal recognition are particularly apt for a challenge to power exercised through the differential scarcities of capacity characteristic of the division of labor.

Habermas (1990, 76–109) offers a quasi-transcendental justification of the ethic, arguing from presuppositions inherent in speech. Whatever the merits of this argument, I do not rely on it for two reasons. First, he justifies the ethic as a general principle of the justification of norms, while I am interested in an ethic specific to the politics of contemporary democracy. Second, so far as this becomes an effective political ethic in foreseeable social circumstances, its demands will have to be compromised considerably, since full participation, real equality of discursive resources, and complete reciprocity cannot be expected in conditions of material shortage. So I am interested in a justification that holds for a modified discourse ethic, one that is genuinely democratic without making the extreme formal demands of Habermas's principle.

Discursive Ethics in Context

At issue is a normative conception appropriate to the tasks of democratic intellectual mediation and to the workings of a democratic culture more generally. It must be a standard that acknowledges the exigencies of shortage without accepting the power relations of scarcity. That is, it must accommodate a certain differentiation of agency consistent with modern conditions while critically identifying ways expertise reproduces systematic power. It would be a normative standpoint appropriate to the formation of capacities and political discussion that constrain experts into democratic responsibility. Let me note in passing that seeking to articulate and defend a discursive standard of this kind does not obviously contradict the arguments or purposes of the normative reflection Habermas pursues with his discourse ethic.

In considering the force of the discourse ethic for the critique of the division of labor, we should first notice more specifically how the discursive values are appropriate for the challenge to power exercised through the scarcity of agency and for practical problems in our historical situation more generally. First, the discourse ethic is attractive because it responds to the evolution of moral discourse by accommodating the decline of consensus around substantive values and norms. Validation now must lie in the process by which social members can reach common understanding. Next, the discursive values provide a critical standpoint regarding issues of knowledge and power. It is in restricting participation, manipulating resources, and shaping and even denying recognition that power exercised in the division of labor often functions. Here we can see that the abstractness of these values allows for their application in a variety of contexts where agency can be made a democratic issue. Third, this ethic coheres with the critical practices of movements that challenge privileged expert standpoints. Such movements demand more participation, access to resources, and recognition of previously ignored voices. Fourth, the discourse ethic provides a general orientation that can guide political discussions in which experts are made responsible. That is, the discursive values state ideals whose observation would require experts to respond to nonexperts in ways consistent with democracy.

Showing that the discourse ethic is appropriate to features of our historical situation is a relevant but not sufficient argument for its justification as a political ethic. Were it possible to achieve a consensus through conversation that fully realized the discursive ideals, the question of justification would be moot. That is, any consensus emerging from a discourse meeting Habermas's ideal would be unassailable from a democratic standpoint, regardless of the philosophical merits of Habermas's philosophical account of it. The issue for us is the standing of agreements that emerge from a process that falls short of the ideal. What kind of a compromise of the discursive ideal is acceptable from a democratic standpoint, and why is it acceptable?

Put differently, the question is, what kind of compromises would not undermine the aim of the critique of the division of labor by permitting the introduction of undemocratic kinds of power? How do we avoid compromises that would allow differentiations of agency that could systematically reintroduce the kinds of power reproduced by the division of labor? How can we regulate the differentiations of agency so that the dangers of scarcity of agency are avoided? From the standpoint of the critique of the division of labor the issue becomes the form and extent to which dependence on specialization is consistent with democracy.

Democratic Conditions

Let me propose two general conditions that must be met for a discourse to be democratic even if it fails fully to meet the ideals of universal participation, equality of resources, and full reciprocity. One has to do with the cultural formation of citizens. It must be such that everyone can question experts sufficiently to locate the blurring of expertise with social power. The second has to do with the representation of claims about latent power. Means must be available for charges of knowledge-power to be considered and discussed by all citizens. Let me elaborate briefly on these requirements and then turn to the issue of their justification.

Real equality of discursive resources is an unrealistic demand, but the requirement of a general level of knowledge sufficient to make specialists responsible may be feasible even if it remains for us a distant ideal. On this requirement, a democratic culture would be one in which every citizen could in principle question experts or easily acquire the ability to do so. I believe that such an ability is presently within the reach of well-educated members of our society, which is to say that we could, but typically do not, have or take the time to equip ourselves to scrutinize the proclamations of economists, highway engineers, physicians, and so on. In effect I am making the empirical claim that, aided by the mediations of critically minded specialists, educated individuals can effectively question experts on their analytical and prescriptive claims. For example, with sufficient time we can usually grasp and assess the reasoning of a physician even if we cannot approximate her or his ability to judge the particulars of a specific case. Such scrutiny usually should be adequate to identify the kinds of mystifications that contribute to illegitimate power in the division of labor.

The second condition for a democratic process that fails to meet the discursive ideal is that it provide for inclusion of the voices of those who historically have struggled against forms of power exercised in the division of labor. The absence of actual discursive equality should be counterbalanced by explicit scrutiny for the legacy of systematic inequalities. The aim here is for a public sphere in which the legacy of class, racism, and sexism remains a theme for reflection carried out by all citizens.

In citing these two conditions for a democratic alternative to the division of labor, I am addressing a matter of historical principles rather than the question of their institutionalization. The point has been to suggest ways compromises with the discursive ideal can sustain its democratic potential. Institutionalization of these principles no doubt raises other questions of compromising the democratic ideal. In general, I am following the principle that only democratic and revocable choice can justify limitations on democracy. Through democratic procedures consistent with the conditions I have discussed, institutional arrangements that accommodate more concretely the requirements of differentiation could be devised and approved.

The compromised discursive standard, then, states that decisions should result from a discourse characterized by participation, equality of resources, and recognition in which the participants possess sufficient cultural formation to question expert claims and in which explicit scrutiny is made for the workings of historic forms of power. This is a standard both for democratic culture in general and for democratic intellectual mediation in particular. That is, it represents an ethos for intellectuals, including philosophers concerned with the kinds of mediation cited in discussing democratic criticism.

Self-Validation of Democratic Norms

Having articulated this version of the discourse ethic, where do we stand with its justification? So far as these conditions preserve the democratic content of the more abstract ethic, they also preserve its justification as a logic of democratic process. So far as they compromise the scrutiny of power that the full ideal implies, they call for further justification. In fact, there is no guarantee that these conditions would suffice to block unrecognized forms of dependence and domination, but such guarantees are not necessary so long as the fears they would forestall are not backed up by concrete analyses and opposition.

More to the point is the question of the standing of such a principle that remains extremely hypothetical even if it is plausible to think that it could be achieved under very different circumstances. From the standpoint of democratic criticism, the democratic norm has a twofold standing. It provides the normative outlines of a democracy that can inform the narrative perspective of contemporary debate. And it represents an ethical standpoint that is relevant to the attempts at democratic mediation within existing relations of power. Let me make a concluding point about justification.

In both its ideal and historically compromised forms, the discourse ethic treats the justification of specific decisions or norms as following from agreements that result from discussions that are democratic, that is, from procedures that meet a certain democratic standard. Because they result from a certain kind of process, these decisions and norms can be considered valid. Philosophers can in turn attempt theoretical arguments to justify these procedures, as Habermas does with his quasi-transcendental arguments about discursive rationality. There is a certain circularity in Habermas's argument, since his own discursive account claims that arguments can only be validated by appropriate consensus. Thus the principle of agreement can be validated only by another agreement. This circularity is not inherently problematic, though it puts the theoretical arguments in a certain context. What is important from the standpoint of democratic reflection is that the democratic principle must itself be validated by democratic agreement. Theoretical arguments are not sufficient, which is not to say that they may not play a necessary role in the process by which the conditions for wider agreement are achieved. In any case, we can draw the inference that no theoretical justification of the modified discourse ethic as a norm for democratic criticism will be forthcoming, but at the same time historical reflection on the course of political discussion can be instructive for theoretical claims about such an ethic. If theoretical justifications imply a hubris that additionally threatens a kind of substitution by intellectuals for actual political evolution, the more modest self-understanding that forgoes theoretical justification by no means denies the need for intellectual criticism regarding impediments to democracy.

Chapter 12

The Project of Democratic Philosophy

In this study I have tried to develop a conception of democratic philosophy that indicates why systematically inclined reflection on rationality is important today and to discuss some of the ways it is possible. I have tried also to say why democracy needs philosophical reflection as well as how some kind of philosophical reflection seems unavoidable when knowledge is as important in society as it is for us today. Philosophers are neither able nor required to provide a system in the traditional sense. Rather, a systematic "inclination" implies an attempt to fashion understandings that make connections, establish relations, and evoke possibilities that transcend the immediacy of fragmentary experience. The need for philosophical reflection follows in part from the fact that the fragmentation of experience is itself historical and results from a contemporary complex of social practices using abstract knowledge.

Philosophy must provide reflection on the intellectual mediations that figure in the specific mix of order and disorder that characterizes contemporary social experience. My thesis has been that the organizing principle for such reflection should be the critique of the division of labor. Though such a principle involves theoretical commitments (outlined in Part Two), it is not itself a theory in the traditional sense of a systematically organized set of theses arranged by what are offered as rationally necessary arguments. A "principle," a "framework," an "approach," a "narrative perspective": these are ways to characterize reflective commitments that serve to organize and orient ongoing intellectual discussion. In contrast to postmodern intellectual irony, these commitments are both open to argument and permanently in need of it. They involve conceptual and historical claims that are open to criticism and improvement.

Aside from presenting this theoretical standpoint as necessary for intellectual and political reflection concerned with thinking about knowledge in democratic terms, I have argued that it offers a way of interpreting reflection that is underway in contemporary debates. In this respect, the argument for the critique of the division of labor is as much an interpretive claim about a tendency in contemporary intellectual work as it is a claim about the coherence and cogency of a philosophical standpoint. Of course, as such an interpretation it is also an argument directed at those whose work it presumes to cast in this particular light.

Knowledge-Power and Critique

The critique of the division of labor establishes a relation to issues of knowledge and power that resists the exclusive predominance of any specific challenge to contemporary hierarchy and inequality, be it that of class, gender, or race. All the same, it does not rest with an abstract pluralism of power relations and struggles over them. Without claiming a predominance of issues proper to the division of intellectual and manual labor, the critique of the division of labor programmatically asserts the importance in the interrelated conflicts over class, gender, and race of questions of expertise, particularly as they bear on the formation of agency.

Because the different kinds of power operate within a common world (however fragmented in organization and experience), we need a way of thinking about what they have in common and how they are in fact connected. The idea of the division of labor as presented here provides a way of thinking of differentiation and interconnection, of fragmentation and shared preconditions, in a way that is itself historical. This is to say not only that the division of labor is undergoing various kinds of evolution but that it exhibits a specific, philosophically pertinent evolution. Within the complex of differentiated power relations and the more general fragmenting qualities of our world, the link between real and thought abstractions addressed by Marx becomes ever more important to the viability of the world itself. In discussing Marx, I showed that the thesis of thought abstractions could extend from an account of the relation between the knowledge proper to political economy and modern practices of exchange to an account of intellectual mediations that employ such abstractions in socially effective ways. Foucault's researches on nineteenth-century forms of knowledge-power in effect show that the practical significance of thought abstractions was greater than Marx realized. With the structural evolution of contemporary society, this significance has only grown greater.

In emphasizing the division of labor in the philosophical sense I have developed in this study, then, I am pointing to a practical dimension of the differentiation and integration of social experience that has arisen in our time. It is not that knowledge-politics is somehow the supreme and encompassing form of power but that it functions within the workings of the various power relations in their evolving complexity, overlap, and interconnection, in their relation to various social challenges, and in their becoming part of conflicts over structural change. Action on the social relations of the division of labor, as well as on the kinds of agency that figure within these relations, bears on all the kinds of power that are sustained by the division of labor.

It is not, then, too much to say that the critique of the division of labor is a kind of philosophical reflection justified by the evolution of the relations and practices of power, made possible by social conflicts and movements, and required by democratic politics. Earlier I argued that this reflection, and the sort of transhistorical perspective it asserts, is made possible by historical characteristics of the present. I have also acknowledged that there is a kind of circularity to the use of the discourse ethic posited by this critique such that its justification is partly dependent on the facts of political evolution. Within the present, the commitment to a democratic overcoming of the division of labor attaches a utopian character to this kind of philosophical critique. This is not an intellectual flaw, since it does not involve dogmatism but in fact contributes to illuminating analyses. Nonetheless, any such democratic standpoint has to be able to explain how it stands in relation to its ideal, particularly in periods of reaction when democratic prospects seem dim.

Democratic Philosophy
and Democratic Multiculturalism

The utopianism of democratic philosophy is justified not only by arguments from objective possibilities but also by the incoherences of the prevailing common sense. Nonetheless, it is fair to ask for more anchoring in contemporary politics than has been provided so far. In fact I have shown some anchor in the politics of social movements and in what follows draw out some implications and possibilities of points made earlier in the discussion. I draw on these to sketch one important complex of issues in which a role for democratic philosophy can be described. I present ways democratic philosophy does and can figure in the politics of multiculturalism. A democratic multiculturalism has yet to be adequately formulated, and philosophy has a role in doing so. The idea of democratic philosophy is helpful in conceiving a distinctively democratic multiculturalism.

Discussing multiculturalism allows us to appreciate some of the advantages of a democratic perspective over what I earlier discussed as liberal knowledge-power. We can contrast liberal and democratic multiculturalisms in a way that brings out limitations of liberalism's commitments to a national organization of social life along with the growth imperative and the centrality of labor to social life.

While multiculturalism is often associated with debates over the curricula of schools and universities, here it is a response to a much wider set of political questions. These have to do not only with the aspirations of various social movements representing minorities, women, and alternative cultural perspectives (e.g., ecology) but also with associated developments in immigration, the international division of labor and changing composition of the workforce, the internationalization and diversification of markets, and so on. Viewed in this light, the context of multicultural debates is a set of significant social and economic changes that raise far-reaching political problems. In the overlap of multiculturalist debates and arguments over postmodernism, one can see some of the ways these debates address the received understandings of intellectual mediators as these understandings are articulated in the philosophical tradition.

The political issues proper to multiculturalism arise in quite different political settings, including already pluralistic settings such as that of the United States and relatively homogeneous political settings such as Germany. I have already made the general claim that liberalism does not respond adequately to these problems. Here I move from the kinds of general claims about liberalism made earlier to difficulties inherent in liberal efforts at forging a multicultural politics. Then I turn directly to the idea of a democratic multiculturalism and its promise for a democratic approach to intellectual mediation.

Liberal multiculturalism sees the historical developments I have mentioned from the standpoint of the vulnerabilities of liberal institutions. I can briefly distinguish two kinds of liberal response, one at the level of theory and one at the level of more specific mediations.

In a recent book on multiculturalism, Charles Taylor (1992) conceives the acknowledgment of minority demands for recognition in a way that sets out their sympathies and tensions with liberal rights and procedures as traditionally conceived. Without disputing the virtues of his argument in its own terms, I want to indicate how it remains within the purview of liberalism as I have been speaking of it. It is limited in this way not because of Taylor's concern with individual rights or universally binding procedures but because of his retaining a nation-centered perspective. This does not follow simply from his main concern with the question of the Quebec minority in Canada, except insofar as he limits the social conflicts affecting its claims to relatively narrow cultural and political aims. Whether or not this is appropriate for his chosen example, it limits the relevance of his discussion to other multicultural conflicts. In Taylor's hands, multiculturalism is a matter of the reconciliation of groups under the umbrella of the liberal nation-state because it does not involve the larger structural developments that both make issues overflow national boundaries and undercut sharp distinctions between political and cultural concerns on the one side and economic concerns on the other. Because he focuses on the issue of recognition, Taylor misses the extent to which multicultural struggles involve overlapping conflicts that have a wider bearing on democratic issues. And given his exclusion of economic aspects of multiculturalism, Taylor can leave unaddressed the problem of liberalism's economistic or productivist presuppositions and how these affect the political options open to multicultural movements.

The relation to labor and growth is not a matter of tacit presuppositions when it comes to the more practical kind of liberal multiculturalism I want to mention. Such a multiculturalism takes place in practices of state institutions and corporations concerned with managing conflicts associated with the kinds of structural changes I cited earlier. In the face of increasingly differentiated workforces employers, seeking to avoid conflict articulated in ethnic, racial, or gender terms, promote a discourse of tolerance and diversity. Facing a similarly differentiated market at home and abroad, corporations promote advertising and products that advance similar values as filtered through the language and symbols of consumerism. While this kind of multiculturalist practice may advance an internationalist rhetoric, it remains firmly rooted in the productivist assumptions of liberalism: multiculturalism is to serve efficient work, higher productivity, and the economic success of all concerned. Moreover, this kind of multiculturalism invests heavily in the kind of action on agency I described as aestheticizing politics. This is not just a matter of the ways it employs techniques of advertising or informs the products of mass culture more generally, but also a matter of the way these initiatives offer aestheticizing interpretations of the conflicts and aspirations that animate the movements to which liberal multiculturalism responds.

From these brief references to liberal multiculturalism, I hope to have indicated what democratic multiculturalism needs to avoid, and to have reviewed the mix of conditions, problems, and movements that provide the possibility for thinking about such a politics.

I make further reference to this historical setting in presenting in a tentative way what I take to be the main features of a multiculturalism inherent in contemporary democratic initiatives. First I present features of this multiculturalism by discussing how it clashes with the commitments of liberalism to nationality and productivism. Then I survey respects in which this multiculturalism contributes to the kind of democracy I have evoked in the discussion of intellectual mediation. On this basis we will be able to see how this idea of democratic multiculturalism can contribute to a political understanding and an approach to mediation that represent a real alternative to traditional liberalism and socialism.

From the standpoint of my discussion, liberalism's significant commitment to nationality is not exclusively its commitment to the nation-state, that is, to a national organization of political power, but also its making the nation the organizing center of economic and cultural as well as political life. Democratic multiculturalism pursues the possibilities inherent in the "de-centering" of all of these spheres. Such a politics is mindful of the extent to which such a centering was always an idealization (as was the separation of the spheres themselves), but it is also responsive to the kinds of trends I have already mentioned that make such an idealization increasingly anachronistic. None of this implies an abandonment of nationality or national states, though it does imply qualifying and supplementing both in appropriate ways. A democratic multiculturalism places the institutional and discursive relations proper to nationality within a more differentiated complex.

This complex can be conceived as a combination of discursive networks that overlap but do not coincide. These networks can be identified by reference to the movements that promote their specific discursive practices while advancing social claims in the larger political setting. To appreciate the sense of overlapping and yet not coinciding networks, we need only cite feminism, minority movements, ecology, gay rights movements, and antiwar movements. In considering the degree of overlap between these movements and their corresponding discursive networks, we should note both the extent of movements' aspirations (e.g., to speak for half of humanity in the case of feminism, but for one part of the citizens of the United States in the case of African American movements) and the extent of their actual achievements (e.g., to speak for mainly white middle-class women in the case of at least some phases of feminism). In considering overlap, we need to consider not only potential coincidence (e.g., minority women) but also corresponding potentials for conflict or mutual exclusion between groups and movements. Such considerations have to do with thinking about why and how multiculturalism is potentially democratic.

In speaking of different discursive networks, I mean to suggest that the various ways specific cultural claims are developed has to do with frameworks of communication in which common understandings and ideals are pursued. These are frameworks that articulate notions of well-being in relation to a political context in which a tradition of goods and universal norms persists. I use Habermas's way of distinguishing specific ethical communities oriented toward shared ideals from morality formulated in norms that in principle are binding for all. The various discursive networks whose political combination is evoked in the term democratic multiculturalism pursue universals specific to their own contexts. The prospects of a democratic multiculturalism turn on the extent to which these various specific networks can intersect, complement one another, and find common ground in the shared elements of a democratic culture they at the same time help construct.

With the idea of discursive networks we think of complexes of movements, constituencies, and intellectuals held together as much by processes of learning as by shared histories. Political and cultural learning here involves at least three dimensions. The first concerns a dialectic between projected and actual constituencies as networks evolve by way of problems and conflicts inherent in their partial successes (e.g., the evolution of feminist discourse beyond its white middle-class condition of the early 1970s in the United States). The second kind of learning involves a dialectic between those within discursive networks and those without: between feminist women and men, between black activists and whites, and so on. Learning here involves the possibility of new kinds of understanding between historically dominant groups (e.g., men who then challenge gender identification of social roles, or whites who come to recognize the specifics of dominant forms of racial consciousness). Finally, learning also takes the form of intersections and fusions of various discursive networks, yielding such hybrids as eco-feminism, or Latina feminism.

The significance for political culture of this complex of overlapping networks is not immediately institutional, but has rather to do with discursive relations proper to a possible democratic culture. It has to do with the generation of meaning in a world that by hypothesis is still reliant on complex formal organizations, differentiation of tasks, and corresponding mediations. The potential discursive networks I have cited have very different histories and stand in relation to different aspects of individual experience. The movements associated with them reflect respects in which their evolution is associated with conflict and thus with questions of power. I cannot attempt here to unravel the corresponding analytical questions but should acknowledge that this way of treating this political and cultural evolution presupposes the irreducibility of power and conflict in gender and racial/ethnic relations. Doing so follows the critique of socialist productivism, though it clearly does not exclude the intersection of kinds of power or the existence of material prerequisites for overcoming racism and sexism.

The feature of this overlapping complex of networks that I do want to emphasize is the prospect it offers of a mutually informing and interlocking differentiation that is quite different from the unification of society conceived by liberalism, even by a liberal theorist of mediation like Hegel, who concretizes the modern atomized individual in increasingly complex organizations leading to the rational whole of the nation-state. Given the absence in this account of corresponding institutions, I can only repeat the assumption by democratic multiculturalism that the nation-state has to be qualified and supplemented by other legal and political frameworks. That is to say, then, that on this democratic conception one promise of the way discursive networks overlap and do not coincide is that it offers a differential relation to social universality. A citizen, whether female or not, stands in political relation to the discursive claims and operations of feminism while also, whether black or not, standing in political relation to the discursive claims and operations of African American movements. A black woman stands in a distinctive relation to both, but what that relation is of course depends on the individual. In any case, the idea of a complex of overlapping networks offers a very different multiculturalism from that I have associated with liberal multiculturalism and a very different political culture from that of more traditional forms of liberalism.

Multiculturalism here is not conceived as a plurality of communities, though it does not exclude thinking about community in various senses of the term. Nor does multiculturalism start from conceptions of identities and values rooted in traditions, though it is compatible with recognizing the role of historical awareness and the dependence of evaluation on inherited understandings. Rather, this kind of multiculturalism is a way of thinking about democratic politics (where the contrast is with thinking about how democracy can be made compatible with various aims associated with movements or traditions). And it asserts that social movements provide possibilities for new kinds of democratic learning precisely because they concretize issues of power in ways that have the potential to generate new evaluative and normative conceptions, new identities and sensibilities that are responsive to the conditions that have brought liberalism to an impasse.

What I am emphasizing with this idea of multiculturalism, then, is the aspect of contemporary changes that opens possibilities of interpretation, evaluation, and identity that coincide with demographic and structural change as confronted and articulated by movements with democratic potential. The "cultural" side of multiculturalism has to do with interpretive initiatives; the "multi" side has to do with the variety of groups and concerns that has been articulated in these initiatives; and the "democratic" side has to do with the respects in which these initiatives confront power relations and inequality in ways that build on existing democratic traditions and institutions and contribute to new democratic understandings. On this conception, the various discursive networks constituting democratic multiculturalism are contexts of learning in which various ethical conceptions are developed against the background of a democratic morality.

A familiar objection to multiculturalism is that it unleashes a cacophony of mutually indifferent, if not always actually conflicting, voices. It runs into conflict with liberal rights and procedures and so in fact erodes democratic culture. There is no denying that there is an experiential basis for such concerns, and movements have paid a political price for not having confronted them adequately. But rather than define multiculturalism, these centrifugal tendencies have their deeper roots in structural changes, power relations, and a range of conflicts associated with them. The conflict over multiculturalism is itself a political and interpretive response to this larger context. Any such response can of course end by making matters worse rather than better, but my claim for democratic multiculturalism is that it makes explicit the conditions of persisting conflict and of potential resolution alike.

While discussing the theme of fragmentation, it may help to notice that the imagery of Balkanization that often accompanies such criticisms does not apply very well even in posing what is at issue here. Multiculturalism is not a matter of unleashing various and potentially competing nationalisms, even if it seems so in the case of some minority movements or in certain separatist strands in feminism. One problem with liberal multiculturalism is that it encourages such an interpretation with its pluralist treatment of movements and groups under the umbrella of the nation-state. My conception of overlapping networks that do not coincide is one way of characterizing what is different about multiculturalism. Another is the argument for the potentially mutually informing character of these overlapping networks. For the most part, the different strands of multiculturalism do not confront one another as competing ethnic or national groups seeking political autonomy. I think this point can be sustained even when these different strands are in fact different ethnic groups. In any case, my point can be more easily seen from those strands which, in addition to ethnic groups, involve women, gays, and ecology and peace movements. The danger of fragmentation here is less one of Balkanization than it is of narrowness of perspective and mutual indifference leading to shared ineffectiveness in the face of wider structural change and growing political cynicism.

To make the same point from the standpoint of positive goals: the aim of democratic multiculturalism is not best grasped as a version of the multiethnic pluralism that is often said to be the alternative to Balkanization. While the different strands or networks joined in democratic multiculturalism may involve different traditions, communities, and identities, their interrelations are not the same as those of diverse ethnic communities in the Central European sense. Even when these strands or networks involve different groups, they have the potential of mutually informing one another in ways that reflect the characteristic background of structure and power, as I have already suggested in referring to ways African American movements can inform the political understanding of nonblacks. But because these strands or networks often do not essentially involve separate groups, they also have other potentials for shaping new understandings in distinctive ways: the imagery, say, of a gay Latina feminist ecology activist may be used to satirize multiculturalism, but it evokes a democratic ideal at the same time. From the standpoint of democratic citizenship, the point here is that multiculturalism raises possibilities not only about relations between groups with different experiences, traditions, and concerns but also about the formation of individuals whose lives are traversed by a variety of backgrounds, conditions, and potentialities. Democratic multiculturalism is as much about appropriate forms of individuality as it is about the claims of self-defining groups.

The conjunction of the possibility of differentiated group memberships and strong individuality was explored by a W.E.B. DuBois, who may be counted among the thinkers who first developed the kind of democratic multiculturalism I am discussing here. DuBois is often thought of as having negotiated, not always successfully, a difficult balance between autonomous black development and integration in the wider society of the United States. What is less often emphasized is his concern for a social identity that could successfully combine black self-assertion with national membership in a way that overcame the oppressive "double-consciousness" suffered by blacks in the wake of slavery. And this twofold membership for DuBois was not to be at the expense of individuality, but rather a condition for it. For DuBois, the communitarian side of politics is not to sacrifice individuals, but rather to be the condition for individuals who then have unfolding options of new and different kinds of memberships proper to an advanced industrial society.[1]

Apart from its relation to nationality, a democratically coordinated multiculturalism offers an alternative to liberalism's acceptance of the growth imperative and the centrality of labor as well. In seeing some respects in which this is so, I also develop themes introduced above, in particular regarding the social learning associated with democratic

multiculturalism. This includes learning about the possibilities of production and consumption where such learning stands in contrast to the
kinds of reforms associated with liberalism so far as it acknowledges
the need for minimum conditions of material well-being to overcome
social conflict. More generally, democratic multiculturalism's relation
to issues of production and consumption in principle can be contrasted
both to liberalism's claims about the possibility of overcoming exces-
sive inequality through economic growth and to socialism's claims
about the supersession of capitalist production relations as the means
for overcoming the various oppressions that characterize modern society. Rather than ignore issues of material life, democratic multiculturalism as I understand it explores conditions for taking advantage
of contemporary levels of productive potential by rethinking the meaning of economic growth and the associated place of labor in social life.

Elements of such an exploration can be seen in the ways social
movements make features of agency a political issue. To be sure, some
feminist and minority struggles over quality of schools, curricula,
training, racial and gender tracking, and more egalitarian hiring and
promotion opportunities can be seen within a liberal framework. But
other initiatives make the democratic potential of any politics of agency
more explicit, for example, when it comes to the relation of child
rearing to the demands of work, the content and function of advertising, the aims of corporations as they affect minority communities, or
the uses and aims of technological change. In a variety of ways such
movements come up against the imperatives of economic growth and
the demands of labor-centered social existence.

Ecology's importance within democratic multiculturalism is clear,
since it provides terms for thinking about social relations and capacities in the setting both of natural constraints and of the possibilities of
alternative ways of conceiving humanity's relation to nature. As a
dimension of multiculturalism, ecology informs a discursive network
that is associated with social movements and that offers alternative
interpretations of social practices and capacities. The way ecology
figures in the complex of overlapping yet not coinciding discursive
networks is unique: it aspires to speak to and for all humanity while
residing in relatively restricted communities of discussion and action
that nonetheless help spark occasional bursts of protest and action. It is
a discursive network that advances distinctive ethical understandings,
both about norms for environmentally responsible action and about

human and natural well-being. The way ecology contributes to social learning provides examples too of the possible intersection of these discursive networks, when minority or women's movements make an issue of the ways environmental damage tends to affect minorities and women most.

Ecology, feminism, and minority movements, then, politicize aspects of a productivist culture that liberalism long treated as possessing a natural necessity. This introduces at least the possibility of what I have called social learning regarding the growth imperative and modern forms of production and consumption. Indeed, these movements sometimes directly confront the practices whose political character I have said contemporary liberalism for the most part leaves unacknowledged: for example, advertising, mass entertainment, and various more or less direct strategies for managing conflict in the workplace, schools, prisons, and so on. To say that this contribution to social learning has provided an alternative to liberal productivism is of course a different matter.

To acknowledge the dimensions of such a task but also to see how it persists as the horizon of our daily political experience, we can refer to what may seem a quite different aspect of multiculturalism. In speaking of the multicultural alternative to nationality I did not pursue the relation between minority movements and their various relations to the diasporas resulting from voluntary and involuntary forms of migration. In the United States, the shift in usage from the term "black" to "African American" reflects how this minority conceives its experience and possibilities in ways that transcend the boundaries of its own country. The aspect of this kind of internationalism I want to mention here is its bearing on the understanding within an advanced industrial society of North/South relations. While the historical relation to Africa points to the legacy of slavery embodied in the inequalities experienced by African Americans, it also brings the experiences and conditions of Africa and of other streams of the diaspora (e.g., Haiti) into political consideration. This aspect of multiculturalism, then, offers a kind of social learning that potentially brings into view the conditions associated with international inequality and transnational divisions of labor.

Obviously here I am evoking what for the most part is only a possibility inherent in the conditions of democratic multiculturalism, particularly as this kind of learning might affect the majority in the United States. But it does indicate one way multiculturalism has a historicizing and politicizing potential regarding conditions of production and consumption; and this is a way that might affect the pursuit of politics through both national and international institutions.

So far I have discussed ways democratic multiculturalism provides an alternative to liberalism's nation-centered and productivist politics. Implicit in many of my examples has been a reference to ways the movements associated with multiculturalism challenge existing forms of intellectual mediation. In so doing they contribute to the kind of democratic mediation that I have argued is necessary for a genuine alternative to received forms of liberalism and socialism. I will try to develop this claim with reference to some of the ways such challenges bear on what I have called the politics of agency.

First I should note ways the politics I associate with multiculturalism challenge existing forms of expertise. Feminist and minority critics have challenged the assumptions and procedures of traditional philosophy, the natural and social sciences, the professions, mass culture, and education. Ecologists have questioned the content and application of technological reason, analyses of economic necessities, and environmental analyses. As these examples indicate, such challenges extend to practices that address elements of agency, in education, mass culture, and the professions. And these initiatives have not been aimed solely at the claims of experts but have figured in attempts to transform specialized practices themselves. Debates within disciplines have frequently included the formation of caucuses animated by the concerns of movements and aiming to transform specialist practice, for example, among social workers, attorneys, and medical doctors.

So far as such tendencies within fields of expert mediation challenge ways power is exercised by their own and other specialties, they contribute to a more general questioning of the division of labor and the scarcity that governs the distribution and formation of agency. In some contexts, issues of scarce agency become explicit, for example, when bias in teaching girls or in advising minority students in school is uncovered, or when gender and racial assumptions are identified in mass culture. No doubt, such criticism is a far cry from developing practices that honor the discursive ideal I presented earlier. But these challenges begin to make the wider themes of the historical formation of agency a political question. And they do so by illustrating how the discursive values of participation, recognition, and equality of discursive resources can function as a standard by which to measure actual practices.

So far as multiculturalist criticism thus addresses ways the division of labor contributes to the reproduction of various kinds of power relations and inequalities, it anticipates one of the conditions I cited earlier for a democratic culture. It develops an understanding of the ways that the distribution of expertise has to be questioned for its contribution to undemocratic operations of power. At best, of course, this is only an anticipation of one of the conditions of a consistently democratic culture. Another condition was what I called a democratic culture of competence that would provide all citizens with the capacity to understand the differences and interconnections of expertise and politics and to question and judge expert claims as they bear on political questions. While this too stands in utopian contrast to existing practices, I can nonetheless also cite contemporary anticipations of such a culture of competence.

Such anticipations take place in the ambiguous trends of mass higher education, communications media, and social information. I can cite democratic experiments in education, attempts to develop alternative uses of mass media, struggles to make information that is in principle available in fact accessible. Such examples by no means prove the feasibility of the wider aims I have associated with democratic multiculturalism, but they do show that this ideal has an operative relevance to actual practices and debates.

On the basis of my earlier discussion of aestheticized politics one could infer that the prospects of the idea of democratic multiculturalism depend significantly on democratic challenges to this aspect of contemporary political life. Aestheticized politics crystallizes the issues I have associated with the critique of contemporary liberalism so far as it involves a kind of mediated relation to politics in which reflexive relations to the scarcity of agency function explicitly. One could argue that many of the democratic initiatives I have cited in fact challenge such a politics. More generally, one can look to the contents of aestheticized politics and find much that responds to multicultural initiative, for example, in the ways minority and feminist questions become translated into the terms of mass entertainment. It is impossible here to offer a balanced assessment of these phenomena. But I believe we have some grounds for concluding that the conflicts pursued by democratic multiculturalism penetrate the elements of aestheticizing politics. This should not be surprising if in fact multicultural struggles have their basis in the most general structural evolution of contemporary society.

Democratic Uncertainty

It is easy to cite contemporary developments that make overcoming the division of labor seem problematic. Two major political economic facts make superseding the specifically capitalist organization of scarcity seem unlikely. The collapse of Communism eliminates attempts at rival forms of organization of production, and the decline of social democratic and welfare-state policies puts efforts to subdue market forces on the defensive. We seem to be in a new period of capitalist evolution, in which the international scale of economic relations compromises political efforts to keep economic value considerations at bay. At the same time, political and cultural developments also work against democratization. The assertion of nationalisms in the former Communist societies and the rise there and elsewhere of so-called religious fundamentalisms undercut efforts at democratic and egalitarian reconstruction. One hardly needs postmodern theory to sense that secular projects of egalitarian and democratizing social change are relics of a past that seems increasingly remote. The language and practices of that past seem to lack all potential for being reactivated.

Democrats, however, are not at a complete loss for countervailing considerations. Despite the triumphalism of the exponents of capitalism, the advanced capitalist economies have exhibited stagnation and increasing unemployment. Inequities within these societies and between them and the poor societies of the "South" have grown. As I noted earlier, the ecological crisis is part of a general inability so far of the wealthy societies to resolve their structural problems. Within these societies one finds a continuing and deepening cultural and moral crisis.

One cannot simply claim that more democracy would resolve these problems, either within or without a capitalist framework. The savagery exhibited in the post-Communist societies has revived yet again pessimistic views of human nature. Even if we take such conservative thought patterns as symptoms of the times, democrats still need to develop conceptions and practices that respond to the experienced dilemmas of the present.

My suggestion is that it is precisely in the light of the concerns that seem to militate against democratic hopes that the critique of the division of labor shows its intellectual promise as a critical framework. Apart from its capacity to draw together existing democratic conceptions, it provides a way of addressing those problematic areas of contemporary experience that seem to make democratic hopes utopian in a hopeless and perhaps dangerous sense. It offers a standpoint on the paradoxical political rise of economics over politics, on the mobilization of social energies over the regulation of agency, on the limits of liberalism, and on postmodern suspicion regarding expertise. It offers a way of furthering the democratic argument while accommodating those concerns that have raised doubts about past democratic arguments and practices, and at the same time it casts critical light on the assumptions and actions of antidemocratic arguments.

Notes

Chapter 4

1. Althusser calls for such a philosophical reading of Marx's texts, but the interpretation I offer is designed to avoid fatal ambiguities about agency in Althusser's work. See Althusser and Balibar 1970.

2. Sohn-Rethel (1977) provides a helpful discussion of the relation between exchange practices and thought abstractions.

3. Marx introduces this idea in "Critique of Hegel's *Philosophy of Right*: Introduction," and seems to hold to it throughout his career.

Chapter 6

1. The following account draws from Habermas's two-volume *Theory of Communicative Action*.

2. An early statement is to be found in Habermas 1970.

3. Thus Foucault sees his work in relation to historical conflicts. Foucault 1983, 211–13.

4. Sohn-Rethel (1977) provides an extensive account of interrelations between thought and real abstractions.

5. Marx 1973, introduction. Althusser's exploration of the epistemological force of Marx's comments in these and related texts remains a fruitful source for reflection on Marx's philosophical suggestions. See esp. Althusser 1970.

6. In the following quote, one can see Hegel employing Schelling's language against him, both in explicit quotations and the use of terminology. The concluding use of a Yiddish proverb illustrates another kind of dialogical appropriation. "Dealing with something from the perspective of the Absolute consists merely in declaring that, although one has been speaking of it just now as something definite, yet in the Absolute, the A = A, there is nothing of the kind, for there all is one. To pit this single insight, that in the Absolute everything is the same, as against the full body of articulated cognition, which at least seeks and demands such fulfillment, to palm off its Absolute as the night in which, as the saying goes, all cows are black—this is cognition naïvely reduced to vacuity" (Hegel 1977, 9).

Chapter 8

1. Former Vice President Walter Mondale's quip at a debate in the 1984 Democratic primary debates.

Chapter 9

1. For an account of dilemmas of economic development in these conditions, see Wolfe 1981.

2. I use quotation marks here to acknowledge that the kind of validity question raised by needs is a point that requires discussion.

Chapter 12

1. For a discussion of this aspect of Dubois's work, see Boxill 1984.

References

Adorno, Theodor W. 1974. *Minima Moralia*. Translated by E.F.N. Jephcott. London: Verso.

Althusser, Louis. 1970. *For Marx*. Translated by Ben Brewster. New York: Vintage.

Althusser, Louis, and Etienne Balibar. 1970. *Reading Capital*. Translated by Ben Brewster. London: New Left Books.

Amin, Samir, Giovanni Arrighi, André Gunder Frank, and Immanuel Wallerstein. 1982. *Dynamics of Global Crisis*. New York: Monthly Review.

———. 1990. *Transforming the Revolution: Social Movements and the World System*. New York: Monthly Review.

Apel, Karl-Otto. 1967. *Analytic Philosophy of Language and the Geisteswissenschaften*. Translated by Harald Holstelilie. Dordrecht: Reidel.

Arendt, Hannah. 1958. *The Human Condition*. Chicago: University of Chicago Press.

Armstrong, Robert, and Janet Shenk. 1982. *El Salvador: The Face of Revolution*. Boston: South End.

Arrighi, Giovanni, Terence K. Hopkins, and Immanuel Wallerstein. 1989. *Antisystemic Movements*. London: Verso.

Asante, Molefi Kete. 1987. *The Afrocentric Idea*. Philadelphia: Temple University Press.

Bakhtin, Mikhail. 1981. *The Dialogical Imagination*. Translated by Caryl Emerson and Michael Holquist. Austin: University of Texas Press.

———. 1984a. *Problems in Dostoevsky's Poetics*. Translated by Caryl Emerson. Minneapolis: University of Minnesota Press.

———. 1984b. *Rabelais and His World*. Translated by Helene Iswolsky. Bloomington: Indiana University Press.

———. 1986. *Speech Genres and Other Late Essays*. Translated by Caryl Emerson and Michael Holquist. Austin: University of Texas Press.

Baudrillard, Jean. 1988. Selected Writings. Edited by Mark Poster. Stanford: Stanford University Press.

Baynes, Kenneth, James Bohman, and Thomas McCarthy, eds. 1987. *After Philosophy: End or Transformation?* Cambridge: MIT Press.

Bell, Daniel. 1960. *The End of Ideology*. Glencoe, Ill.: Free Press.

———. 1976a. *The Coming of Post-Industrial Society*. New York: Basic Books.

_____. 1976b. *The Cultural Contradictions of Capitalism*. New York: Basic Books.

Benhabib, Seyla, and Fred Dallmayr, eds. 1990. *The Communicative Ethics Controversy*. Cambridge: MIT Press.

Benjamin, Walter. 1969. "The Work of Art in the Age of Mechanical Reproduction." In *Illuminations*, edited by Hannah Arendt. New York: Schocken.

_____. 1982. "The Author as Producer." In *The Essential Frankfurt School Reader*, edited by Andrew Arato and Eike Gebhardt. New York: Continuum.

Bernstein, Richard J. 1983. *Beyond Objectivism and Relativism*. Philadelphia: University of Pennsylvania Press.

Boston Women's Health Collective. 1984. *Our Bodies, Ourselves*. New York: Simon & Schuster.

Boxill, Bernard R. *Blacks and Social Justice*. Totowa, N.J.: Rowman & Allenheld, 1984.

Brown, Lester, Christopher Flavin, and Hal Kane. 1992. *Vital Signs, 1992*. New York: Norton.

Burke, Edmund. 1969. *Reflections on the Revolution in France*. Baltimore: Penguin.

Butler, Judith. 1990. *Gender Trouble: Feminism and the Subversion of Identity*. New York: Routledge.

Clark, Katerina, and Michael Holquist. 1984. *Mikhail Bakhtin*. Cambridge: Harvard University.

Cohen, Jean L. 1982. *Class and Civil Society*. Amherst: University of Massachusetts Press.

_____, ed. 1985. *Social Movements*. Special issue of *Social Research* 52 (winter).

Commoner, Barry. 1979. *The Politics of Energy*. New York: Knopf.

Crozier, Michael, Samuel Huntington, and Joji Watanuki. 1975. *The Crisis of Democracy*. New York: New York University Press.

Derrida, Jacques. 1976. *Of Grammatology*. Translated by Gayatri Chakravorty Spivak. Baltimore: Johns Hopkins University Press.

_____. 1978. *Edmund Husserl's "Origin of Geometry": An Introduction*. Translated by John P. Leavey Jr. Stony Brook, N.Y.: N. Hays.

_____. 1989. *Of Spirit*. Translated by Geoffrey Bennington and Rachel Bowlby. Chicago: University of Chicago.

Dews, Peter. 1987. *Logics of Disintegration*. London: Verso.

Diamond, Irene, and Lee Quinby, eds. 1988. *Feminism and Foucault*. Boston: Northeastern University Press.

Dreyfus, Hubert L., and Paul Rabinow. 1983. *Michel Foucault: Beyond Structuralism and Hermeneutics*. 2d ed. Chicago: University of Chicago Press.

Edelman, Murray. 1988. *Constructing the Political Spectacle*. Chicago: University of Chicago Press.

Elias, Norbert. 1978. *The Civilizing Process*. Oxford: Blackwell.

Engels, Frederick. 1969. *Anti-Dühring*. Moscow: Progress Publishers.

Esquith, Stephen L. 1994. *Intimacy and Spectacle: Political Education at the Hands of Liberal Theory*. Ithaca, N.Y.: Cornell University Press.

Feyerabend, Paul. 1988. *Against Method*. London: Verso.

Foucault, Michel. 1972. *Archaeology of Knowledge: Includes the Discourse on Language.* Translated by A. M. Sheridan Smith. New York: Irvington.

———. 1977. *Discipline and Punish.* Translated by Alan Sheridan. New York: Vintage.

———. 1980a. *A History of Sexuality.* Vol. 1. Translated by Robert Hurley. New York: Vintage.

———. 1980b. *Power/Knowledge.* Edited by Colin Gordon. New York: Pantheon.

———. 1983. "The Subject and Power." In *Michel Foucault: Beyond Structuralism and Hermeneutics,* edited by Hubert L. Dreyfus and Paul Rabinow. 2d ed. Chicago: University of Chicago Press.

———. 1984. *Foucault Reader.* Edited by Paul Rabinow. New York: Pantheon.

Foucault, Michel, and Giles Deleuze. 1977. "Intellectuals and Power." In *Language, Counter-Memory, Practices,* translated by D. F. Bouchard and Sherry Simon. Ithaca, N.Y.: Cornell University Press.

Frank, André Gunder. 1980. *Crisis: In the World Economy.* New York: Holmes & Meirer.

Fukuyama, Francis. 1992. *The End of History and the Last Man.* New York: Free Press.

Gadamer, Hans-Georg. 1975. *Truth and Method.* New York: Seabury.

Giddens, Anthony. 1982. "Labour and Interaction." In *Habermas: Critical Debates,* edited by John B. Thompson and David Held. Cambridge: MIT Press.

Gorz, André. 1968. *Strategy for Labor.* Translated by M. A. Nicolaus and V. Ortiz. Boston: Beacon.

———. 1980. *Ecology as Politics.* Boston: South End.

———. 1982. *Farewell to the Working Class.* Boston: South End.

———. 1985. *Paths to Paradise.* Boston: South End.

Gouldner, Alvin. 1976. *The Dialectic of Ideology and Technology.* New York: Seabury.

———. 1979. *The Future of Intellectuals and the Rise of the New Class.* New York: Continuum.

Green, Philip. 1985. *Retrieving Democracy.* Totowa, N.J.: Rowman & Allanheld.

Habermas, Jürgen. 1970. "Technology and Science as Ideology." In *Toward a Rational Society,* translated by Jeremy J. Shapiro. Boston: Beacon.

———. 1971. *Knowledge and Human Interests.* Translated by Jeremy J. Shapiro. Boston: Beacon.

———. 1973. *Theory and Practice.* Translated by John Viertel. Boston: Beacon.

———. 1975. *Legitimation Crisis.* Translated by Thomas McCarthy. Boston: Beacon.

———. 1982. "A Reply to My Critics." In *Habermas: Critical Debates.* Edited by John B. Thompson and David Held. Cambridge: MIT Press.

———. 1984. *The Theory of Communicative Action.* Vol. 1. Translated by Thomas McCarthy. Boston: Beacon.

———. 1987a. *The Philosophical Discourse of Modernity.* Translated by Frederick Lawrence. Cambridge: MIT.

_____. 1987b. *The Theory of Communicative Action.* Vol. 2. Translated by Thomas McCarthy. Boston: Beacon.

_____. 1990. *Moral Consciousness and Communicative Action.* Translated by C. Lenhardt and S. W. Nicholson. Cambridge: Polity.

Harding, Sandra. 1986. *The Science Question in Feminism.* Ithaca, N.Y.: Cornell University Press.

Hegel, G.W.F. 1956. *The Philosophy of History.* Translated by J. Sibree. New York: Dover.

_____. 1977. *Phenomenology of Spirit.* Translated by A. V. Miller. Oxford: Clarendon.

_____. 1990. *Preface and Introduction to the Phenomenology of Mind.* Edited by Lawrence S. Stepelevich. New York: Macmillan.

_____. 1991a. *Elements of the Philosophy of Right.* Translated by A. Wood. Cambridge: Cambridge University Press.

_____. 1991b. *The Encyclopedia Logic.* Translated by T. F. Geraets, W. A. Suchting, and H. S. Harris. Indianapolis: Hackett.

Heidegger, Martin. 1977. *Basic Writings.* Edited by David Krell. New York: Harper Collins.

Herman, Edward S., and Frank Broadhead. 1984. *Demonstration Elections.* Boston: South End.

Hessen, Boris. 1974. "The Social and Economic Roots of Newton's *Principia.*" In *Science, Technology, and Freedom,* edited by Willis H. Truitt and T. W. Graham Solomons. Boston: Houghton Mifflin.

Horkheimer, Max. 1972. *Critical Theory: Selected Essays.* Translated by Matthew J. O'Connel and others. New York: Herder & Herder.

Horkheimer, Max, and Theodor W. Adorno. 1972. *Dialectic of Enlightenment.* Translated by John Cummings. New York: Herder & Herder.

Husserl, Edmund. 1970. *The Crisis of European Sciences and Transcendental Phenomenology.* Translated by David Carr. Evanston, Ill.: Northwestern University Press.

Jaggar, Alison M. 1983. *Feminist Politics and Human Nature.* Sussex: Harvester.

Jameson, Fredric. 1991. *Postmodernism, or the Cultural Logic of Late Capitalism.* Durham, N.C.: Duke University Press.

Jay, Martin. 1984. *Marxism and Totality.* Berkeley and Los Angeles: University of California Press,

_____. 1985. "Habermas and Modernism." In *Habermas and Modernity,* edited by Richard Bernstein. Cambridge: MIT Press.

Kant, Immanuel. 1956. *The Critique of Practical Reason.* Translated by Lewis White Beck. Indianapolis: Bobbs-Merrill.

_____. 1965. *The Critique of Pure Reason.* Translated by Norman Kemp Smith. New York: St. Martin's.

_____. 1983. "What Is Enlightenment?" In *Perpetual Peace and Other Essays.* Translated by Ted Humphrey. Indianapolis: Hackett.

_____. 1987. *The Critique of Judgement.* Translated by Werner S. Pluhar. Indianapolis: Hackett.

Konrad, Gyorgy, and Ivan Szelenyi. 1979. *The Intellectuals on the Road to Class Power.* Translated by Andrew Arato and Richard E. Allen. New York: Harcourt Brace Jovanovich.

Kornbluth, Peter. 1987. *Nicaragua: The Price of Intervention.* Washington, D.C.: Institute for Policy Studies.

Kuhn, Thomas. 1962. *The Structure of Scientific Revolutions.* Chicago: University of Chicago Press.

Lindblom, Charles E. 1977. *Politics and Markets.* New York: Basic Books.

Locke, John. 1980. *Second Treatise of Government.* Indianapolis: Hackett.

Lukács, György. 1971. *History and Class Consciousness.* Translated by Rodney Livingstone. Cambridge: MIT Press.

Lyotard, Jean-François. 1984. *The Postmodern Condition: A Report on Knowledge.* Translated by Geoff Bennington and Brian Massumi. Minneapolis: University of Minnesota Press.

MacIntyre, Alasdair. 1981. *After Virtue.* Notre Dame, Ind.: University of Notre Dame Press.

Marcuse, Herbert. 1960. *Reason and Revolution.* Boston: Beacon.

————. 1964. *One-Dimensional Man.* Boston: Beacon.

Marx, Karl. 1964. *The Economic and Philosophical Manuscripts of 1844.* Translated by Martin Milligan. New York: International Publishers.

————. 1967. "Toward the Critique of Hegel's Philosophy of Law: Introduction." In *Writings of the Young Marx on Philosophy and Society,* edited by Loyd D. Easton and Kurt H. Guddat. New York: Anchor.

————. 1973. *Grundrisse.* Translated by Martin Nicolaus. Harmondsworth, Middlesex: Penguin.

————. 1976. *Capital.* Vol. 1. Translated by Ben Fowkes. New York: Vintage.

————. 1977. Preface to *A Contribution to the Critique of Political Economy.* In *Karl Marx: Selected Writings,* edited by David McLellan. Oxford: Oxford University Press.

Marx, Karl, and Frederick Engels. 1970. *The German Ideology.* Edited by C. J. Arthur. New York: International Publishers.

————. 1971. *Writings on the Paris Commune.* Edited by Hal Draper. New York: Monthly Review.

————. 1978. *Manifesto of the Communist Party.* In *The Marx-Engels Reader,* 2d ed., edited by Robert C. Tucker. New York: Norton.

Mill, John Stuart. 1972. *Utilitarianism, On Liberty,* and *Considerations on Representative Government.* Edited by H. B. Acton. London: Everyman's Library.

Morson, Gary S., and Caryl Emerson. 1990. *Mikhail Bakhtin: Creation of a Prosaics* Stanford: Stanford University Press.

North American Congress on Latin America (NACLA). 1984. *Report on the Americas* (Special issues on Guatemala), vol. 17, nos. 1 and 2.

O'Connor, James. 1984. *Accumulation Crisis.* New York: Basil Blackwell.

Offe, Claus. 1985. *Disorganized Capitalism.* Cambridge: MIT Press.

Pittman, John, ed. 1992–93. *African-American Perspectives and Philosophical Traditions.* Special issue of *Philosophical Forum* 24, nos. 1–3 (fall–spring).

Polanyi, Karl. 1957. *The Great Transformation.* Boston: Beacon.

Rawls, John. 1971. *A Theory of Justice.* Cambridge: Harvard University Press.

Rorty, Richard. 1979. *Philosophy and the Mirror of Nature.* Princeton: Princeton University Press.

_____. 1982. *Consequences of Pragmatism.* Minneapolis: University of Minnesota Press.

_____. 1983. "Postmodern Bourgeois Liberalism." *Journal of Philosophy* 80:553–69.

_____. 1985. "Habermas and Lyotard on Postmodernity." In *Habermas and Modernity,* edited by Richard Bernstein. Cambridge: MIT Press.

_____. 1987. "Pragmatism and Philosophy." In *After Philosophy: End or Transformation?* edited by Kenneth Baynes, James Bohman, and Thomas McCarthy. Cambridge: MIT Press.

Sohn-Rethel, Alfred. 1977. *Intellectual and Manual Labor: A Critique of Epistemology.* Atlantic Highlands, N.J.: Humanities.

Steinfells, Peter. 1979. *The Neoconservatives.* New York: Simon & Schuster.

Taylor, Charles. 1989. *Sources of the Self.* Cambridge: Harvard University Press.

_____. 1992. *Multiculturalism and "The Politics of Recognition."* Princeton: Princeton University Press.

Thompson, E. P., and Dan Smith, eds. 1981. *Protest and Survive.* New York: Monthly Review.

Thompson, John, and David Held, eds. 1982. *Habermas: Critical Debates.* Cambridge: MIT Press.

Volosinov, V. N. 1973. *Marxism and the Philosophy of Language.* Translated by Ladislav Matejka and I. R. Titunik. Cambridge: Harvard University Press.

_____. 1976. *Freudianism: A Critical Sketch.* Translated by I. R. Titunik. Bloomington: Indiana University Press.

Weber, Max. 1958. *The Protestant Ethic and the Spirit of Capitalism.* Translated by Talcott Parsons. New York: Scribner.

Wolfe, Alan. 1981. *America's Impasse.* New York: Pantheon.

Wood, Neal. 1983. *The Politics of Locke's Philosophy.* Berkeley and Los Angeles: University of California Press.

Index

Adorno, Theodor W., 8, 122, 126, 256
advertising, postmodern politics and, 222–30
aestheticized politics: democratic multiculturalism and, 324–25; democratic philosophy and, 295–99; growth and, 277–79; rationality and, 252–56
agency: aestheticized politics and, 296–99; aestheticizing politics and, 257–61; alienated politics and, 210–15; citizen as client and, 231–34; citizenship, postmodernism and, 230–31; conflict and politics of, 158–61; constitutive practices and, 152–55; critique of division of labor and, 108; culture of democratic competence and, 290–94; disaster entertainment and, 236–37; in Foucault's language theory, 143–46; Habermas's communications theory and, 121–22, 124–29; liberal metaphysics and, 241–42, 246–52; passivity and aestheticized politics, 254–56; postmodernism and, 204–5; role of, in popular culture, 226–30; scarcity of, 268–69; spectatorship and, 234–38; terrorism and, 247–48; transhistorical perspective on, 302–3. *See also* social practices and movements; state institutions
alienation, postmodern politics and, 210–15
Althusser, Louis, 327n.1
Anti-Dühring, 88
anti-ideological ideology, postmodernism and, 197–98
a priori knowledge, in Foucault's language theory, 139–40
archaeological perspective, in Foucault's language theory, 139–41, 145–46
Arendt, Hannah, liberalism critiqued by, 32, 34
argumentation, democratic philosophy and, 47
Armstrong, Robert, 247
audience, role of, in popular culture, 224–30
authoritative voice (Bakhtin), 129

Bakhtin, Mikhail: democratic philosophy and, 49, 284; dialogical analysis of, 130–35; critique of division of labor and, 150, 159, 161; Foucault's language theory and, 138–39, 143, 146; genre concept of, 172–73; language theory of, 49, 120, 129–37, 157, 159–61, 171, 174–76; Marx's political economy and, 165; philosophy as social practice, 14; rationality and, 153–54
Baudrillard, Jean, 199
Bell, Daniel, 20, 190
Benjamin, Walter, 252
Broadhead, Frank, 240
Brown, Lester, 273
Butler, Judith, 190

Capital, 81, 163, 166–68
capitalism, Marx's theory of political economy and, 81–84, 163–68
carnival theme, in Bakhtin's language theory, 136–37
citizenship: aestheticized politics and, 252–56; client-citizens, 231–34; culture of democratic competence and, 291–94; democratic multiculturalism, 317–18; liberal metaphysics and, 238–52; postmodernism and, 210–15; postmodern politics and, 230–52; spectatorship and, 234–38. *See also specific types of citizenship,* e.g., aestheticized citizenship
"civilizing process," division of labor and, 103–4
class structure: Foucault's language theory and, 145–46; Marx's theory of knowledge-power and, 85–87; Marx's theory of political economy and, 83–84, 327n.3; specialization of knowledge and, 20
client citizenship: contemporary politics and, 210–15; postmodern politics and, 231–34
cognition, Kant's critique of reason and, 65–68
Cold War perspective, postmodern politics and, 241–44, 249–52, 257–61